Introduction to
Contractors' All Risks Insurance

Introduction to Contractors' All Risks Insurance

Frank Eaglestone

LLB (Lond), FCII, FCIArb, Barrister

Series editor: RM Walmsley

Croner Publications Ltd
Croner House
London Road
Kingston upon Thames
Surrey KT2 6SR
Tel: 01-547 3333

Copyright © 1990 F Eaglestone
First published 1990

Published by
Croner Publications Ltd,
Croner House,
London Road,
Kingston upon Thames,
Surrey KT2 6SR
Telephone 01-547 3333

While every care has been taken in the writing and efiting of this book,
readers should be aware that only Acts of Parliament
and Statutory Instruments have the force of law,
and that only the courts can authoritatively
interpret the law.

British Library Cataloguing in Publication Data
Eaglestone, F.N. (Frank Nelson) *1916–*
Introduction to contractors' all risks insurance.
(Insurance in practice series)
1. Great Britain. Buildings. Construction. Building
construction. Contractors. Insurance.
I. Title
368

ISBN 1-85452-061-X

Printed by Whitstable Litho, Whitstable, Kent

Contents

Series preface

The day to day practice of insurance involves making decisions in relation to the interpretation of contract documents.

It is a practical job concerned with real problems for real people, and the books in this series are primarily intended to give essential basic information to insurance and professional students which will enable them to understand the principles involved in their work.

In addition, people insured in a private capacity and officials of insured companies need to understand those principles underlying the contracts into which they have entered. Thus this series should also be of value to them, both in the negotiation stage of arranging insurance cover and later when questions arise in relation to a claim.

The various authors are engaged in the claims field and thus the texts are based on practical experience.

R M Walmsley
Birmingham
July 1989

Preface

This is one of a series of insurance books published by Croner Publications Ltd and edited by R M Walmsley.

While each book has as its base a specific insurance policy which forms the structure for comment, explanation and presentation of information, the intention is that the books should appeal not only to insurance students but also to other business or profession students. In addition they should interest the business person and professional practitioner who needs some general practical guidance on the subject.

The policy which is the subject of this book appears under various names according to the views of the underwriter or market manager of the insurer issuing the policy. However, the most popular terms (not necessarily the most descriptive names) used in the insurance industry are the "contractors' all risks policy" or "contract works policy". Possibly the former is the favourite, if only because the abbreviation CAR indicates to the majority that a material damage policy covering property in the course of erection or installation, in the widest form, is concerned. This leads to the immediate criticism that the term "all risks" has caused the insurance industry some trouble in that, like the term "comprehensive", it implies that there are no exclusions to the policy. But it is becoming known, even to the "man in the street" that "all risks" and "comprehensive" policies do have their limitations, thus these terms are not as misleading as once they were considered to be, bearing in mind also that the policy in question is usually issued to business people. Therefore, although "construction and erection policy" may be more descriptive of the policy cover, this book will stay with the well-known title "contractors' all risks policy".

It is a peculiarity of insurance publications that the CAR policy usually appears as part of a book on building contracts and thus there is no publication, as far as the author is aware, which regards this policy as its main subject. Inevitably the policy must be bound up with building contract conditions. In fact, before the 1939–1945 war there was no such policy generally sold by insurers as it is now. The Institution of Civil Engineers' Conditions of Contract led to the birth of the CAR policy, which is why the excepted risks in subclause 20(3) form the basis of the exclusions in the CAR policy. One of the first CAR policies to be issued covered the building of Lambeth Bridge and more recently a more sophisticated cover was provided for the Thames Barrier and now there is the Channel Tunnel policy.

It must be appreciated that the CAR policy often has two other sections, namely a liability section (covering public and even employers' liability) and a consequential loss (loss of profits) section. To avoid clashing with other books in this series, liability insurance will not be discussed but some aspects of the consequential loss section will be considered as such losses are bound up with material damage cover. While liability will not be considered, the JCT (Standard Form of Building Contract 1980, as amended in 1986) clause 21.2.1 insurance policy will be included in this book for the reason mentioned later in this preface.

The only insurance examination directly involving this policy (although the Chartered Insurance Institute in their third draft for the 1992 examination scheme include "construction insurance" as a subject) is held by the Chartered Institute of Loss Adjusters and their syllabus (dated June 1989) for the subject entitled "Contractors' All Risks Claims" includes the following:

(f) The candidates should have studied the following contract forms together with all subsequent amendments thereto:-

JCT Standard Form of Building Contract (1980)

JCT Agreement for Minor Building Works (1980)

JCT Nominated Sub-Contract (NSC/4) (1980)

JCT Non-Nominated Sub-Contract (DOM/1 (1980)

JCT Fixed Fee Form of Prime Cost Contract (1976)

JCT Intermediate Form of Building Contract for Works of Simple Content (1984 Edition)

GC/WORKS/1 — General Conditions of Government Contractors for Building and Civil Engineering Works.

GC/WORKS/2—General Conditions of Government Contracts for Building and Civil Engineering Minor Works.

ICE Conditions of Contract (Fifth Edition)

Federation of Civil Engineering Contractors Form of Sub-Contract (Blue Form, revised September, 1984).

Model Form of General Conditions of Contract recommended by The Institute of Mechanical Engineers — Home Contracts — with Erection (Model Form A)

It must be remembered that the main reason for the existence of the insurance protection of the works, etc is that requirement in the contract concerned for the employer (the person or organisation commissioning the work), contractor or sub-contractor to protect itself so far as loss or damage to the works, etc is concerned. The CAR policy, and it is usually this type of policy that is required, would be useless if it did not reflect the needs of the contract. It therefore follows that those dealing with contract works claims should be fully conversant with the terms and conditions of the contract, as well as those of the policy.

These contracts either call for, or in order to comply with the contract terms the prudent employer of contractor would require, a CAR policy. It is the intention of this book to deal with those sections of the syllabus concerned with contract works, temporary works (including any unfixed materials or other things delivered to the site for incorporation therein), constructional plant, site huts and employees' tools. As stated earlier this means that the clauses of the above contracts dealing with liability for personal injury and damage to property of third parties and those clauses requiring employers' and public liability policies are not dealt with as these aspects would overlap with the area covered by another book in this series. However, the insurance required by JCT clause 21.2.1 is considered as it covers the property of the employer which is adjacent to the works. In that respect it is a material damage policy, although basically it is a public liability policy, also it is included in the above syllabus.

While the legal cases mentioned in the text are considered therein, there is an Appendix which gives further details of some cases where it is considered that this is required. There is a chapter on the Construction Plant Hire Association's Model Conditions for the Hiring of Plant, as this is relevant to the subject of this book and this contract is also included in the above syllabus.

The international contract FIDIC has been included as it is mentioned in the Chartered Insurance Institute's proposed new examination subject "Construction Insurance" and contractors involved in overseas contracts will be interested.

Acknowledgements are made to the Independent Insurance Company Ltd and the Trinity Insurance Company Ltd for allowing their policies to be used by way of illustration or comment.

Frank Eaglestone
August 1989

CHAPTER 1

The general law of contract related to insurance

What is a contract?

A contract has been defined as "an agreement and promise enforceable at law" and to some extent this is correct, although it is necessary to warn that while a contract may exist it may not be enforceable because of some disability of one of the parties to that contract. Also, there must be two elements for a contract to be enforceable at law, namely an agreement and an obligation.

To constitute an agreement there must be an accord between two or more persons in one and the same intention, which lawyers refer to as "consensus ad idem". However, it is clear that something more than a mere agreement is required before a contract can be made enforceable at law. Agreements are being made all the time, eg a business appointment or a social engagement. Such agreements are really "arrangements" and cannot be regarded as legal contracts otherwise the default by one party might give rise to a legal action and this is not in the minds of either party.

The essence of a contract lies in the important fact that there is an intention on the part of those entering into the agreement to create a legal obligation, ie that the parties can turn to the courts, or arbitration, if the contract so provides, in the event of a breach on one side or the other.

The essential elements are:

(a) offer and acceptance resulting in a legal relationship;

(b) capacity to contract;

(c) legality;

(d) form or consideration;

(e) absence of fraud, misrepresentation, mistake, duress or undue influence.

If one of these elements is missing the contract may be:

(a) Unenforceable, which means it is valid in itself but cannot be proved in a court. This occurs when written evidence cannot be produced and which is required in some cases. For example, a contract for the deposition of an interest in land cannot be enforced except against a party who has signed it or a note or memorandum of it. Coming closer to the subject of this book, a performance bond is required to be in writing, signed and under seal to be enforceable.

(b) Void, ie having no validity and the parties have no rights there-under, as occurs in the case of contracts with infants (persons under the age of 18, more fashionably known as minors), for the sale of goods other than necessaries (such as insurance contracts) and those which are binding unless repudiated, see (c) below.

(c) Voidable, capable of being affirmed or rejected at the option of one of the parties, eg in the case of continuous contracts with infants.

The law relating to the insurance contract

An insurance contract is one where the insurer agrees in return for a consideration, called the premium, to pay to the insured a sum of money or its equivalent upon the happening of a certain event. Insurers are either insurance companies or underwriters of Lloyds of London.

There are three main principles which distinguish the formation of the contract of insurance dealt with in this book. (There are others which will be mentioned later.)

In the first place there must be present what is known as insurable interest to make the contract valid.

Secondly, the transaction must be supported by what is called "the utmost good faith".

Thirdly the contract must be one of indemnity.

What is the meaning of insurable interest?

In the case of a contract of indemnity (which will be dealt with in detail later), such as a fire policy or the contractors' all risks policy, it was stated in *Lucena v Crawfurd* (1890) that a person has an insurable interest in a thing "where he is so circumstanced with respect to it as to have benefit from its existence, or prejudice from its destruction". Insurable interest also includes the legal liability of the policyholder to pay damages.

Examples of insurable interest

(a) An insurance company in its commitments: thus it can reinsure.

(b) A contractor for the goods, works, plant and site in his or her possession.

(c) The employer of the contractor as legal owner of the site and usually by virtue of a contractual right to the goods on site.

(d) An owner of property, whether movable or otherwise.

From an indemnity aspect, to uphold an insurable interest:

(a) there must be a physical object capable of suffering loss or damages;

(b) the physical object must be stated as the subject matter of the insurance;

(c) the person named as the insured must have an interest in the subject matter, in accordance with the definition mentioned earlier.

It must be remembered that it is the insured's interest in the property which is covered and, strictly speaking, it is incorrect to say that the property is covered against loss or damage. Consequently, as it is the insured's interest that is covered, the policy is a personal contract with the insured.

When the interest ceases, no claim to indemnity can be made by another person, unless by operation of law, or by reason of an endorsement by which the personal interest has been substituted by consent of the insured and the insurers.

Difference between insurance and gambling

There is some similarity in that there is an agreement to pay a sum of money on the happening of certain events. However, the fundamental differences are as follows.

(a) The party effecting the insurance must have an interest in the subject matter, but the interest of those who participate in gambling is solely confined to the stake lost or won in the wager.

(b) In an insurance contract only the insured is immune from loss, but in a wager either party may win or lose.

(c) The occurrence of the event insured against is not in the interest of either party to the policy, since under it, the insured is only indemnified and the insurer loses, while in a gamble, the winner benefits.

(d) In an insurance contract it is clear from the inception of the contract who is immune from loss, but in a wager this is not known until the event has taken place.

(e) An insurance contract is subject to the principle of the utmost good faith but this principle does not apply to a wager.

(f) A contract of insurance is enforceable at law, but a wager is not recognised by the courts because the Gaming Act 1845 s. 18 rendered all contracts by way of gaming or wagering void.

Utmost good faith

The common law principle of entering into contracts is based on the fact that the parties contract at their peril, because the legal maxim "caveat emptor" (let the buyer beware) prevails. Thus if you sell your house you do not have to tell the buyer that the roof lets in the snow and when the thaw comes the ceilings will leak, unless you are asked. Also, while certain Acts have been passed, such as the Sale of Goods Act 1979, through which some protection is afforded to contracting parties influenced by these Acts, even this protection does not bring such contracts within the sphere of the privileged classes (there are a very few others) of which insurance is the main one, which enjoy the benefit of the principle of utmost good faith.

The principle arises from the fact that "the underwriter knows nothing and the man who asks him to insure knows everything". Hence the latter is, as a general rule, bound to declare all facts which are material to the risk. The following extract from the case of *Carter v Boehm* (1766) gives more detail.

The special facts upon which the contingent chance is to be computed lie most commonly in the knowledge of the insured only. The underwriter trusts to his representations, and proceeds upon confidence that he does not keep back any circumstances in his knowledge to mislead the underwriter into a belief that the circumstance does not exist, and to induce him to estimate the risk as if it did not exist.

The keeping back of such circumstance is a fraud, and therefore the policy is void. Although the suppression should happen through mistake, without any fraudulent intention; yet still the underwriter is deceived, and the policy is void; because the risk is really different from the risk understood and intended to be run at the time of the agreement.

The policy would be equally void, against the underwriter if he concealed: as if he insured a ship on her voyage, which he privately knew to be arrived: and an action would lie to recover the premium.

The last paragraph of this extract has been emphasised in the recent case of *La Banque Financiere de la Cite SA (formerly Banque Keyser Ullman SA) v Skandia (UK) Insurance Co and Others* (1988). In this case the facts known to the underwriter were material to the recoverability of a claim under the first policy and if disclosed would have been taken into account by a prudent insured in deciding whether to place the further insurance with the underwriter. It followed, therefore, that the underwriter had been in breach of his duty of disclosure in relation to the further contracts of insurance and the insured, on discovering the non-disclosure, would have been entitled to rescind that contract and demand a return of the premium. However, the case was primarily about whether such duty gave rise to an action in tort for damages. (In the reverse situation, ie non-disclosure by the insured, insurers have the remedy of avoidance not damages.) It was decided that the principle of utmost good faith could not, by itself, justify the awarding of damages, although it must be admitted that to rescind the contract and obtain a return of the premium does not help the insured a great deal in these cases.

Therefore, it is clear that the reason for the principle of the utmost good faith by both parties to the contract is to prevent fraud and to establish this. Full disclosure must be wedded to material facts.

A material fact is one which would influence the judgement of a prudent insurer in fixing the premium, or determining whether he or she will accept the risk. S. 18(2) of the Marine Insurance Act 1906. Certain facts have come to be recognised as being material to a risk and these are usually obvious, eg facts showing that the subject matter of the insurance is exposed to more than usual danger from the peril proposed to be insured against, or where there is a moral or physical hazard in the proposer's history or his or her approach to the insurance. However, in the case of a dispute, it is always a question for a court to decide.

Facts which need not be disclosed by the proposer

During the passage of time it has been established that the following facts need not be disclosed.

(a) Non-material facts and those which improve the risk.

(b) Facts which the insurer ought to know in the ordinary course of his or her business.

(c) Information which is waived by the insurer.

(d) Facts which ought to be deduced from the information given by the proposer.

(e) Facts common to the knowledge of the insurer, eg matters of public knowledge.

(f) Facts which should be brought to light by making the usual enquiries, apart from the information already given.

Proposal forms

Questions on proposal forms must be truthfully answered and this is emphasised by the declaration at the foot of the form. However, the duty of the utmost good faith is not necessarily discharged by the proposer who replies truthfully to all the questions on the proposal. Any other material facts which might affect the insurer's mind in considering the risk must be disclosed. This means any material facts not covered by questions on the proposals. See *Hair v Prudential Assurance Company Ltd* (1982).

The following list, which is not exhaustive, should assist in the completion of the proposal form.

(a) All questions should be answered fully and completely honestly. Although this may seem elementary, it is often not complied with. Even if questions are not applicable, this should be stated, explaining why the question does not apply unless it is obvious.

(b) All matters should be disclosed which a prudent insurer would wish to consider in deciding whether to offer cover. If in doubt the matter should be disclosed.

(c) A specimen of the policy required should be obtained. A check should be made that the exclusions and conditions are understood and are acceptable.

(d) Any special explanations required concerning the cover should be obtained in writing and the correspondence retained; similarly in the case of policy extensions.

(e) Sums insured and limits of indemnity must be adequate.

(f) A copy of the completed proposal should be kept.

Throughout the policy period:

(a) any change in risk should be notified which is basic to the cover provided, eg an extension of geographical, or the type of, activity;

(b) claims should be notified immediately. If in doubt, the circumstances concerning a possible claim should be notified;

(c) in the case of liability insurance claims, no admission, offer, promise or payment to the third party should be made and relevant correspondence should be passed to the insurer immediately.

On renewal the proposal answers should be checked and all the changes or requirements notified.

If the above points are followed, repudiation of policy liability by the insurer on the grounds of non-disclosure is unlikely.

If the proposal form is completed by an agent the position is usually governed by the case of *Newholme Bros v Road Transport and General Insurance Company* (1929) where it was decided that if the agent fills in the proposal at the request of the proposer, for that purpose he or she must be considered the agent of the proposer. Also, Scrutton LJ said:

> I have great difficulty in understanding how a man who has signed, without reading it, a document which he knows to be a proposal for insurance, and which contains statements in fact untrue, and a promise that they are true and the basis of the contract, can escape from the consequences of his negligence by saying that the person he asked to fill it up for him is the agent of the person to whom the proposal is addressed.

There are exceptions in the case of proposers who are illiterate and even
those of little education and, possibly, where the agent is more than a mere
commission agent, but ostensibly has some authority to vary the contract.
The authorities for these exceptions are *Bawden v London, Edinburgh &
Glasgow Assurance Co* (1892) and *Stone v Reliance Mutual Insurance Society*
(1972).

The duty upon the proposer to disclose material facts only applies to
the proposer before the contract or renewal is concluded. There is no duty
at common law to disclose material facts which occur during the period
of insurance. However, some policies include an alteration in risk condition which in effect extends the common law duty of disclosure
throughout the period of insurance should the risk increase. For example,
in a contractors' all risks policy such a condition would call for notification
to the insurer should any defects or conditions of working render the risk
more than usually hazardous (see *Mitchell Conveyor and Transport Co Ltd
v Pulbrook* (1933). This would not include variations of the works allowed
by a provision in the construction contract. If the insured fails to comply
with the condition then the policy is voidable at the option of the insurer
from the date of the breach.

Indemnity

On the happening of the event insured against, the insured shall not be
paid more in money than the value he or she has lost, subject to the sum
insured. In *Castellain v Preston* (1883), Brett LJ, said:

> The very foundation, in my opinion, of every rule which has been applied to
> insurance law is this, namely, that the contract of insurance contained in a
> marine and fire policy is a contract of indemnity, and of indemnity only, and
> that this contract means that the assured shall be fully indemnified, but shall
> never be more than fully indemnified.

Although an insured, under normal circumstances, is entitled to be placed
in the same financial position which he or she occupied before the
happening of the event insured against, this need not mean precisely the
same position, but only that which is reasonably possible. Whether the
damage is total or partial, and in the case of a building in course of erection
it is usually the latter, the insured is entitled to reconstruction cost in the
case of a total destruction (within the sum insured), and to the cost of
repair where a partial loss has taken place. In this way the insured will get
an indemnity but it is not always as simple as this, particularly in the case

of buildings which are some years old. In *Harbutt's Plasticine v Wayne Tank Co Ltd* (1970) Lord Denning said:

> The destruction of a building is different from the destruction of a chattel. If a secondhand car is destroyed, the owner only gets its value; because he can go into the market and get another secondhand car to replace it. He cannot charge the other party with the cost of replacing it with a new car. But, when this mill was destroyed the plaintiffs had no choice. They were bound to replace it as soon as they could, not only to keep their business going, but also to mitigate the loss of profit (for which they would be able to charge the defendants). They replaced it in the only possible way without adding any extras. I think they should be allowed the cost of replacement. True it is they got new for old, but I do not think the wrongdoer can diminish the claim on that account. If they had added extra accommodation or made extra improvements, they would have to give credit. But that is not this case.

The following points about this statement should be appreciated. In the first place, *Harbutt's* case was not an action to determine the value of an indemnity under a material damage insurance policy, but an action in negligence for damages, and the failure to allow deductions of new for old is not unusual in such actions.

However, it is well established that in providing an indemnity under an insurance policy the liability of insurers is subject to any necessary deductions for prior wear and tear. The difficulty in the case of buildings is that certain damaged items are considered to last the life of the building, eg the roof (subject to the condition of the tile nails), and some insurers may consider that no allowance should be deducted for betterment in such cases.

Secondly, in the case of the CAR policy it is very unlikely that betterment has to be considered as the goods and materials used in the erection or installation are obviously new. Nevertheless, as betterment is an important aspect in dealing with indemnity claims under material damage policies, the point had to be made.

Subrogation

The principle of subrogation is a corollary of the principle of indemnity. Subrogation is the right which the insurer has of standing in the place of the insured and availing himself or herself of all the rights and remedies of the insured, whether already enforced or not, but only up to the amount of the insurer's payment to the insured. This right of subrogation is exercisable at common law after the insurer has paid the claim, subject to a condition in the policy which may entitle the insurer to exercise the right before the payment is made.

In the construction industry it is sometimes the practice to insure many of the parties involved in the construction project as "joint insureds" under the one policy. In this event the principle of subrogation cannot operate to allow the insurer, after paying one insured, to recover from a joint insured. See *Petrofina (UK) Ltd v Magnaload* (1983) in Appendix 4.

Another point insurers, contemplating the right of subrogation, should consider is the decision in *MH Smith (Plant Hire) v DL Mainwaring (t/as Inshore)* (1986). From this case it is clear that insurers should consider whether their insureds are likely to remain solvent before suing a third party in their insured's name. In this case the insurer's recovery action failed as the insured had ceased to exist when the action was taken in the insured's name, as a non-existent party could not be a party to an action.

It seems from this case that there are steps the insurers can take to protect themselves against this situation. They could include a conditional assignment in the proposal declaration, or better still in the declaration on the claim form, thus obtaining the insured's signature to the assignment. Alternatively, if it was known that the insured was going into liquidation, a separate document of assignment could be obtained. Unfortunately, the insured's fate would probably not be known until it was too late, as in *Smith's* case.

The final choice, suggested in the judgement of *Smith's* case, is to make use of s. 651 of the Companies Act. Under this section the court may at any time within two years of the date of the dissolution of the company, on an application made for the purpose by the liquidator of the company or by any other interested person, make an order, on such terms as the court thinks fit, declaring the dissolution to have been void. Thereupon, such proceedings may be taken as might have been taken if the company had not been dissolved.

Contribution

Like subrogation this principle is a corollary of the principle of indemnity, but it only applies between insurers. It is the right of an insurer who has paid under a policy to call upon other insurers equally or otherwise liable for the same loss to contribute to the payment. Before the principle can be applied, the insurances called into contribution must cover:

(a) the same interest;

(b) the same subject matter;

(c) against the same peril, and

(d) the policies must be legally enforceable, as a policy which is not legally binding cannot give rise to a claim for contribution.

Contribution will not operate if one policy clearly states that it only applies after any other double insurances (other insurances complying with the rules above) have been exhausted, and provided the other insurance(s) does (do) not contain the same wording. In practice, policies usually contain a non-contribution condition of some kind, but some are more strictly worded than others, as already indicated. See the New Zealand Court of Appeal case of *State Fire Insurance General Manager v Liverpool and London and Globe Insurance Co Ltd* (1952).

It must be appreciated that the omission of a contribution condition in the policy does not destroy the doctrine. A contribution condition merely precludes an insured from selecting any insurer to indemnify him or her and thus leaving that insurer to collect rateable proportions from his or her co-insurers. Consequently it compels the insured to claim from each insurer the rateable proportion due to him or her in order to obtain an indemnity.

The statements made above have been verified in the Scottish appeal case of *Steelclad Ltd v Iron Trades Mutual Insurance Co Ltd* (1984). However, the interesting part of that case was the court's view of the words in the contribution condition of the policy of the defender which refers to loss or damage insured by any other policy *"effected by the insured . . . on his behalf"* when the defender would not be liable except in respect of any excess beyond the amount payable under such other policy. The pursuer was the insured under the Iron Trades policy and was a subcontractor on a project policy covering the employer, all contractors and all sub-contractors. The contribution clause in that policy was worded exactly the same as the Iron Trades policy except for the phrase mentioned above in quotes. The court considered the project policy was not a policy effected by the insured *on his behalf*. Because the phrase was ambiguous, it was construed *contra proferentum* against the insurer who had refused to contribute. The project policy insurer had already paid almost half of the claim. The court did not have to go any further, having come to a decision on this wording. However, they did in effect say that even without this phrase or if the project policy had been effected on the pursuer's behalf, they *would still not allow the two policy conditions to cancel the cover given* (by ignoring in each case the condition which was worded exactly the same way in the other policy), with the result that if the loss is covered elsewhere, it is covered nowhere.

The correct decision, and surely the intention, is that each policy should contribute subject always to a rateable proportion condition. Basically, an insured must get an indemnity whether he or she insures once or twice the same subject matter against the same peril, subject always to the other terms and conditions of the policy or policies. It is rather strange that the matter should ever have been in doubt.

The insurance contract

An insurance contract is formed when one party has made an offer and the other party has accepted it, both parties being in agreement as to the terms.

The contract is normally contained in a policy. This document is evidence of the contract which has usually come into existence before the policy is issued. Policies vary with different classes of insurance, and those dealt with in this book can be divided into the following sections.

(a) Recital clause, which refers to a schedule for details (see below). This clause also refers to the proposal form and its declaration as being the basis of the contract. However one qualifies "the event", it must be uncertain.

(b) Operative clause, which describes the cover which is the subject matter of the insurance.

(c) Exceptions which help to describe the cover by stating what is excluded.

(d) Signature clause on behalf of the insurer.

(e) Schedule, which contains the names of the parties, the address of the insured, the period of insurance, possibly the business of the insured, the sums insured or limit(s) of indemnity (in liability insurance), and the premium payable.

(f) Conditions, which limit the insured's legal rights, stipulate the various things the insured may or may not do and sometimes express or amend the common law or indicate an agreed state of affairs. It is usual to classify conditions (whether expressed or implied) as:

(i)   conditions precedent to the policy, eg all material facts must be disclosed during negotiations preceding the insurance contract;

(ii) conditions subsequent of the policy, eg notice by the insured of a change of risk during the period of the policy;

(iii) conditions precedent to liability, eg the notice of loss by the insured.

The following is the result of this classification:

(a) conditions precedent to the policy must be observed for the insurance to be valid from the beginning;

(b) conditions subsequent of the policy refer to matters arising after the contract has been completed and affect the validity of the policy from the date of breach of the condition;

(c) conditions precedent to liability only affect the claim which the breach of the condition concerns, the policy remaining in force.

A condition by which the insured undertakes that some particular things will be done or not done or that a state of affairs exists or shall continue to exist is referred to as a warranty or a continuing warranty. Breach of such condition will probably allow the insurer to repudiate liability, as a warranty must be complied with strictly and literally.

Occasionally a so-called condition in the policy has been held to be a mere stipulation. Thus it has been stated that the condition in the employers' and public liability policies requiring the insured to keep a proper wages book in order to return his or her annual wage roll on which the premium is based is a mere stipulation, a breach of which results in the insurer possibly obtaining damages as compensation but not allowing him or her to repudiate policy liability.

There is a general rule of evidence (among many) concerning the interpretation of the insurance policy, which occasionally arises. It is called the *contra proferentum* rule and states that in the event of ambiguity a document will be construed strictly against the party who has drawn it up. Thus the interpretation less favourable to the insurer will be taken.

From what has been said under the last few headings concerning non-disclosure and breach of warranty, it will be appreciated that insurance law is tilted in favour of the insurer. However, the Law Commission's Working Paper No 73 entitled *Insurance Law, Non-disclosure and Breach of Warranty* recommended reforms to improve the insured's position. This was followed by a Final Report on the same subject and on the same lines, with a draft Insurance Law Reform Bill annexed. This report is dated October 1980 and the matter has not been pursued since.

However, British insurers endeavour to behave reasonably and in 1977 they agreed to the publication of statements of their practice (all to the advantage of the insured), but this applied to insurances effected by individuals resident in the United Kingdom but insured in their private capacity only. Nevertheless, this tends to "rub off " onto the practice of other kinds of insurance such as those required in the construction industry.

It has often been considered a material fact that a proposer has been convicted of a criminal offence and thus non-disclosure thereof invalidates the insurance. This is because the non-disclosure either directly concerns the risks insured or it shows a degree of dishonesty making a prudent insurer reluctant to give cover on normal terms, or at all.

Now the main purpose of the Rehabilitation of Offenders Act 1974 is to rehabilitate offenders who have not been reconvicted of any serious offence for a number of years and prima facie entitles such persons to deny the existence of certain convictions. This Act does not apply to sentences of imprisonment of more than two and a half years. Where the Act applies, there is a rehabilitation period after which the conviction is considered spent and s. 4 of the Act provides that a spent conviction is to be treated for all purposes in law as though it had never happened. Therefore, a proposer whose conviction is spent need not disclose it to the insurer concerned. Furthermore, the publisher of a spent conviction could be liable in a defamation action if the publication was made with malice. See s. 4 of the 1977 Act and *Herbage v Pressdam* (1984). Thus many insurers refuse to disclose spent convictions within their knowledge to third parties.

Introduction to standard forms of contract

The law of the United Kingdom provides that parties are usually free to choose their own terms. In practice parties tend to use a standard form of contract because they have not the desire or ability to draft their own. Also, if certain provisions are not stated implied terms, imposed by statute, could operate and drafting one's own terms can result in uncertainty and disputes. In any event, responsibility for the works under a contract usually calls for a CAR policy.

Sometimes, particularly in the construction industry, standard conditions are imposed by the employer who is having the work done, so there is no choice for the contractor. These conditions often place responsibility for the works on the contractor as well as a requirement to insure them. The works are usually set out in drawings and a bill of quantities or a specification. The use of standard forms is partly due to the impossibility of writing new conditions for each contract and the fact that the courts have interpreted the more ambiguous clauses of the more common forms, such as the JCT (Joint Contracts Tribunal for the Standard Form of Building Contract) and ICE (Institution of Civil Engineers Conditions) contracts, so their meaning is no longer in doubt. Furthermore, the wording of these contracts is normally agreed by the representative bodies of both parties to the contract which is a better situation than in a unilateral agreement drawn up by the employer alone, whose sole aim is to protect his or her own interests. This can be seen in some of the motor manufacturers' building and engineering contracts as exemplified in the case of *Smith v South Wales Switchgear* (1978).

While a standard contract can be altered by the parties to it to suit their requirements, the difficulty of such an approach is that the alteration of one clause involves making alterations to others on which the first clause depends, and this may be difficult to agree. To some extent this explains why it takes such a long time for the representative bodies to agree how an ambiguity or controversy should be resolved. This was seen in the alteration to the JCT form changing the required insurance cover for the works in 1986 from a fire and special perils insurance to an all risks insurance. Failure to make all the necessary alterations throughout a contract can produce ambiguities.

Reference should be made to Chapters 4 to 12 which deal with certain provisions relevant to the subject of this book, in standard contracts used by the construction industry.

The parties to construction contracts

Main construction contracts concern two parties: the employer (the person or organisation commissioning the work) and the contractor. The contract work involves many parties. Some of these parties are appointed by the contractor and others by the employer. Thus the employer appoints an architect and/or consulting engineer, who, *inter alia*, nominates sub-contractors. The contractor employs domestic subcontractors to assist in completing the work.

Subcontract forms govern the subcontract work but often the liability and insurance clauses in the subcontract forms follow fairly closely the wording used in the main contract, except that "contractor" takes the place of "employer" and "subcontractor" replaces "contractor". At least in the JCT contracts this is so. Also, under the JCT subcontract forms NSC/4 and DOM/1, by various tendering procedures the subcontractor effectively enters into a contract with the employer for certain purposes.

By the JCT 1986 amendment of the 1980 main contract, clause 22(3), concerning responsibility for the works, provides for any nominated subcontractor to be regarded as an insured under the joint names policy, or to include a waiver of subrogation rights against any subcontractor in respect of the relevant perils.

Both the contractor and the subcontractor may hire plant in order to carry out the contract and this means that these parties have to enter into a hire contract, which is usually the Model Conditions for the Hiring of Plant issued by the Contractors' Plant Hire Association.

Exclusion, indemnity and limitation clauses

Exclusion and indemnity clauses are not easily accepted by the courts, thus the construction of these clauses is all important. If they are poorly drafted they will be construed against the drafters. One of the most recent examples of this occurred in *Smith v South Wales Switchgear* (1978), where an indemnity against "any liability whatsoever in respect of personal injury" . . . "of any person whomsoever" was considered not to include negligence, as the word "negligence", or a synonym for it, was required to include negligence.

An exclusion clause means any term in a contract restricting, excluding or modifying a liability arising out of breach of a contractual obligation. The use of these clauses is limited by the Unfair Contract Terms Act 1977 (see Appendix 2).

An indemnity clause exists where one party to the contract stipulates that the party with whom he or she is in contract should indemnify him or her in respect of loss or damage he or she sustains. An example is the building contract where the contractor usually has to indemnify the employer in respect of injury or damage.

In the case of a limitation clause one party to the contract limits his or her liability to an agreed amount. For example, in the *Harbutt's Plasticine* case, mentioned earlier, the agreed amount was the value of the contract itself.

General practice concerning the insurance contract

(a) Unless the construction contract concerns minor works the insurers require all details including plans.

(b) The insurer may wish to insist upon safety aspects, and in order to consider the risk may require a survey and periodical reports. Sometimes the broker concerned will carry out these tasks.

The position of the insurance broker

The placing of insurances for the construction industry is a specialised business and only specialised brokers should be consulted.

The responsibility of the broker for insurers' repudiations based on the completion of proposal forms for insurance by a broker, has to some extent already been discussed when considering the cases of *Newsholme Bros* and *Bawden* earlier in this chapter.

As regards any recovery action against the broker in the above circumstances, success from the insured's point of view will depend on whether the broker provided the incorrect (or failed to provide full) details, which only he or she knew, or, whether when the insured signed the proposal he or she failed to read the answers and check them for correctness, assuming he or she had the information to do so. Thus in *O'Connor v BDB Kirby & Co and Another* (1972) a question on the proposal was incorrectly answered and a policy was issued on the basis that the insured vehicle was kept in a locked garage at night, although it was not. The broker handed the proposal form back to the insured for checking; the insured merely glanced at it, but did not spot the error and signed it. When a claim occurred and was repudiated on the above grounds the insured failed in his action of recovery against the broker.

On the other hand in *Dunbar v A & B Painters Ltd and Economic Insurance Co and Whitehouse & Co* (1986) the insured were not aware of the higher premium required by the then holding insurers, and at the time of signing the proposal form would not know (and rightly left to the brokers) details of the estimated cost of outstanding claims. The fact that the insurers were entitled to repudiate flowed directly from the conduct of the brokers, so the insured were able to recover their outlay, in respect of this employers' liability claim, from the brokers.

CHAPTER 2

The contractors' all risks policy

The material damage cover (the contractors' all risks cover) is set out in section 3 of a contractors' policy which is printed in full in Appendix 1, but this is a combined policy which also includes in section 1 employers' liability, and in section 2 public liability cover, as well as section 4 entitled "21.2.1" (a clause of the JCT contract) cover. The employers' and public liability covers will not be considered as these go beyond the scope of this book as set out in the preface, but the clause 21.2.1 cover will be dealt with in another chapter. However, the whole contractors' policy is included in Appendix 1 in order to show how the various sections of the policy are considered by those parts of the policy which apply to more than one section, ie the parts entitled "Definitions", "Extensions", "General Exceptions", "Conditions of the Policy", "Endorsements" and the "Schedule".

Taking the recital clause, section 3 of the policy, and the appropriate parts by clauses in the order in which they appear in the document, the following comments are relevant. Note that a reference to "the CAR policy" in this book refers only to the parts just mentioned of the contractors' policy all of which is set out in Appendix 1, unless otherwise stated.

Recital clause

In consideration of the payment of the premium the Independent Insurance Company Ltd (the Company) will indemnify the Insured in the terms of the Policy against the events set out in the Sections operative (specified in the Schedule) and occurring in connection with the Business during the Period of Insurance or any subsequent period for which the Company agrees to accept payment of premium.

The Proposal made by the Insured is the basis of and forms part of this Policy.

The premium is the consideration for which the insurers issue the policy.

The insured, business, premium and period of insurance are all set out in the policy schedule (see Appendix 1).

"Proposal" appears in the "Definitions" section as follows:

Proposal shall mean any information provided by the Insured in connection with this insurance and any declaration made in connection therewith.

Absolute accuracy of the answers on the proposal form is required as it is made the basis of the contract and legally the slightest inaccuracy will entitle the insurers to avoid liability. Whether they do so is another matter and if the incorrect answer is not material to the risk, the fact that the insurer is unlikely to take the point is irrelevant to the insurer's right to do so. See Chapter 1 under the heading "Proposal Forms".

Damage to the works

In the event of Damage to the property Insured the Company will by payment or at its option by repair reinstatement or replacement indemnify the Insured against such Damage

Provided that
1. The Company shall not indemnify the Insured in any one Period of Insurance for any amount exceeding the Limit of Indemnity in respect of each item of Property Insured

2. the Property belongs to or is the responsibility of the Insured

3. the Property is
    a) on or adjacent to the site of the Contract Works or
    b) being carried by road rail or inland waterway to or from the site of the Contract Works
    within the Territorial Limits.

This is the insuring or operative clause which indicates the cover given.

In the even of damage to the property insured

Under the heading "Definitions" damage includes loss and property means material property.

The property insured appears in the schedule of the policy as follows:

Item 1 — Contract Works

Item 2 — Constructional Plant Tools and Equipment owned by the Insured.

Item 3 — Temporary Buildings and Site Huts (including fixtures and fittings therein)

Item 4 — Hired – in Property described in Items 2 and 3 not exceeding £....... any one item.

Item 5 — Personal Effects and Tools of the Insureds Employees not exceeding £....... any one Employee.

The policy defines contract works as follows:

Contract Works means the temporary or permanent works executed in course of executing by or on behalf of the Insured in the development of any building or site or the performance of any contract including materials supplied by reason of the contract and other materials for use in connection therewith.

The Company will ------------indemnify

The alternative methods of indemnity to a payment, ie repair, reinstatement or replacement, will in practice be a payment to the insured for the cost of repairing or replacing the damage to the insured property.

The insured

To comply with most construction contracts the insured will be the employer and the main contractor although other parties such as subcontractors may be included as the insured in the schedule of the policy. However the prudent contractor will insure his or her property including the works even when not required to do so by contract conditions. Further, the "all risks" cover could well be more extensive than the perils required to be insured by contract.

Against such damage

Damage is defined as including loss, and all forms of loss or damage are covered subject to the policy exceptions and conditions (see later).

Proviso 1

Clearly the intention here is to limit the maximum amount payable in respect of each item of property to the amount stated in the schedule in each period of insurance which is also stated in the schedule.

Proviso 2

Obviously all the property listed in the items 1 to 5 of the schedule either belongs to or is the responsibility of the insured under the construction contract otherwise there would be a lack of insurable interest and the property concerned could not be insured by those named as insured in the policy schedule.

Proviso 3

Unlike proviso 2 it is not so obvious that all the property listed in the items 1 to 5 is either on or adjacent to the site of the contract works or is being carried by road, rail or inland waterway to or from the site of the contract works within the territorial limits. Some materials or goods might be stored off site and it will be seen later that if they have been certified for payment under the contract terms the indemnity provided by the policy is extended to apply to such goods or materials as being intended for incorporation in the contract works.

The territorial limits are defined in the policy as follows:

Territorial Limits shall mean
(a) Great Britain Northern Ireland the Isle of Man the Channel Islands or off shore installations within the continental shelf around those countries
(b) member countries of the European Economic Community where the Insured or directors partners or Employees of the Insured who are ordinarily resident in (a) above are temporarily engaged on the business of the Insured
(c) elsewhere in the world where the Insured or directors partners or Employees of the Insured who are ordinarily resident in (a) above are on a temporary visit for the purpose of non-manual work on the Business of the Insured.

Transit anywhere within the territorial limits of the policy is covered. It should be noted that transit by sea or air is not included, because of the heavier risks involved, which in turn call for specialised underwriting considerations.

It is difficult to visualise how paragraphs (b) or (c) can apply to a CAR policy other than possibly to the personal effects and tools of an employee travelling abroad on business for the insured. In fact, as the definition of territorial limits applies to the whole of the contractors' policy no doubt the insurers' intention is to apply these paragraphs to the employers' and public liability sections of this policy. If the insured does not send employees overseas these paragraphs do not apply.

Additional covers

1. Professional fees

The Company will indemnify the Insured for architects' surveyors' consulting engineers and other professional fees necessarily incurred in the repair reinstatement or replacement of Damage to the Property Insured to which the indemnity provided by this Section applies

Provided that
(a) such fees shall not exceed that authorised under the scales of the appropriate professional body or institute regulating such charges
(b) the company shall not indemnify the Insured against any fees incurred by the Insured in preparing or contending any claim.

It is important that the limit of indemnity (sum insured) estimated by the insured for the contract works, including temporary works, should make provision for these fees. Some construction contracts such as clause 22 of the JCT 1980 contract and clause 21 of the ICE conditions require this risk to be covered by the contractors' all risks policy.

Proviso (a) is self-explanatory and proviso (b) emphasises the fact that insurers are not going to pay to assist the insured by financing claims against themselves.

The words "professional fees necessarily incurred in the repair reinstatement or replacement of Damage to the Property Insured" emphasise that the cost of a site investigation will be claimable under the policy if it is related to the repair reinstatement or replacement of damage to the property insured to which the indemnity provided by the policy applies.

Sometimes professional fees are duplicated. Thus a surveyor or architect dealing with the repair of subsidence damage involving the employment of a consulting engineer to advise on, and prepare a scheme for, underpinning, can result in the architect or surveyor submitting the full professional scale fee on all the work, in addition to the engineer's fees, as if the latter had not been appointed. In the first place if additional work, over and above the repair reinstatement or replacement of the original work, is necessary, the cost of such additional work and fees connected with it are not covered by the policy. The policy does not cover defective or incorrect workmanship, design or specification, or materials or goods installed, erected or intended for incorporation in the contract works. See exception 1 later in this chapter.

Secondly, even if the work does only involve the repair reinstatement or replacement of existing work and the surveyor or architect does not perform the complete duties specified in the RICS or RIBA scales of professional charges, because the engineer does some of the work, the surveyor or architect is not entitled to the complete percentage scale fee.

The onus of proof is on the insured that the costs relate to the repair, reinstatement or replacement of damage to the property insured as these words come from the operative clause of the policy. They must provide evidence which will mean incurring costs. However, if they employ a claim maker or adviser, such as an assessor, the fees will not be covered. See proviso (b).

2. Debris removal

The Limit of Indemnity provided in respect of Item 1 of the Property Insured shall include the cost and expenses necessarily incurred by the Insured with the consent of the Company in

a) removing and disposing of debris from or adjacent to the site of the Contract Works
b) dismantling or demolishing
c) shoring up or propping
d) cleaning or clearing of drains mains services gullies manholes and the like within the site of the Contract Works

consequent upon Damage for which indemnity is provided by this Section

Provided that the Company shall not be liable in respect of seepage pollution or contamination of any Property not insured by this Section.

The reason for the existence of "debris removal" cover is to allow the insured to recover costs that would otherwise have been outside the protection of the CAR policy. If debris removal is not covered difficulties can arise as to what is an act of debris removal and what is an act of repair. See Chapter 3 under "Debris removal".

The expense of removing debris can be very high. There is not only the possibility of rubble from a collapsed building but debris spread over the

site following a storm. This rubble and debris cannot be dumped anywhere but may have to be transported to a suitable and permitted place.
Note that the insurers' permission for such expense to be incurred must
be obtained and it is important to include a sum within item 1 of the
schedule (contract works) to cater for such costs.

This cover includes both dismantling and demolishing, shoring and
propping up as well as cleaning or clearing of drains and the like, the cost
of which can be considerable in the case of flooding of the site. In any event
shoring or propping done in order to minimise damage to the works, etc
would be covered and would not need the permission of insurers. The
proviso is understandable and merely emphasises that this policy is a
material damage one and does not cover third party property or even the
insured's extraneous property not within the definition of, and listed as
insured property in the schedule.

3. *Off-site storage*

> The indemnity provided by this Section extends to apply to materials or goods
> whilst not on the site of the Contract Works but intended for incorporation
> therein where the Insured is responsible under contract conditions provided
> that the value of such materials and goods has been included in an interim
> certificate and they are separately stored and identified as being designated for
> incorporation in the Contract Works.

The important point about this cover is that apart from the value to the
contractor no CAR policy should be accepted by an architect or engineer
on behalf of a client (the employer) without this cover being given in some
shape or form, as the JCT 1980 contract requires it under clauses 16 and
30.3 (see below) and the ICE conditions under clause 54. The above clauses
of the JCT contract provide as follows:

Clause 16 Materials and goods unfixed or off-site

16.1   Unfixed materials and goods delivered to, placed on or adjacent to
        the Works and intended therefor shall not be removed except for use
        upon the Works unless the Architect has consented in writing to such
        removal which consent shall not be unreasonable withheld. Where
        the value of any such materials or goods has in accordance with
        clause 30-2 been included in any Interim Certificate under which the
        amount properly due to the Contractor has been paid by the
        Employer, such materials and goods shall become the property of the
        Employer, but, subject to clause 22B or 22C (if applicable), the

Contractor shall remain responsible for loss or damage to the same.

16.2   Where the value of any materials or goods intended for the Works
         and stored off-site has in accordance with clause 30-3 been included
         in any Interim Certificate under which the amount properly due to
         the Contractor has been paid by the Employer, such materials and
         goods stored shall become the property of the Employer and there-
         after the Contractor shall not, except for use upon the Works, remove
         or cause or permit the same to be moved or removed from the
         premises where they are, but the Contractor shall nevertheless be
         responsible for any loss thereof or damage thereto and for the cost of
         storage, handling and insurance of the same until such time as they
         are delivered to and placed on or adjacent to the Works whereupon
         the provisions of clause 16-1 (except the words "Where the value" to
         the words "the property of the Employer, but") shall apply thereto.

Clause 30 Certificates and Payments Off-site materials or goods

30.3   The amount stated as due in an Interim Certificate may in the
         discretion of the Architect include the value of any materials or goods
         before delivery thereof to or adjacent to the Works (in clause 30-3
         referred to as 'the materials') provided that:

30.3   .9 the Contractor provides the Architect with reasonable proof that
         the materials are insured against loss or damage for their full value
         under a policy of insurance protecting the interests of the
         Employer and the Contractor in respect of the specific Perils,
         during the period commencing with the transfer of property in
         the materials to the Contractor until they are delivered to, or
         adjacent to, the Works.

4. Final contract price

This term is probably better known as an escalation clause. It reads:

> In the event of an increase occurring to the original price the Limit of Indemnity
> in respect of Item 1 of the Property Insured shall be increased proportionately
> by an amount not exceeding 20%.

In this way the insurers have built into the policy a 20% inflation factor
but this does not protect the contractor and employer from the necessity
to ensure that the limit of indemnity (or sum insured) is always adequate,
ie of a sufficient sum to cover the cost of repairing any damage which may
occur plus debris removal costs and professional fees. Incidentally it is

usual to use the term "limit of indemnity" to apply to the policy limit in liability policies and the term "sum insured" is used in the case of material damage policies to indicate a policy limit.

5. Tools, plant, equipment and temporary buildings

The wording of this clause reads:

> The Limit of Indemnity in respect of Items 2, 3 and 5 of the Property Insured is subject to average and if at the time of any Damage the total value of such Item of the Property Insured is of greater value than the Limit of Indemnity the Insured shall be considered as being his own insurer for the difference and shall bear a rateable share of the loss accordingly.

Incidentally, this clause would read more correctly if the letters, "ie" were substituted for the word "and" in the second line. Average only applies to items 2, 3 and 5 of the property insured as listed in the policy schedule. Once average is applied all claims are affected if the limit of indemnity (sum insured) is inadequate as the claim is scaled down in proportion to the amount the sum insured bears to the full value at risk. Thus, if property worth £40,000 is only insured for £30,000 the insured is under-insured and the amount payable under the policy is calculated as follows:

$$\frac{\text{Sum insured £30,000}}{\text{Value at risk £40,000}} \times \text{Loss sustained}$$

6. Speculative housebuilding

> The insurance in respect of Item 1 of the Property Insured shall notwithstanding Exception 4(b) for private dwelling houses flats and maisonettes constructed by the Insured for the purpose of sale continue for a period up to 180 days beyond the date of practical completion pending completion of sale.

> Practical completion shall mean when the erection and finishing of the private dwelling house are complete apart from any choice of decoration fixtures and fittings which are left to be at the option of the purchaser.

The reason for this additional cover is to protect the insured contractor between the completion of the construction work (in accordance with the second paragraph above) and the sale of the premises to a purchaser, for a period of about six months beyond the date of such completion. This is a useful addition which is not usually included in the basic cover of a CAR policy. It is especially useful in relation to theft and malicious damage.

7. Local authorities

This clause reads:

The Indemnity provided by this Section shall include any additional cost of reinstatement consequent upon Damage to the Property Insured which is incurred solely because of the need to comply with building or other regulations made under statutory authority or with bye-laws of any Municipal or Local Authority.

Provided that
1. the Company shall not indemnify the Insured against the cost of complying with such regulations or bye-laws

    (a) in respect of Damage which is not insured by this Section
    (b) if notice has been served on the Insured by the appropriate authority prior to the occurrence of such Damage
    (c) in respect of any part of the Insured Property which is undamaged other than the foundations of that part which is the subject of Damage.

2. the Company shall not indemnify the Insured against any rate tax duty development or other charge or assessment arising out of capital appreciation which may be payable in respect of the property by its owner by reason of compliance with such regulations or bye-laws

3. reinstatement is commenced and carried out with reasonable despatch.

Local authorities have their own bye-laws which allow them to require the owners of property to reinstate damage or destroyed buildings in a way which is acceptable to them. This clause (often included in fire policies as an extension) covers the extra cost incurred by the insured in complying with these requirements. The wording emphasises that the insured cannot claim for the extra cost of improvements *he or she decides* to carry out whilst the reinstatement of the damage is being done nor even for changes which are recommended by the authorities. Only when the insured has no alternative but to have the addition or different work done because of the local authority's requirements, which has the legal power to enforce such requirements, does the clause impose liability on the insurers to pay for this extra expense incurred by the insured.

In the event of this clause being involved in a claim the insurer will obtain confirmation from the authority of the date on which the insured was informed that the extra cost was to be incurred. If this date was prior to the occurrence of the damage resulting in the claim the extra expense is not recoverable from the insurers, even though the notice did not require any alteration or addition to be carried out before the date of the damage. This extra cost and cover is still subject to the limit of indemnity.

The remaining exclusions are self-explanatory.

8. *Immobilised plant*

The indemnity provided in respect of Items 2 and 4 of the Property Insured shall include the cost of recovery or withdrawal of unintentionally immobilised constructional plant or equipment provided that such recovery is not necessitated solely by reason of electrical or mechanical breakdown or derangement.

This clause draws attention to the fact that although plant may be covered under items 2 and 4 in the schedule there is an exception 3 (see later under the heading "Exceptions") which excludes damage to plant, tools or equipment due to its own explosion, breakdown or derangement. However, whereas the exception 3 wording only applies to the part responsible and does not extend to other parts of the plant, tools or equipment which sustain direct accidental damage therefrom, this clause excludes the whole of the plant, tools and equipment (including hired-in plant, etc) immobilised solely by reason of electrical or mechanical breakdown or derangement.

9. *Free materials*

Property for which the Insured is responsible shall include all free materials supplied by or on behalf of the Employer (named in the contract or agreement entered into by the Insured).

Provided that the total value of all such materials shall be included in the Limit of Indemnity for Item 1 of the Property Insured and also included in the declaration made to the Company under Condition 2.

As under the majority of construction contracts involving a standard form the employer would be included as an insured in the policy schedule; this wording is again merely for emphasis. However, the proviso should prevent the value of such materials being overlooked when deciding the limit of indemnity for item 1 of the property insured in the policy schedule. The insured must insure the property for its full value (under the JCT form for its reinstatement value).

Condition 2 is a premium adjustment condition when the premium is based on estimates. Consequently it is important to include the value of free materials in making the return at the end of the policy period as required by this condition.

Exceptions

The Company shall not indemnify the Insured against

Exception 1

the cost and expenses of replacing or making good any of the Property Insured which is in a defective condition due to faulty defective or incorrect

(a) workmanship
(b) design or specification
(c) materials goods or other property installed erected or intended for incorporation in the Contract Works

but this exclusion shall not apply to accidental Damage which occurs as a direct consequence to the remainder of the Property Insured which is free of such defective condition.

This exception concerns in (a) and (c) defective workmanship and materials which insurers consider to be a trade risk. Consequently they will not pay for the expense of remedying, repairing, or making good defective materials or workmanship. This policy does not cover the insured's competency in this respect. However, the exclusion is qualified making it clear that consequential damage to the remainder of the property insured is covered as the latter damage is free of such defective condition. Nevertheless difficulties can arise as it is not always possible to indicate what is and what is not a defective part, and what cost should be excluded.

The meaning of part (b) is clear, namely to exclude the professional negligence risk as the professionals concerned should carry this risk and they should insure accordingly. If this part of the exclusion did not carry the later qualification (as some policies do) it would dispose of most difficulties but with the qualification which excludes only the defective part there can be controversy in identifying the part which is defectively designed. For example defective piling can result in a complete rebuild.

The JCT contract, by clause 22.2 in the 1986 amendment, sets out the meaning of "all risks insurance" in that contract and the same type of exclusion reads as follows:

> any work executed or any Site Materials lost or damaged as a result of its own defect in design plan, specification, materials or workmanship or any other work executed which is lost or damaged in consequence thereof where such work relied for its support or stability on such work which was defective.

Now this exclusion is wider than the exception under discussion as it excludes "work [which] relied for its support or stability on such work which was defective" as well as excluding the defective part. So if a beam supporting a ceiling is held up by a defective bolt and the beam collapses because of the defective bolt and the beam falls through the two floors underneath, there is damage to the bolt, to the beam and to the floors (all part of the contract works). The exception under discussion, as it only excludes the defective part, would only exclude the bolt, but the JCT exclusion would exclude the bolt and the beam as the latter relied for its support on the defective bolt.

This indicates that the policy exception under discussion would only exclude work which is not of much value to remedy, ie the bolt, whereas the JCT form would exclude both the cost of the beam replacement as well as the bolt which is more expensive. Neither exception would exclude the damage to the floors below, which would be the major expense involved.

The Canadian case of *Pentagon Construction (1969) Co Ltd v United States Fidelity and Guarantee Co* (1978) illustrates the difficulties in differentiating between defective workmanship and defective design, although that case did not concern the limited cover given by United Kingdom insurers for defective material or workmanship. The interpretation of the following wording was considered.

> This insurance does not cover:
>
> (a) Loss or damage caused by:
>   (i)   faulty or improper material or
>   (ii)   faulty or improper workmanship or
>   (iii) faulty or improper design.

In this case Pentagon was a building contractor engaged to construct a sewage treatment plant which included a concrete tank. The plans and specifications required a number of steel struts to be laid across the top of the tank with each end welded to a plate let into the concrete wall beneath it. The purposes of the struts were to strengthen the tank by holding the sides together and to hang equipment from them. The contract required Pentagon to test the tank. Pentagon insured the work under a contractors' all risks policy.

After the concrete work of the tank was completed and the struts laid across the tank, but before the end of the struts had been welded, the tank was tested by filling with water. The tank bulged and a claim was lodged under the policy and repudiated by the insurers who relied on the above exclusion.

At the court of first instance it was held that the design of the tank was not faulty or improper and there was no faulty or improper workmanship. The insurers appealed, and argued that the word "design" included the plans and specifications and that they were faulty in that they omitted to state that the tank should not be tested until after the struts had been welded.

All three judges in the appeal court decided that as the evidence clearly established that the wall of the tank failed because of the failure to weld the steel struts to the top of each side of the wall before testing; this amounted to improper workmanship. This led one judge to decide it was unnecessary for him to consider the question of faulty or improper design. The other two judges reached different opinions on the meaning of "design".

The conclusions to be drawn from this case are that:

(a) Workmanship is not limited to the work or result produced by a worker. It includes the combination or conglomeration of all the skills necessary to complete the contract, including, in this case, the particular sequence necessary to achieve the performance of the contract. Failure to follow that sequence could constitute faulty or improper workmanship and in this case did so.

(b) It is not known whether:

(i) detailed instructions on the plans and specifications on how the work of construction is to be carried out are not part of the design, which was one judge's view (he added that if he were wrong he did not think it was necessary for the plans and specifications to warn that the tank should not be filled with water before the struts were welded); or

(ii)   design includes the drawings and specifications, which was
       the other judge's view.

Thus on the meaning of "design", with the third judge abstaining, the case
is unsatisfactory.

Defective workmanship is a contract hazard normally accepted by
contractors. The cost of doing such work twice is not properly a matter
for insurers (but the cost of rebuilding other parts of the insured property
is), and if the use of defective materials is not due to the negligence of the
contractor, he or she will probably have a remedy against the suppliers.

Nothing is said in the policy about the cost of dismantling or exposure
work necessary to get at a defective part. It is arguable both ways, ie it is
part of the cost of rectifying the property excluded by the policy or it is
part of the insured property not excluded. The same position can arise
when a limited form of design cover is given, ie who pays for the cost of
getting at the defectively design part? In practice, an insurer may be
prepared to pay for half of such costs on the grounds that a court might
hold that it is an ambiguous matter, and therefore decide against the
insurer *contra proferentum*. See Chapter 1 under "The insurance contract".

Some policies will exclude "intentional damage". None will pay if no
damage occurs at all but purely a defect comes to light.

A case on the meaning of "faulty design" as used in the exclusion to
this policy is *Queensland Government Railways and Another v Manufacturers'
Mutual Insurance Ltd* (1969). A railway bridge in Australia was being
constructed by Electric Power Transmission Pty Ltd for QGR (railway
authority) to replace the bridge built in 1897 which had been swept away
by flood waters. Prismatic piers (similar to the original piers, but streng-
thened) were being erected when they were overturned by flood waters
after exceptionally heavy rains. EPT and QGR claimed to be indemnified
by the insurers under a contractors' all risks policy, which provided *(inter
alia)*:

> . . . this insurance shall not apply to or include:
> (vii) cost of making good faulty workmanship or construction . . .
> (xi) loss or damage arising from faulty design and liabilities arising therefrom.

The insurers denied liability, contending that the loss was due to faulty
design of the piers. The arbitrator found that, in the state of engineering
knowledge at that time, the design of the new piers was satisfactory.
However investigations into the cause of failure of the piers showed that
during floods they were subjected to greater transverse forces than had

been realised, and that the loss was not due to faulty design, in that "faulty design" meant that "in the designing of the piers there was some element of personal failure or non-compliance with the standards which would be expected of designing engineers". Therefore, the insurers were liable. They applied to have an award set aside or remitted on the ground that the arbitrator misconstrued the term.

It was held by the Supreme Court of Queensland that, in the context, "faulty design" implied some element of blameworthiness or negligence, which had been negatived by the arbitrator's findings; that subsequently acquired knowledge revealing that the piers were not strong enough could not convert the design, which would at the time have been accepted by responsible and competent engineers, into a "faulty design", and that, therefore, the insurer was liable.

On appeal the decision of the Queensland Supreme Court was reversed. It was held that "faulty design" did not imply an element of blameworthiness or negligence; the loss of piers through the inadequacy of their design to withstand an unprecedented flood was outside the policy, notwithstanding that the design complied with the standards that would be expected of designing engineers according to engineering knowledge and practice at the time of their design.

Exception 2

Damage due to
(a) wear, tear, rust or other gradual deterioration
(b) normal upkeep or normal making good
(c) disappearance or shortage which is only revealed when an inventory is made or is not traceable to an identifiable event.

(a) Wear, tear, rust or other gradual deterioration as trade risks would probably constitute cover that would not be expected by the insured contractor, who, in any event, cannot insure for such risks as the policy is not a maintenance contract but an indemnity contract. See Chapter 1. Also, these are inevitable risks; they are not fortuitous and thus are not a suitable subject for insurance.

(b) Normal upkeep and making good is in the same position as wear, tear, rust and other gradual deterioration as the former are usually the remedial work necessary to rectify the latter risks.

(c) Although theft losses are covered, the object here is to exclude short-ages not arising out of a specific identifiable incident but due to regular pilfering — general losses over a period of time. Condition 6 requires notice as soon as possible after the occurrence of *any event* which may give rise to liability under the policy. It is not intended to cover shortages discovered at the time of stocktaking, ie unexplained shortages. Contract sites suffer minor pilferages which in themselves are difficult to detect and virtually impossible to investigate, although over a period they can amount to a considerable sum. So this risk has also an inevitable or non-fortuitous aspect to it.

Exception 3

Damage to
(a) machinery plant tools or equipment due to its own explosion breakdown or derangement but this exception shall be limited to that part responsible and shall not extend to other parts which sustain direct accidental Damage therefrom
(b) aircraft hovercraft or watercraft other than hand propelled watercraft not exceeding 20 ft in length
(c) any mechanically propelled vehicle licensed for road use including trailer attached thereto other than Damage which occurs to plant whilst it is on the site of the Contract Works or it is being carried to or from such site or it is stored in a premises or compound of the Insured
(d) bank notes cheques securities for money deeds or stamps
(e) structures (or any fixtures fittings or contents thereof) existing at the time of commencement of the Contract Works.
(f) Item 1 of the Property Insured in respect of any contract or development
    (i) the value or anticipated cost of which at the time of its commencement exceeds the Limit of Indemnity for Item 1
    (ii) the period for which at the time of its commencement exceeds the Maximum Period.

(a) Loss of or damage to plant, etc due to its own explosion, etc is a risk which can be covered by an engineering policy, and is not covered here, but the exception does not exclude damage to other parts of the plant, etc caused by the explosion, etc and this follows the principle mentioned in exception (1) above concerning defective workmanship and materials.

(b) and (c)
These concern exclusions in respect of loss of or damage to mechanically propelled vehicles which are licensed for road use, aircraft, watercraft (except hand propelled craft not exceeding 20 feet in

length), or hovercraft. These risks are properly the subject of more specialist insurances such as motor, engineering, aviation and marine, although special arrangements can be made where individual types of such plant are required to be covered by this policy. Regarding mechanically propelled vehicles, clearly the Road Traffic Act risk is excluded from the policy cover while the tool of trade risk is covered. In this policy the cover for plant is wide as carriage to and from the site and storage in the insured's premises are covered. In some policies there can be difficulty in deciding what risks are covered by the motor policy and the CAR policy, eg when moving by its own power on a road works site, as some policies only cover the plant when used as a tool of trade.

(d) The policy excludes bank notes, etc as there are likely to be large sums on the site at the time of payment of wages and this property should be more correctly covered under a money insurance policy. Furthermore, there is a doubt whether this exception is necessary since this type of property does not come within the items in the schedule under the heading "Property Insured". As with a number of terms in policies this exception merely emphasises the basic position under the policy which is stated elsewhere.

(e) The exclusion of existing structures which are not part of the contract works are clearly not covered by the policy. Nevertheless what is not always clear is what are works and what are existing structures when there is an extension of an existing structure or an alteration of an existing structure.

In the JCT 1980 edition the "Works" are defined in clause 1.3 as those "briefly described in the First recital and shown and described in the Contract Drawings and in the Contract Bills". Loosely, "works" in the same contract means the work done by the contractor and not yet handed over and also the unfixed materials and goods, delivered to, placed on or adjacent to the work done and intended for incorporation therein in accordance with clause 22. On the other hand in the JCT contract clause 22C.1 the existing structures which are the responsibility of the employer as well as the contents thereof owned by him or her must be insured. Therefore although the employer is required by that clause 22 C.1 to take out a joint names policy covering those responsibilities against specified perils it is clear that the wording under discussion would not cover the existing structures.

(f) Both parts of this exception seem almost unnecessary as it can only emphasise what is already stated in the policy schedule.

Exception 4

Damage to the Contract Works or any part thereof
(a) caused by or arising from use or occupancy other than for performance of the contract or for completion of the Contract Works by or on behalf of the Insured

(b) occurring after practical completion or in respect of which a Certificate of Completion has been issued unless such Damage arises
   (i) during any period (other than the Maintenance Period) not exceeding 14 days following practical completion or issue of such Certificate in which the Insured shall remain responsible under the terms of the contract for the Contract Works or the completed part thereof
   (ii) during the Maintenance Period and from an event occurring prior to the commencement thereof
   (iii) by the Insured in the course of any operations carried out in pursuance of any obligation under the contract during the Maintenance Period.

This exception concerns loss or damage after the contract works (or any part thereof) have been completed and delivered to or taken into use or occupation by the principal (employer), except to the extent that the insured may remain liable:

(a) under the maintenance conditions of the contract;

(b) during a period not exceeding fourteen days after the issue of a certificate of completion and which is the responsibility of the insured to insure.

So far as the JCT 80 form is concerned, sub-clause 22A requires the contractor to insure until "the date of issue of the certificate of Practical Completion". In any event, once the works have been completed and delivered, it is arguable that the contractor no longer has an insurable interest in the works, assuming he or she has been paid and subject to the contract terms. Sometimes insurers are asked to cover occupation before completion, and they may be prepared to do so for an additional premium.

Any occupation will usually involve a change of information on which the insurance business was placed and thus a probable change of rate for premium purposes. In case of failure to notify the insurer, the fact of the employer's or his or her tenant's occupation is rarely in doubt but the part of the property occupied can be in contention. However, once notification takes place, in most cases the problem is resolved quite easily.

At practical completion the risk of loss or damage passes to the employer who is responsible for arranging his or her own insurances. Clause 18 of the JCT 80 form deals with "partial possession by the employer" and reads as follows:

18   Partial possession by Employer

Employer's wish – Contractor's consent	**18.1**	If at any time or times before the date of issue by the Architect of the certificate of Practical Completion the Employer wishes to take possession of any part or parts of the Works and the consent of the Contractor (which consent shall not be unreasonable withheld) has been obtained, then notwithstanding anything expressed or implied elsewhere in this Contract, the Employer may take possession thereof. The Architect shall thereupon issue to the Contractor on behalf of the Employer a written statement identifying the part or parts of the Works taken into possession and giving the date when the Employer took possession (in clauses 18, 20.3, 22.3.1 and 22C.1 referred to as "the relevant part" and "the relevant date" respectively).
Practical * Completion – relevant part	**18.1** .1	For the purposes of clauses 17.2, 17.3, 17.5 and 30.4.1.2 Practical Completion of the relevant part shall be deemed to have occurred and the Defects Liability Period in respect of the relevant part shall be deemed to have commenced on the relevant date.
Defects etc – relevant part	**18.1** .2	When in the opinion of the Architect any defects, shrinkages or other faults in the relevant part which he may have required to be made good under clause 17.2 or clause 17.3 shall have been made good he shall issue a certificate to that effect.
Insurance – relevant part	**18.1** .3	As from the relevant date the obligation of the Contractor under clause 22A or of the Employer under clause 22B.1 or clause 22C.2 whichever is applicable to insure shall terminate in respect of the relevant part but not further or otherwise; and

where clause 22C applies the obligation of the Employer to insure under clause 22C.1 shall from the relevant date include the relevant part.

Liquidated   **18.1** .4 In lieu of any sum to be paid or allowed by the
damages –   Contractor under clause 24 in respect of any period
relevant part   during which the Works may remain incomplete
                         occurring after the relevant date there shall be paid
                         or allowed such sum as bears the same ratio to the
                         sum which would be paid or allowed apart from the
                         provisions of clause 18 as the Contract Sum less the
                         amount contained therein in respect of the relevant
                         part bears to the Contract Sum.

It is arguable that "possession" in this clause is not the same or may not be the same as "caused by or arising from use or occupancy" which is the expression used in the policy, as merely use for storage may not involve taking possession.

Nevertheless, such use would fall foul of the policy wording. Secondly, the question arises as to the effect of such use or occupancy. Does it just affect the cover for that part of the site used or occupied, or is the whole of the policy cover prejudiced? Probably the answer depends on the additional risk the use or occupance imposed on the remainder of the site which is not used or occupied. If the whole site risk is increased then it will affect the whole policy cover. For example the storage of inflammable material could affect the whole site.

The responsibility to insure in the case of sectional completion was considered in *English Industrial Estates Corporation v George Wimpey & Co Ltd* (1972) although this was a case of *alleged* sectional completion.

A factory owned by English Industrial Estates Corporation was leased to Reed Corrugated Cases Ltd. In 1969 Reed wanted to extend the factory, while continuing to make corrugated cardboard, to install a large new machine and have storage space for hundreds of reels of paper.

George Wimpey & Co Ltd tendered for the contract and was successful. The tender was on the pre-1980 JCT form incorporating the bills of quantities. Wimpey had a blanket contractors' all risks policy which provided the cover required by sub-clause 20(A)(1), now sub-clause 22A.1 under JCT 80.

By January 1970, a great deal of the work had been carried out by Wimpey, and Reed had installed the machine and had stored 1500 reels in the new reel warehouse. On 18.1.70 much of the new factory was gutted by fire and the damage was estimated at £250,000. At that time the contractors had not finished their work.

The Corporation argued that, as the works had not been completed, it was Wimpey's duty to insure, and that the loss, therefore, should fall upon it or its insurers.

Wimpey, however, argued that the Corporation, through Reed, had taken possession of several parts of the works and that, under clause 16, the risk had passed to the Corporation in respect of those parts. For the wording of clause 16 see clause 18 of JCT 80.

The question before the court was, had the employer before the date of the fire "taken possession" of any parts or parts of the works? If it had, that part was at the employer's risk. If it had not, then the contractor was at risk.

The facts showed that the car park, for example, was accepted for handover by the employer's architect in September, 1969, when he issued a certificate on a RIBA printed form which certified that "a part . . . of the works, namely, car park, the value of which I estimate to be £10,000 was completed to my satisfaction and taken into possession on 22 September, 1969 . . .".

An architect gave evidence that that form of certificate was normal for sectional completion.

The matter was complicated by special provisions in the bills of quantities showing that Reed would install plant and equipment and would occupy and use part of the works, but that the contractor was still to keep the works covered by insurance. Lord Denning was prepared to consider clause 16 without placing any reliance on the provisions just mentioned. In his opinion the words "taking possession" of a part of the works must be so interpreted as to give precision to the time of taking possession and in defining the part, because of the important consequences which followed on it.

To achieve this precision, the parties themselves had evolved suitable machinery to determine it by way of a definite handing over of the part by the contractors to the employers. The practice was for the contractors to tell the architect that a part was ready for hand-over. The architect would inspect it and, if satisfied, would accept it on behalf of the employers. He would give a certificate defining the part, its value and the date of taking possession. The hand-over was thus precise and definite. It was the accepted means of defining the hand-over.

In Lord Denning's view, the contractor at the time of the fire had not handed over to the employer the responsibility for the board machine house, the reel warehouse or the two extensions. Although Reed was using those places, it was the contractor's responsibility to insure them until actual hand-over. The risk remained with it and its insurers must bear the loss.

The other two judges in the Court of Appeal came to the same conclusion as Lord Denning, but they merely considered that some formality was required in interpreting clause 16.

Clearly there are dangers for contractors in allowing use or possession of the works which they are insuring for all risks under clause 22A without clarifying responsibility for insurance of their part of the works concerned. However, if, before practical completion of any part of the works is reached, and consequently clause 18 could not apply, the employer requires to use part of the works, then this should not be allowed without the insurance position being agreed. Incidentally, it is just as important that the party responsible for the insurance of the partly occupied premised should agree the position with their insurers.

It seems from the above case that whatever type of construction contract applies some clear cut and final formalised conduct by the parties must be shown, evidencing the transfer of possession so that the parties are in no doubt that the various consequences of taking possession have come into effect. Care must be taken to deal with the various consequential matters including, and particularly, those relating to insurance.

Exception 5

> Damage for which the Insured is relieved of responsibility under the terms of any contract or agreement.

In some construction contracts the contractor is relieved of responsibility for loss or damage to the works in certain circumstances. Thus, under the optional clauses 22B and 22C of JCT 80 (as amended in 1986) the employer is responsible for the works and site materials (as defined), in that he or she is to take out and maintain a joint names insurance policy (in the joint names of the main contractor and the employer) for all risks insurance.

Under the fifth edition of the Institution of Civil Engineers Conditions of Contract the "excepted risks" (those for which the main contractor is not responsible) so far as the contract works is concerned, include damage due to use or occupation by the employer, his or her agents, servants or other contractors (not employed by the main contractor) or due to fault, defect, error or omission in the design of the works (other than a design provided by the contractor pursuant to his or her obligations under the contract) as well as war and kindred risks, nuclear risks, and sonic waves.

Exception 6

(a) liquidated damages or penalties for delay or non-completion
(b) consequential loss of any nature

Regarding (a) insurers prefer to work on an indemnity basis when paying claims under a material damage policy and are reluctant to enter into payments on an agreed value basis. Apart from this, penalty payments as defined are consequential losses and the following remarks apply.

Turning to (b) the operative clause of the CAR policy is usually worded so that without this exclusion it would cover consequential loss. The danger for the insurer is that legally "consequential loss or damage" has been held to mean loss which does not result directly and naturally from the act concerned or, in the situation under discussion, the perils covered by the policy. The point is that the type of loss which (within the insurance industry) is considered by insurers (in their terminology) to be consequential loss is not in fact considered by the courts to be consequential because it is a direct and natural result, eg loss of profit from loss of use, increased cost of working, and loss arising from delay in completing contracts. Therefore, a safer way is for the insurer to state specifically what he or she intends to exclude by the words "consequential loss", otherwise the legal interpretation of "indirect or consequential" will not include those heads of damage intended by the insurer to be excluded from the policy cover of the CAR policy. However, this could result in a lengthy list, which even then may not exclude everything intended to be excluded from the policy. Possibly the best way is to confine the operative clause to physical or material loss or damage, which the policy in Appendix 1 does. For the legal authorities on this aspect see the line of cases from *Millar's Machinery Co Ltd v David Way & Son* (1934) to *Croudace Construction Ltd v Cawoods Concrete Products Ltd* (1978). A combination of both methods may be even more satisfactory to all concerned, specifically excluding the financial losses mentioned above.

Some consequential losses may be covered under special policies; sometimes the employer (principal) is the insured. These policies normally give cover against the same perils as the material damage policy required for the protection of the works and subject to such a policy operating. Consequential loss policies can be obtained covering:

(a) *Advance profits*
     The protection provided by this policy is in respect of financial loss through delay by damage to the works or at the supplier's premises

of important plant or equipment or during transit. Payment under this policy does not start until the date the business would have commenced but for the damage, and is in respect of the anticipated income, ie the gross profit of a manufacturer or the rent of a property developer which is not earned at the estimated date. See further details in Chapter 5 and Appendix 6.

(b) *Additional cost of working*

This is an expense incurred by the contractor and can be an extension of the contractors' all risks policy as it follows a claim under that policy and involves costs beyond those incurred in making good that damage. For example, the basis of claims settlements in the case of payment to workmen by reason of guaranteed time or such agreements is by calculating the difference between the amount paid to the workmen and the amount which would have been payable had no such agreement been in force. In the case of plant standing idle, the calculation for hired plant as the amount payable for the affected period and for the contractors' own plant, is based on an allowance in respect of loss of working time, say 66% of the rates for such plant in either of the publications applicable (*Definition of Prime Cost of Daywork carried out under a Building Contract*, published jointly by the RICS and BEC (formerly the NFBTE), or the *Schedules of Dayworks carried out incidental to Contract Work*, issued by the Federation of Civil Engineering Contractors). Sometimes the expense is difficult to identify, especially when time has also been lost on the contract before the damage.

(c) *Fines and damages*

This is also a possible extension to the contractors' all risks policy covering fines and damages payable by the contractor under the construction contract, following loss or damage due to some or all of the perils covered by this all risks policy. This cover is not easily obtainable and the rate of premium is high.

(d) *Additional or extended interest charges*

Where the subject matter of the contract is to be sold on completion, in the case of damage there could be delay in receipt of the money from the sale. The cover can give the agreed amount of interest on the new amount of the sale to the extent that it is delayed subject to a limitation of the indemnity period. On the other hand, the actual interest on a loan could be insured so far as it is extended due to the damage.

Exception 7

Damage occasioned by pressure waves caused by aircraft or other aerial devices travelling at sonic or supersonic speeds.

Material damage and loss of profits policies were never intended to cover loss, destruction or damage directly occasioned by sonic waves and, as will be seen when dealing with sub-clause 1.3 in chapter 5, the JCT 80 contract specifically excludes sonic waves in the definition of "excepted risks". Furthermore, the United Kingdom Government indicated that if such damage were to result from Concorde's flights it would pay compensation. In fact this does not appear to have been necessary. The material damage policies concerned would include not only the CAR policy but also the specified perils policy mentioned in Chapter 5 plus the "damage to own vehicle" section of the comprehensive motor vehicle policy.

Exception 8

the Excess specified in the Schedule

The CAR policy can have an overall excess of £250, however the loss or damage arises, and/or a higher excess for whatever the underwriter considers the more hazardous perils.

Exception 9

Damage in Northern Ireland caused by or happening through or in consequence of

(a) civil commotion

(b) any unlawful wanton or malicious act committed maliciously by a person or persons acting on behalf of or in connection with any unlawful association

For the purpose of this exclusion

(i) unlawful association means any organisation which is engaged in terrorism and includes any organisation which at the relevant time is a prescribed organisation within the meaning of the Northern Ireland (Emergency Provisions) Act 1973

(ii)   terrorism means the use of violence for political ends and includes any use of violence for the purpose of putting the public in fear

In any suit action or other proceedings where the Company alleges that by reason of this Exception any Damage is not covered by this Section the burden of proving that such Damage is covered shall be on the Insured.

This is an insurance market clause the reason for which is obviously as a result of the unrest in Northern Ireland. It should be noted that whereas normally the burden of proving that an exception applies is on the insurer, in this particular exception the burden is placed on the insured.

Extension

Indemnity to Principal.
Where any contract or agreement entered into by the Insured for the performance of work so requires the Company will

(a)   indemnify the Principal in like manner to the Insured in respect of the principal's liability arising from the performance of the work by the Insured

(b)   note the interest of the Principal in the Property Insured by Section 3 to the extent that the contract or agreement requires such interest to be noted.

"Principal" means the employer who commissions the work in a construction contract. By making the principal an insured party with the contractor the policy complies with the obligation under clause 22 of the JCT 80 contract (as amended in 1986), and under clause 21 of the ICE conditions for the insurance of the works to be in the joint names of the employer and the contractor. The advantage of "joint insureds" is seen in the commentary under the heading "Subrogation" in Chapter 1.

General Exceptions

All the following exceptions are subject to the introductory paragraph reading "The Company shall not indemnify the Insured".

Exception 1

(i)   for loss destruction of or damage to any property whatsoever or any loss or expense whatsoever resulting or arising therefrom or any consequential loss

(ii) for any legal liability of whatsoever nature

directly or indirectly caused by or contributed to or arising from

(a) ionising radiations or contamination by radioactivity from any nuclear waste from the combustion of nuclear fuel

(b) the radioactive toxic explosive or other hazardous properties of any explosive nuclear assembly or nuclear component thereof

In respect of Bodily Injury caused to an Employee this Exception shall apply only when the Insured under a contract or agreement has undertaken to indemnify a Principal or has assumed liability under contract for such Bodily Injury and which liability would not have attached in the absence of such contract or agreement.

This is an insurance market clause which appears on all policies because the risks are so great as not to be suitable for ordinary commercial insurance.

The Nuclear Installations Acts 1965 and 1969, together with the Energy Act 1983, make the operator of a nuclear installation solely liable for injury to any person or damage to any third party property. Only the operator is liable, notwithstanding that other parties such as contractors may be liable in tort for the consequences of a nuclear accident on the licensed site. Because the operator alone is liable, he or she only is required to provide insurance, and the United Kingdom Pool policy meets the operator's nuclear legal requirements. This policy is a type of liability insurance written through the British Insurance (Atomic Energy) Committee and, *inter alia,* covers the operator's nuclear liabilities under the statutes mentioned for an overall indemnity figure of £20 million (in relevant cases £5 million) for the current "cover period". Above £20 million the Government is responsible up to £190 million. The cover period in practice means the lifetime of a licensed installation subject to certain information.

Exception 2

This general exception as can be seen from Appendix 1 does not apply to the CAR policy, ie section 3 of the Contractors' Policy.

Exception 3

under Section 2, 3 or 4 for any consequence of war invasion act of foreign enemy hostilities (whether war be declared or not) civil war rebellion revolution insurrection or military or usurped power.

This again is an insurance market clause as it deals with matters that a commercial insurance policy could not underwrite for this type of cover. War risks were handled by the Government in the First and Second World Wars.

So far as kindred risks "invasion, act of foreign enemy, hostilities (whether war be declared or not)" are concerned, they all imply the existence of a state of war with a foreign power, and the pattern of international events during and since the last world war is reflected in the qualification "whether war be declared or not". The exclusion is worded so that it applies not only to losses due to enemy acts but also to those incurred through the steps taken to oppose the enemy, as shown in the Falklands crisis. Clauses 32 and 33 of JCT 80 deal respectively with the procedure in the event of an outbreak of hostilities and how war damage is to be handled. Civil war implies something in the nature of organised acts of warfare.

Rebellion in *Lindsay and Pirie v General Accident, etc Corp Ltd* (1914) was defined as the taking up of arms traitorously against the Crown, whether by natural subjects or others when subdued. It can also mean disobedience to the process of the law as applied by the courts. Revolution is very similar.

Insurrection is a stage short of rebellion and is defined in *Jowitt's Dictionary of English Law* as a rising of the people in open resistance against established authority with the object of supplanting it.

The term "military power" includes acts done by the Crown's military forces in opposition to subjects of the realm in open rebellion and organised as a military force. "Usurped power" applies to an organised rebellion which is acting under some authority and has assumed the power of government by making laws and enforcing them. In *Curtis v Mathews* (1919), Banks LJ said:

Usurped power seems to me to mean something more than the action of an unorganised rabble. How much more I am not prepared to define. There must probably be action by some more or less organised body with more or less authoritative leaders.

It has been suggested that the last four words of the kindred risks to war, namely "military or usurped power" come within the exclusion of nuclear weapons material used outside the United Kingdom.

Conditions of the policy

This heading has an introductory paragraph which reads:

> This policy and the Schedule shall be read together and any word or expression to which a specific meaning has been attached in any part of this Policy or of the Schedule shall bear such meaning wherever it may appear.

Condition 1. Alteration in risk

> The Company shall not be liable under this Policy if the risk be materially increased without the written consent of the Company.

The duty of disclosure comes to an end when the policy is issued and does not apply again until renewal since this is, in effect, the negotiation of a new contract.

In order to protect itself against a substantial increase in the risk during the policy period the insurance company uses the above condition. From the wording it is clear that the company is not on cover in respect of any such material change or risk until it has agreed to accept the change. Insurers normally regard as material a basic alteration in design, or an increase in value which considerably exceeds the original estimated contract price, or the amount already provided for in any automatic provision for increasing the sum insured (see heading 4 under "Additional Covers" in this chapter).

Condition 2. Premium adjustment

> If the premium for this Policy is based on estimates an accurate record containing all particulars relative thereto shall be kept by the Insured.
>
> The Insured shall at all times allow the Company to inspect such records and shall supply such particulars and information as the Company may require within one month from the expiry of each Period of Insurance and the premium shall thereupon be adjusted by the Company (subject to the Minimum Premium chargeable for the risk being retained by the Company).

This condition sets out the requirements concerning returns the insurance company requires in order to estimate its premiums which are adjustable at the year end when the correct figure is available. The second paragraph allows the company to examine the insured's records concerning wages or turnover on which the premium is based, and reinforces the actions required by the insured in the context of the duty of disclosure within the doctrine of the utmost good faith.

Condition 3. Duties of the insured

The Insured shall take all reasonable care

(a)   to prevent any event which may give rise to a claim under this Policy

(b)   to maintain the premises, plant and everything used in the Business in proper repair

(c)   in the selection and supervision of Employees.

(d)   to comply with all statutory and other obligations and regulations imposed by any authority.

The insurers are entitled to expect their insureds to behave with the same care as they would if they were uninsured. However, as the insureds can reasonably expect to be covered when they have failed to take some precautions on the grounds that these circumstances give rise to the very situation for which they arranged insurance, the insurers cannot take too literal an interpretation.

Insurers should not attempt to apply this condition when the insured's employees are negligent as this condition is imposed upon the insured, ie the proprietor, whether an individual or a board of directors. Failure to take reasonable care has to be a deliberate, wilful or blatant action on the part of the insured before the insurer can be certain that any attempt to operate the condition will be upheld by a court.

In *Duncan Logan (Contractors) Ltd and Others v Royal Exchange Assurance Group* (1973) where a contractors' all risks policy required the insured to take all reasonable precautions for the safety of the property, an attempt was made under the policy to argue that the company was vicariously responsible for its employees' negligence, which is so in the case of negligence claims. However, the interpretation of an insurance policy, between the parties to the contract, was considered to involve different arguments. The court considered it would be curious to find that an all risks policy was worded so as to exclude negligence on the part of the insured's own officers and servants. Thus when insureds undertake to

take reasonable care and precautions, they do not, as a condition precedent to the policy operating, undertake that none of their employees,
officers or servants will be negligent. In other words the insured does not
warrant that all employees will behave reasonably. The court did not think
it right to consider the standing of the employee who has failed to take
care. It was decided that the duty to take care lay upon the insured and
in this they could fail by appointing incompetent officers or by failing to
take proper procedures or give adequate instructions regarding any
danger of which the board of directors ought to have been aware. In any
event the policy did not by its wording attempt to apply the duty to the
insured's officers.

Condition 4. Make good defects

> The Insured shall make good or remedy any defect or danger which becomes
> apparent and take such additional precautions as circumstances may require.

This condition is self-explanatory and follows from (a) and (b) of the
previous condition. For example it may become necessary to insert longer
piles if it becomes obvious that the piles inserted or suggested are
inadequate.

Condition 5. Maximum payments

> This condition is not set out as it only refers to the legal liability sections of the
> policy and not to the CAR section 3.

Condition 6. Claims

> The insured or his legal personal representatives shall give notice in writing to
> the Company as soon as possible after any event which may give rise to liability
> under this Policy with full particulars of such event. Every claim notice letter
> writ or process or other document served on the Insured shall be forwarded to
> the Company immediately on receipt. Notice in writing shall also be given
> immediately to the Company by the Insured of impending prosecution inquest
> or fatal inquiry in connection with any such event. No admission offer promise
> payment or indemnity shall be made or given by or on behalf of the Insured
> without the written consent of the Company. In the event of Damage by theft
> or malicious act the Insured shall also give immediate notice to the police.

So far as CAR claims are concerned the only circumstance where an
insured might think that he or she need not comply with this condition

would be if the policy contained a large excess (deductible) and the insured decided to handle the repair cost himself or herself as the amount concerned was well within the excess. Nevertheless on the policy wording the insurer should still be notified. In any event costs can be substantially under-estimated in their initial stages, and it would be prudent to advise insurers of the incident.

Condition 7. Subrogation

> The Company shall be entitled if it so desires to take over and conduct in the name of the Insured the defence or settlement of any claim or to prosecute in the name of the Insured for its own benefit any claim for indemnity or damages or otherwise and shall have full discretion in the conduct of any proceedings and in the settlement of any claim and the Insured shall give all such information and assistance as the Company may require.

This condition increases the insurers' common law rights of subrogation (whereby an insurer can stand in the place of the insured and claim in his or her name after indemnifying him or her) by giving such rights before indemnifying the insured. It also gives the insurer the control of proceedings and settlement of any claim and reminds the insured of his or her duty to give all information and assistance that the company may require.

Condition 8. Contribution

> If at the time of any event to which this Policy applies there is or but for the existence of this Policy there would be any other insurance covering the same liability or Damage the Company shall not be liable under this Policy except in respect of any excess beyond the amount which would be payable under such other insurance had this Policy not been effected.

This wording adopts the more modern approach of not merely stating that if there is another insurance in operation covering the same subject matter against the same risk in respect of the same insured, it will not apply, as in addition it emphasises that it will only pay any excess beyond the amount which would be payable under such other insurance. Without this emphasis the effect is the same as if the clause had said it would only pay its rateable proportion assuming both insurers say they are not going to contribute and both their policies are in operation. The authority for this is *Gale v Motor Union and Loyst v General Accident Fire and Life Assurance Corporation Ltd* (1928). The courts will not allow the two non-contribution policy conditions (which are exactly the same) to cancel the cover given with the result that if the loss is covered elsewhere it is covered nowhere. The correct decision must be that each policy should contribute its rateable proportion. However, once the wording is different so that one policy contains, as here, an excess wording in the contribution condition stating that it will not operate until the second policy is exhausted and the second policy does not contain such a clause, then the common law principle of contribution will not operate between the two policies. See the New Zealand Court of Appeal decision in *State Fire Insurance General Manager v Liverpool and London and Globe Insurance Co Ltd* (1952).

On the other hand, from the Scottish appeal case of *Steelclad Ltd v Iron Trades Mutual Insurance Co Ltd* (1984) where *both* policies contained an excess wording it is clear that both will have to contribute on a rateable proportion basis. However, the interesting part of that case was the court's view of the words in the contribution condition of the policy of the defender (the Iron Trades) which refers to loss or damage insured by any other policy "effected by the insured . . . on his behalf" when the defender would not be liable except in respect of any excess beyond the amount payable under such other policy. The pursuer (Steelclad) was the insured under the Iron Trades policy and was a subcontractor on a project where the employer having the work done had arranged a project policy covering the employer, all contractors and all subcontractors. The contribution clause in that project policy was worded exactly the same as the Iron Trades policy except for the phrase mentioned above in quotes. The court considered the project policy arranged by the employer was not a policy effected by the insured *on his behalf*. The phrase was ambiguous and was therefore construed *contra proferentum* against the insurer who had refused to contribute. The project policy insurers had already paid almost half the claim and while the court did not have to go any further having come to a decision on this wording, they did in effect say that even without this phrase or if the project policy had been effected on the insured's behalf it *would still not allow* the two policy conditions to cancel the cover given.

An illustration of the basic rule that for contribution to apply the same risk and the same property must be covered for the same interest, appears in the case of *Petrofina (UK) Ltd and Others v Magnaload Ltd and Others* (1983) which concerned a contractors' all risks policy.

In this case an attempt was made to draw the CAR policy into contribution with a liability policy provided by another insurer. It was said that the insurances were not therefore insurances on the same property and against the same risk and it followed that there was no possibility of double insurance in the true sense. See Appendix 4.

Condition 9. Cancellation

The Company may cancel this Policy by giving thirty days' notice by recorded delivery letter to the last known address of the Insured. The Company shall make a return of the proportionate part of the premium in respect of the unexpired Period of Insurance or if the premium has been based wholly or partly upon estimates the premium shall be adjusted in accordance with condition 2.

Those policies which contain a cancellation clause give the insurers, but not the insured, the right to cancel. However, a cancellation clause is not usually contained in policies dealing with a single project (see below). Normally contractors have annual blanket (or floater) policies covering all their work during the policy year provided that work comes within the business description in the policy schedule (see below). In respect of new contracts' blanket policies, the cancellation condition normally applies to work not yet commenced, thus allowing cover to continue until completion of contracts already being performed. This limits the use of this condition to new contracts not yet commenced.

(1) *Single contract policy*
The contractors' all risks policy can be arranged on a "contract by contract" basis. However, this may be considered undesirable because of the danger of overlooking the necessity to insure and also in view of the greater administrative work involved in costing insurance for each contract. Another danger of this type of contract is that cover ceases when the policy terminates. The contractor therefore needs to have a separate "residual risks" policy (a separate annual policy to cover minor works, including going back to work on lapsed contracts). On the other hand this type of cover gives the underwriter more details of the insured's method of construction and any special hazards of a particular site.

(2) *Blanket (or floater) policy*
Contractors frequently find it prudent to arrange this type of contractors' all risks policy, particularly where a considerable number of contracts are undertaken each year. This policy is renewable annually and charged at fixed premium rates against the annual turnover. Although there is usually an exclusion of hazardous operations, eg foundation work on existing structures, bridges, viaducts, tunnelling, work in water, the policy has the following advantages:

(a) As the cost is known, tendering is simple.

(b) There is a minimum number of policies and minimal admin-
     istrative work.

(c) There is automatic cover on almost, if not all, contracts, ie
     without notification to insurers, subject to contracts exceeding
     a predetermined value.

(d) An estimated premium is paid at the beginning of each year
     and that premium is adjusted at the pre-fixed rate at the year
     end according to the total insured sums involved.

(e) The policy can be extended to cover all constructional plant
     and equipment used on all the sites throughout the policy
     year.

(f) The policy is usually issued to a contractor to insure him or
     her, and his or her employer and subcontractors also, in
     respect of accidents occurring in connection with the work
     described in the policy. A blanket policy may also be issued
     to an industrial, commercial or other type of employer who
     frequently employs contractors for construction, extension or
     alteration of its own property.

(g) Underwriters can monitor claims and adjust premiums.

Condition 10. Disputes

Any dispute concerning the interpretation of the terms of this Policy shall be
resolved in accordance with the jurisdiction of the territory in which this Policy
is issued.

This is an unusual wording as most policies contain an arbitration condition which applies to disputes on amount only, the insured being allowed
to use the courts in cases of disputes abroad as well as for those which
arise concerning cover provided in the United Kingdom. However, as the
policy is not likely to be issued in a territory other than the United
Kingdom, it probably only means that United Kingdom law will apply.

Condition 11. Rights

In the event of Damage for which a claim is or may be made under Section 3

(a) The Company shall be entitled without incurring any liability under this Policy to

    (i)   enter any site or premises where Damage has occurred and take and keep possession of the Property Insured

    (ii)   deal with any salvage as they deem fit

    but no property may be abandoned to the Company

(b) if the Company elects or becomes bound to reinstate or replace any property the Insured shall at their own expense produce and give to the Company all such plans and documents books and information as the Company may reasonably require. The Company shall not be bound to reinstate exactly or completely but only as circumstances permit and in reasonably sufficient manner and shall not in any case be bound to expend in respect of any one of the items of Property Insured more than the Limit of Indemnity in respect of such item.

In a number of aspects this seem to be a "belt and braces" condition in that it merely emphasises a right which would exist without this condition. Thus:

(a) while the onus of proof is primarily on the insured, the insurers could hardly be expected to pay a claim without investigation which must involve entering the site and at least examining property insured. However, the abandoning of property to the insurers is not a situation the insurers would want as they might become liable for potential third party liabilities, cost of removal, etc. In any event, the insured's claim is basically for the loss of value, ie after salvage value has been considered.

(b) The insurers similarly are entitled to all information to support a claim which they may reasonably require, and the insurers in complying with the principle of indemnity would not be expected to reinstate exactly or completely but only as circumstances permit and in a reasonably sufficient manner up to the limit of indemnity stated in the policy schedule.

Condition 12. Observance

The due observance and fulfilment of the terms exceptions conditions and endorsements of this Policy in so far as they relate to anything to be done or complied with by the Insured and the truth of the statements and answers in the proposal shall be conditions precedent to the liability of the Company to make any payment under this Policy.

It has been mentioned earlier that the recital clause makes the proposal completed by the insured, the basis of, and states that it forms part of, the policy. In addition this condition makes the observance of the terms exceptions conditions and endorsements, conditions precedent to the liability of the insurer to pay any claim. This is in accordance with the explanation of a "condition precedent to liability" given in Chapter 1 under the heading "The Insurance Contract". Consequently, as well as inaccuracies on the proposal form, failure to observe or fulfil all the terms, exceptions, conditions and endorsements of the policy gives the insurers an opportunity to avoid the claim if they so wish.

Endorsements

1. Limitation of Work
    For the purposes of this Policy the Business of the Insured is restricted to work on or in connection with private dwellings blocks of flats shops offices public houses guest houses or hotels not exceeding four storeys in height (including the ground floor) and attic.

This is an underwriting restriction in a positive form for use with an annual policy where necessary, ie it states what type of work is covered which is usually stated in the policy schedule. Work involving five or more stories would have to be referred to the insurers for special underwriting consideration.

2. Hazardous Premises Exclusion
    The Company shall not indemnify the Insured under Sections 1, 2 or 3 against liability or Damage arising from any work in or on or in connection with

    (a) towers steeples chimney shafts blast furnaces dams canals viaducts bridges or tunnels

    (b) aircraft airports ships docks piers wharves breakwaters or sea walls

    (c) collieries mines chemical works gas works oil refineries or power stations

    (d) offshore installations or bulk oil petrol gas or chemical storage tanks or chambers.

This is an underwriting restriction in a negative form for use with an annual policy when considered necessary, ie it states the type of work which is not covered (largely of a civil engineering nature). Hence it is in the form of an exclusion.

3. Automatic Reinstatement
    The Limits of Indemnity under Section 3 will not be reduced by the amount of any claim.
    Provided that the Insured shall pay an additional premium at a rate to be agreed on the amount of each claim from the date Damage occurs to the date of the expiry of the Period of Insurance and that any such additional premium will be disregarded for the purpose of any adjustment of premium under Condition 2.

The property section (section 3 Contract Works in the policy under discussion) usually in the policy schedule indicates that the liability of the insurers in respect of loss or damage to any item of property insured shall not exceed the sum insured (the limit of indemnity in the policy schedule of the policy in Appendix 1). Exception 3 (f) (mentioned earlier) also emphasises this point. The insured buys a certain amount of insurance, ie up to the amount of the sum insured which is the limit of indemnity. Some of this is used up by payment of a claim and the insured would need to restore the maximum cover available. The policy also normally contains a type of clause or endorsement providing for reinstatement of the sums insured after a loss. This condition requires the insured to pay an additional premium calculated *pro rata* from the date of the loss or damage to the expiry of the period of insurance, it being understood that the additional premium should be disregarded for the purpose of the adjustment of the premium to be made on expiry of the period of insurance.

4. Showhouses
    Exception 4 (b) of Section 3 shall not apply to showhouses showflats or showmaisonettes including the contents thereof the property of the Insured or for which they may be responsible until completion of sale takes place. Provided that the liability of the Company shall not exceed £500,000 in any one Period of Insurance nor £100,000 in respect of any one showhouse showflat or showmaisonette.

Exception 4 (b) terminates the insurers' liability when the contract works have been completed and delivered to or taken into use or occupation by the employer subject to a limited extent (maintenance conditions and fourteen days after the issue of the certificate of completion). In the case

of showhouses the developer, whether he or she is the contractor or
employer, will require the insurance to continue beyond the terms of
termination mentioned both for the building and the contents and this
endorsement arranges that cover subject to the limits of indemnity stated
in the endorsement. The insured already has some protection in this
respect under the Additional Covers heading number 6 "Speculative
housebuilding".

5.   Negligent Breakdown
     Exception 3(a) of Section 3 shall not apply to explosion breakdown or
     derangement of machinery plant or tools hired to the Insured under the
     Model Conditions for the Hiring of Plant of the Contractors Plant
     Association or other similar conditions

     Provided that
     (a)   such explosion breakdown or derangement is due to the negligence
           misuse or misdirection of the Insured or any Employee

     (b)   the liability of the company shall not exceed £50,000 for any one item

     (c)   The Company shall not provide indemnity against the first £250 of
           each and every occurrence.

Exception (3) limits the exclusion of damage to machinery plant tools or
equipment *due to its own explosion breakdown or derangement* thus other
parts of the contract works so damaged are covered. However, by this
endorsement the exception just mentioned does not apply to hired-in
plant, etc under the Model Conditions for the Hiring of Plant of the
Contractors Plant Association or other similar conditions subject to the
provisos mentioned. This is necessary because these conditions may place
responsibility for such damage on the insured, thus he or she needs the
cover. See Chapter 11.
     Nevertheless the insurers do not intend to provide cover to the plant
owner which is not transferred to the insured hiring-in making him or her,
or any employee responsible for their negligence, misuse or misdirection.
Hence proviso (a). The other two provisos are self-explanatory.

6.   Continuing Hire Charges
     The Company will indemnify the Insured under Section 3 in respect of
     liability assumed by the Insured under Clause 9 (d) of the Model Condi-
     tions for the Hiring of Plant of the Contractors Plant Association (or similar
     conditions) for the payment of hire charges arising from explosion break-

down or derangement of machinery plant or tools hired to the Insured

Provided that
(a)   such explosion breakdown or derangement is due to the negligence
       misuse or misdirection of the Insured or any Employee

(b)   the liability of the Company in any one Period of Insurance shall not
       exceed £10,000

(c)   the company shall not provide indemnity against the first £250 of
       each and every occurrence or the hiring fee for the first 48 hours
       following each and every occurrence whichever is the greater.

Reference to the CPA conditions clause 9(d) in Chapter 11 shows that as
in the previous endorsement the intention is to cover the hirer's liability
for negligence, etc under that subclause 9 (d), subject to the limit of indemnity in any one period of insurance as stated and the excess applicable to
each and every occurrence or the hiring fee for the first 48 hours following
each and every occurrence whichever is the greater.

7.   Plant Immobilisation
      It is a condition precedent to the liability of the Company under Section 3
      in respect of Damage caused by theft to plant insured by Items 2 and 4 of
      the Property Insured that such plant shall be immobilised when left
      unattended.

This is a precautionary requirement for security purposes.

8.   Plans
      Section 3 shall extend to indemnify the Insured in respect of the cost and
      expenses necessarily incurred in re-writing or re-drawing plans drawings
      or other contract documents following Damage thereto
      Provided that the liability of the Company shall not exceed £25,000 in
      respect of any one contract or development.

It should be noted that only the cost and expenses (presumably limited to
labour and materials) necessarily incurred in re-writing or re-drawing
plans, drawings or other contract documents are covered, not the other
financial consequential losses (due, for example, to delay in pursuing the
contract work) which could be considerable. There is also a limitation of
£25,000 in respect of any one contract or development, which could prove
to be too low on some contracts.

Schedule

This section of the policy document can be seen in Appendix 1.

The operative or insuring clause of the policy does not identify the insured, the property insured, etc so the identification, description, definition and limitations in amount of certain particulars of the individual risk and terms of the insurance are normally presented in a compact way in a policy schedule. The policy schedule is usually the only typewritten part of the policy (the remainder being printed).

This document is largely self-explanatory but where an explanation is necessary it has been given when proceeding through the policy wording in this chapter.

Section 4, concerning the JCT clause 21.2.1, is considered in Chapter 4.

CHAPTER 3

The presentation and handling of CAR claims

It is intended that this chapter should be a link between the previous chapter on the CAR policy and the following chapters dealing with the various construction contracts calling for the CAR policy, other than Chapter 4.

Notification of claims to insurers

The wording of the policy condition number 6 requiring notification of a claim, etc immediately it comes to the knowledge of the insured or their representatives, is given in chapter 2. Condition 6 not only requires notification in writing as soon as possible after any event which may give rise to liability (a claim) under the policy with full particulars of such an event, but also of impending prosecution in connection with any such event, and damage by theft or malicious act must be notified to the policy immediately. Condition 11 also reminds the insured of the obligation to give all information and assistance to the insurers to enable them to handle the claim properly.

Insurers usually impose upon themselves a test before invoking such conditions, ie before refusing to protect the insured. They ask themselves whether they have been prejudiced by the delay or failure to comply with the condition. Legally, the insurers do not have to be prejudiced before operating such conditions. The cases of *Farrell v Federated Employers' Insurance Association Ltd* (1970) and *Pioneer Concrete (UK) Ltd v National Employers' Mutual General* (1985) illustrate this. See Appendix 4.

Does the policy apply?

The insurers have to determine whether the policy was in force at the time of the claim and whether it covers the claim. While this is elementary it can easily be overlooked. The first stage is to ask the insured to complete a claim form. The following list, which is not exhaustive, should assist the insured in the presentation of a claim:

(a) All questions on the claim form should be answered fully and completely honestly. If questions are not applicable, this should be stated, explaining why the question does not apply (unless it is obvious). Questions should not be ignored.

(b) Any relevant matter should be disclosed; if in doubt disclose it.

(c) The names and addresses of witnesses of the damage to property which is the subject of a claim can be very important, even if they only saw the aftermath of the occurrence, and should be supplied to the insurers.

The insurer will have to check the facts of the claim against the policy insuring (or operative) clause and the policy exclusions and conditions in deciding whether the policy applies. See Chapter 2 for these details.

The loss or damage must be fortuitous (see Condition 3 (a) regarding "Duties of the Insured" in Chapter 2), ie it must be accidental not inevitable or deliberate. The principle of indemnity (see Chapter 1) imposes a requirement that the insured should be placed in the same financial position after the loss as he or she was in before it occurred. While the insured may be the contractor, more usually the contractor and the employer are joint insureds, thus both can benefit from the policy. Both the JCT contract (otherwise known as the Standard Form of Building Contract) and the ICE conditions, in allocating responsibility for the projects (particularly for contracts overseas), may involve package insurance where the employer, the contractor, the subcontractors and occasionally even the architects and consulting engineer are all jointly indemnified.

Claims presentation

Some contractors tend to perform poorly in their method of claims presentation under the CAR policy. CAR claims should be presented under clear and precise headings of claim supported by authenticated daywork sheets or other approved site documents and plant and material allocation forms which will enable claim settlements to proceed smoothly. Poor presentation can involve delays due to misunderstandings with insurers or loss adjusters.

The remedial works must be the subject of as detailed a specification as possible and a bill of quantities. At the earliest possible stage daywork areas must be indicated and a basis of costing agreed. Valuation as "daywork" arises when additional or substituted work cannot be valued by measurement. See clause 13.5.4 of JCT 1980 edition or clause 52(3) of the ICE conditions.

The cost of remedial works is dependent, *inter alia*, on the time involved. Thus it is necessary to have a programme of works arranged from the start. This may involved site demolition and clearance before the remedial works proper can commence. Specialist subcontractors may undertake this type of work as it may be more economic from a direct cost viewpoint, leaving the main contractor free to concentrate on work on other areas of the contract.

It is relevant to remind contractors that under the ICE conditions (see Chapter 7) clause 21 requires them to insure the permanent works, the temporary works (including unfixed materials, etc) and the constructional plant to their full value. Furthermore under clause 8 contractors are required to construct, complete and maintain the works, etc. Therefore the adequacy of the insurance is largely their problem.

On the other hand under JCT 80 as amended in 1986 (see Chapter 5) by clause 22A.1 the insurance cover must be for the full reinstatement value of the works plus a percentage for professional fees, and while before 1986 temporary buildings, plant, tools and equipment were specifically excluded it must be assumed that this is still the position. In any event these other items of property, eg temporary works, constructional plant, scaffolding, tools, equipment, site huts and other temporary buildings in practice will also be insured by the contractor.

Therefore, under clause 22A.1, bearing in mind that the contractor also still has his or her obligation under clause 2.1 to carry out and complete the works in the contract documents, the problem of adequacy of insurance becomes the contractor's problem. If either of the optional clauses 22B or 22C apply then the insurance of the works becomes the employer's responsibility but more detail of these requirements will be found in Chapter 5.

The costs submitted, so far as they relate to the repair or reinstatement of the permanent or temporary works, will consist basically of labour costs, material and plant costs and overheads. Incidentally it is usually the loss adjuster who recommends the payments on account. The payment being in the joint names of the employer and contractor, subject to the wording of the construction contract concerned.

Labour costs

The labour costs are supported by daywork sheets which record the type of labour employed, the number of hours entered for each class of labour, usually the tasks performed, a rate and the extent to which that rate is varied by on-costs such as bonuses, subsistence or lodging, travelling, etc. The daywork sheets should be authorised by a responsible official on site and/or should as far as possible have been approved by the loss adjuster during interim site visits.

On general building work there can be two methods of calculating the main contractor's labour costs. The first is the unit rate included in the original main contract bill of quantities, used for tender purposes. This method can be used where the damaged areas are easily recognised as part of the original bill. Where the items of damage were not included in the original bill there is no alternative but to adopt a daywork basis or agree a unit figure. In the case of hourly-paid labour, questions sometimes arise concerning waiting time for either the arrival of materials, or plant, or just for an improvement in the weather. Provided the labour has been properly and reasonably brought to the site and cannot be employed elsewhere either on-site or at other nearby sites such costs are usually recoverable. Overtime working would not normally be paid by insurers on the grounds that the insured benefits in that he can avoid other liabilities, but in some circumstances such overtime has the effect of reducing on-costs such as travelling and lodging by reducing the repair period overall and this may be recoverable under the policy. Also there may be other acceptable reasons why overtime payments should be allowed.

The Conditions of Contract (revised 1979) 5th edition used in civil engineering work make reference to daywork. Clause 52(3) indicates reference to the "Schedules of dayworks carried out incidental to Contract Work" issued by The Federation of Civil Engineering Contractors. There are very detailed rules on how labour rates are to be built up from the productive working hours and the base rates. The amount of wages are defined as:

Wages, actual bonus paid, daily travelling allowances (fare and/or time) tool allowance and all prescribed payments including those in respect of time lost due to inclement weather paid to workmen at plain time rates and/or at overtime rates.

All payments shall be in accordance with the Working Rule Agreement of the Civil Engineering Construction Conciliation Board for Great Britain Rule Nos I to XXIII inclusive or that of other appropriate wage-fixing authorities current at the date of executing the work and where there are no prescribed payments or recognised wage-fixing authorities, the actual payments made to the workmen concerned.

Regarding the building and allied trades, a method of calculation of hours worked and the calculation of labour costs is published annually by the Building and Allied Trades Joint Industrial Council (BATJIC). There are also complementary wage awards applicable within other allied industries such as mechanical, electrical, heating and ventilation engineering.

Material costs

The cost of materials should be straightforward provided that the nature and amount of the materials is in accordance with the particular loss or damage. The claim must be supported by invoices. The main contractor is permitted to charge the invoiced price of all materials after deducting VAT including delivery to site and accounting for trade discounts.

Major changes to the VAT status of supplies of goods and services by contractors came into effect on 1.4.89. It is clear that on and from that date the majority of work supplied under contracts on JCT contracts and ICE conditions will be chargeable on the contractor at the standard rate. The VAT status of the employer will have a bearing on the declared contract value and possibly the valuation of claims.

The National Economic Development Office (NEDO) Price Adjustment Formula is used throughout the construction industry for up-grading prices to current value. The NEDO statistics are published in most of the construction industry journals and these are used to act as multiplication factors to change the rates quoted for particular items, in any specific category of building work from the date of origin to the date on which the work was carried out.

Overheads

The most common overheads are site overheads which are included as preliminary items in the bill of quantities, ie the cost of setting up and operating the site including temporary site buildings, electricity, water and telephone supply, and site security. It should be borne in mind that preliminaries are a capital cost to the contract and may not be increased if indemnifiable damage under a policy occurs, unless there is an extension of the contract period.

Another type of overhead arises in the form of administration in placing and processing orders for replacement materials and is added to the invoice value. Although there are no guidelines concerning overheads in the building industry, there are in the civil engineering industry.

There is a percentage addition, currently 133%, to the amount of wages paid to workmen which provides for statutory charges and other charges including:

(a) National Insurance and surcharge;

(b) normal contract works, third party, and employers' liability insurances;

(c) annual and public holidays with pay;

(d) non-contributory sick pay scheme;

(e) industrial training levy;

(f) redundancy payments contribution;

(g) Contracts of Employment Act;

(h) site supervision and staff including foremen and walking gangers, but the time of the gangers or charge hands working with the gangs is to be paid for as for workmen;

(i) small tools such as picks, shovels, barrows, trowels, hand saws, buckets, trestles, hammers, chisels and all items of a like nature;

(j) protective clothing;

(k) head office charges and profit.

All *labour only* subcontractors' accounts to be charged at full amount of invoice (without deduction of any cash discounts not exceeding 2 1/2%) plus 64%.

Subsistence or lodging allowances and periodic travel allowances (fare and/or time) paid to or incurred on behalf of workmen are chargeable at cost plus 12 1/2%.

The charges referred to above are as at date of publication and will be subject to periodic review.

Claims submitted to insurers will usually include profit, and provided the insured contractor can show that had his or her resources not been employed on the repair and replacement work they would have been employed elsewhere, this profit is justified. The cost of preparing and presenting the claim is not a cost recoverable under the policy.

The main risks causing claims

The risks here are endless and claims can vary according to the nature of the construction involved, particularly in the case of civil engineering work.

Fire damage

This is probably the most common cause of loss or damage and is often the most costly. Fires frequently destroy site offices and canteens with all their contents, because these temporary buildings are timber built. A common cause of fires on contract sites is the use of oxy-acetylene cutting and welding equipment, especially in confined spaces. Hence the use of a fire precautions endorsement used by some insurers, although it appears more frequently in the public liability policy than in the CAR policy.

Flood damage

Insurers have defined "flood", whether resulting from storm or tempest or otherwise, as:

(a) the escape of water from the normal confines of any natural or artificial water course (other than water tanks, water apparatus or pipes) or lake, reservoir, canal or dam, or

(b) inundation from the sea.

Incidentally the exclusion in brackets is made on the assumption that these risks are covered as a separate item under the policy. It is difficult for a contractor to apply satisfactory protective measures if the contract is a flood protection scheme. However, the Thames Barrier Scheme was carried out under a specially arranged CAR policy, and incidentally that scheme illustrates what can be achieved by project (package) insurance for a very large contract even as long ago as the early 1970s.

The CAR insurance was placed with a leading office and eight other United Kingdom insurers plus Lloyds. The policy covered the contract works, temporary works, materials and non-marine construction plant (marine hull insurance had to be effected elsewhere) tools and equipment, together with a public liability section.

The main points of this insurance were:

(a) All subcontractors were covered as joint insureds.

(b) Cover was for all operations anywhere in the United Kingdom including storage and transit risks whether by land or water.

(c) Indemnity for loss or damage caused by defective design, materials or workmanship *without* exclusion of the defective part.

(d) Indemnity for increased cost of working sustained in expediting the reinstatement of loss or damage to the insured property in order to avoid or reduce a delay in completing the contract, subject to a limit of £2 million.

(e) Cover for the cost of professional fees, removal of debris, shoring up etc, without separate lower limits.

(f) Cover for permanent buildings on the site used by the contractors in relation to the contract.

(g) Deductibles (excesses) of:

  (i) £25,000 each claim for defective design, materials or workmanship,

  (ii) £10,000 each claim for property in the river or dock,

  (iii) £500 each claim for all others.

  Currently these excesses would be very much higher.

Bearing in mind that the insurance market when this contract was placed was less competitive than it is nowadays, it is felt that at the time of writing it would be easier to place the insurances with possibly lower rates and wider coverage. For example, it is possible that a separate marine hull insurance could be arranged in one omnibus policy with the CAR, etc cover.

It is interesting to note that in this contract there were problems with ground conditions but the costs of overcoming these were paid for under the equivalent clause to clause 12 of the ICE Conditions of Contract dealing with adverse physical conditions and artificial obstructions which could not reasonably have been foreseen by an experienced contractor. See Appendix 7 for a modern example of project insurance, ie the Eurotunnel project construction policy.

Computer & Systems Engineering plc v John Lelliott (Ilford) Ltd and Others (1989) concerned building operations at the plaintiff's premises when a metal purlin was dropped on to a sprinkler system pipe so that water escaped and damaged the plaintiff's property. The plaintiff was the "employer" under a JCT contract, where the interpretation of clause 22C.1 was considered. The question was whether the water damage was caused by "flood" or "bursting . . . of . . . pipes" within the definition of "clause 22 perils". "Clause 22 perils" since the 1986 Amendment have been defined as "specified perils". It was decided that the proximate cause of the water damage was the negligent dropping of the purlin and not flood or a burst pipe for which the employer would have been responsible. Consequently the subcontractor who was responsible for dropping the purlin had to pay for the damage to the plaintiff's goods and there was no liability on the plaintiff. Further details of this case can be found in Appendix 4.

Storm damage

Buildings in the course of erection are more likely to be damaged by storm and strong winds than is a completed and occupied building. While the word "storm", used in the insured perils clause of an insurance policy, might involve an element of violence in the sense of rapid movement of air or liquid, it is also properly used where the precipitation is of an extreme or unusual intensity. Lord Clyde so held in the Outer House of the Court of Session in the case of *Glasgow Training Group (Motor Trade) Limited v Lombard Continental plc* (1988). He found that the insurer under a policy, which included such a clause, was liable to indemnify the policyholder in respect of damage caused to a building by a heavy fall of snow. For further details see Appendix 4.

Debris removal

The reason for the existence of this extension to the CAR policy is to enable the insured to recover expenses that would otherwise be outside the scope of the policy cover. The test as to whether a true act of debris removal is involved or whether it is an act of repair depends on whether it is necessary to carry it out before reconstruction can begin or not. In the latter event (not before reconstruction) it is an act of repair and covered by the policy without the debris removal extension, whereas in the former event it is not covered by the policy without the extension.

Wet risks

Risks involving potential sea and river damage, which are referred to as "wet" risks, can result in very expensive claims and thus insurers tend to impose large excesses for this kind or risk. On civil engineering contracts, with the construction of sea defences, there is a danger that the works will be damaged by the force of the sea. Site cabins can be swept out to sea and plant ruined by submersion in salt water.

Other risks

Bursting and overflowing of water apparatus, especially if undetected, can cause severe damage.

One of the most hazardous risks in civil engineering work is tunnelling. Claims can arise from rockfalls, collapse of the sides of tunnels, inrush of water, fire and explosion, and subsidence or heave of the ground surface.

Theft on contract sites is an almost continuous occurrence, consequently insurers have an exclusion of damage due to disappearance or shortage which is only revealed when an inventory is made or is not traceable to an identifiable event, apart from the general excess under the CAR policy which would exclude a series of small thefts spread over the insurance period.

Malicious damage and vandalism is another constant source of worry for the contractor. Fires arising from this source are said to account for 30% of all such incidents and more than 50% of all large fires. Site security, to be effective, is costly.

Subsidence and heave claims can be troublesome to handle because of the complicated legal and technical issues involved (see *Building Subsidence — Liability and Insurance* by Frank Eaglestone and James Apted, published by Blackwell Scientific Publications).

Risks affecting plant

Due to the amount of plant being used on sites, claims for damage to or loss of these items of equipment are common. Even when, for example, an excavator sinks into a marsh, apart from the damage, the cost of extricating it is considerable. Cranes, particularly tower cranes, have a habit of toppling over, and apart from the damage to the crane there is also damage to the works, other equipment on the site and third party injury and property damage.

Plant may be insured on a specified sum basis and some insurers may impose an average condition to ensure they receive adequate premium. Otherwise, there may be no definite sum insured for plant, leaving all plant used for the contract insured up to its full value. The CAR policy will not normally cover breakdown risks, which is left to the engineering policies, but the CAR policy does cover accidental extraneous damage.

The Model Conditions of the Contractors' Plant Association for the Hiring of Plant impose onerous liabilities on the hirer (see Chapter 11). Hirers should insure their liabilities on an all risks basis.

Insurers have been concerned by the increasing frequency of theft of contractors' plant and equipment of all types. While primarily this concerns a CAR policy the problem also involves engineering, plant and motor policies. See the end of Chapter 11. Within the term "theft" it is necessary to include malicious damage and vandalism.

Official and unofficial estimates of annual losses range from £40 to £400 million per annum, ie over £1 million per day. Whatever are the correct figures, it is clear that very large amounts are involved. It has been said that as much as 45% by numbers of all claims under CAR policies relate to theft and malicious damage, of which the vast majority concern plant.

The police apparently are very conscious of the low detection rate for this type of loss due to a number of reasons, one of which is the inability of plant owners/users to be able to describe or identify plant properly. The police would like to see manufacturers adopting a new identification system for all new plant and equipment other than hand tools. It follows that insurers may be required to undertake to pay claims for relevant plant and equipment only where evidence of ownership in the form of a certificate or log book is produced at the time of a claim. However, it may be many years before such a requirement could be mandatory.

It is hoped that insurers in their own interests, as well as a matter of public policy, will support all such measures put forward by the Government, police and industry to improve the position. Perhaps an EC directive will eventually appear.

Both the Home Office and the Association of British Insurers have had working parties reporting on this problem and the above remarks are taken from the latter's report.

The role of the loss adjuster

Small contract works claims are usually settled by insurers as soon as possible with a minimum of investigation. In any event the policy excess will often eliminate the very small claim. Where, however, there is a larger claim involved it is common practice to employ loss adjusters, and this method is also favoured where a risk is scheduled and there are several different insurers involved. The adjuster will investigate the circumstances of the claim and consider the respective liabilities of the parties under the contract conditions. He or she will assess the damage caused and evaluate the cost of repair if necessary in conjunction with a quantity surveyor or other professional help which may be necessary. Sometimes insureds may make arithmetical mistakes in formulating a claim, sometimes they include items which have not been damaged in the particular incident. Occasionally items are overlooked and have to be added.

Although the adjuster is engaged by and paid by the insurers, he will act impartially and do his best to settle the claim on a basis which is fair and equitable to all parties. He will take instructions from the insurers on the scope of their policy cover and will negotiate as required to bring about a just settlement.

There can sometimes be a problem regarding the disclosure of reports. In *Waugh v British Railways Board* (1979) the House of Lords held that in order to establish privilege it is not sufficient that a document should come into existence for a series of purposes, one of which is obtaining legal advice. It is necessary that the dominant purpose for which the report came into existence was the purpose of obtaining legal advice. This question arose in *Victor Melik and Co Ltd v Norwich Union Fire Insurance Society Ltd* (1980) where, following a burglary, the plaintiff (the insured) sought disclosure of an adjuster's report. It was held that the dominant purpose of the report was to enable the insurer to ascertain the facts so that it could reach a decision as to whether or not it should rely on a clause of the policy to repudiate liability. Obtaining advice from solicitors was a secondary purpose. In the circumstances of the case the claim for privilege was not made out and the report therefore had to be disclosed.

In this case a question also arose on the interpretation of the term "without prejudice". The insurer argued that discussions between the insured and the adjuster had been on a "without prejudice" basis and that the assessor's report ought not to be admitted as evidence. The judge considered that the discussions were not part of the investigations into liability and the report was not therefore subject to privilege. The use of the term "without prejudice" by the insurer had meant it wished to avoid it being thought that by investigating the claim it was not reserving its right to repudiate.

CHAPTER 4

Clause 21.2.1 of the Standard Form of Building Contract (JCT) 1986

While basically this sub-clause calls for a liability insurance policy reference to it is included in this book for two reasons.

In the first place this insurance, required under clause 21.2.1, is a hybrid in the sense that it covers the insured's (the employer's) property, although not the works, just as much as it does his or her legal liability for damages to third party property.

Secondly, at least one insurance examination syllabus (that of the Chartered Institute of Loss Adjusters) mentioned in the Preface of this book includes this clause 21.2.1 policy under the subject "Contractors All Risks Claims".

Clause 21.2.1 under JCT 85 reads as follows:

21.2.1 Where it is stated in the Appendix that the insurance to which clause 21.2.1 refers may be required by the Employer the Contractor shall, if so instructed by the Architect, take out and maintain a Joint Names Policy for such amount of indemnity as is stated in the Appendix in respect of any expense, liability, loss, claim or proceedings which the Employer may incur or sustain by reason of injury or damage to any property other than the Works and Site Materials caused by collapse, subsidence, heave, vibration, weakening or removal of support or lowering of ground water arising out of or in the course of or by reason of the carrying out of the Works excepting injury or damage:

   .1.1   for which the Contractor is liable under clause 20.2;

   .1.2   attributable to errors or omissions in the designing of the Works;

   .1.3   which can reasonably be foreseen to be inevitable having regard to the nature of the work to be executed or the manner of its execution;

.1.4   which is the responsibility of the Employer to insure under clause 22C.1 (if applicable);

.1.5   arising from war risks or the Excepted Risks.

Sub-clause 21.2.1 replaces the previous clause 19 (2) (a) under the JCT 1963 Edition which was introduced following the decision in *Gold v Patman and Fotheringham Ltd* (1958). In that case the contract was the 1939 Standard Form of Building Contract, 1952 revision, where clause 15 required the contractors, Patman & Fotheringham, to "effect . . . such insurances . . . as may be specifically required by Bills of Quantities". The risks required to be insured by the bills included "insurance of adjoining properties against subsidence or collapse". A neighbouring owner brought a claim against the employer, Gold, in respect of subsidence caused by the building operations. The contractor had taken out a policy covering its own liability for subsidence, but not that of the plaintiff. The contractor had not been negligent (hence there was no right of action against the contractor by the neighbour) but Gold was liable for removing the support to his neighbour's land (however this was done). He tried to recover from the contractor but the Court of Appeal held that the company was not in breach of its obligations under the contract. It was clear from this decision that employers could not rely on the liability and indemnity clause of the JCT contract (now clause 20) for their complete protection where a claim was made in these circumstances. The Court of Appeal regarded the contract shown by the specific provision for fire insurance (now clause 22) being in the joint names of the employer and contractor, and the requirement for the policies now referred to in clause 21.1, as significant. Thus, where the contract requires the employer to be insured by the contractor, it expressly so provides.

It was decided to introduce a clause into the contract whereby insurance would be required to protect the employer for losses caused otherwise than by negligence of the contractor. However, the first wording used in 1963 was unsatisfactory as it did not set out the perils which were to be covered, nor did it exclude the works or mention exceptions. The amendment in 1968 listed the perils mentioned above, excluded the works and listed exceptions. Nevertheless, there was still some doubt as to exactly how the insurance was to be requested, ie whether a provisional sum specifying limits of indemnity in the bills was sufficient or a specific instruction by the architect was required.

The introductory wording in the current clause of the 1986 amendment reads:

> Where it is stated in the Appendix that the insurance to which clause 21.2.1 refers may be required by the Employer the Contractor shall, if so instructed by the Architect, take out and maintain a Joint Names Policy.

The doubt as to whether a provisional sum in the bills is sufficient to implement this insurance, or whether instructions are also required from the architect, has now been resolved by the 1986 amendment. The correct procedure is now stated in the introduction to the clause. Both a statement in the Appendix that this insurance may be required by the employer and also an instruction by the architect are necessary. The requirement for a provisional sum to be included in the contract bills has been omitted.

The clause continues as follows:

> for such amount of indemnity as is stated in the Appendix in respect of any expense, liability, loss claim or proceedings which the Employer may incur or sustain.

A new 1986 entry in the Appendix is provided for the amount of indemnity which may be for any one accident or series of accidents arising out of one event or an aggregate amount.

The architect should consult the employer before work is begun as to the amount of indemnity required, bearing in mind that the risks referred to in clause 21.2 arise mainly when the works are adjacent to existing buildings or main services, and it is the value of these that is at risk and covered by this insurance. The object is for the contractor to obtain a quotation for the employer for the issue of a policy in the joint names of the employer and contractor which the architect, with the employer's approval, can instruct the contractor to accept. Probably the quickest way for this to be done is for the architect, contractor and insurance official to meet on the site so that the risks can be examined and ideally a quotation obtained and accepted on that occasion assuming the architect and insurance official have the necessary authority.

It is clear that the contractor is only an agent required to arrange the insurance to indemnify the employer, and although the contractor is a joint insured, he or she is not required to indemnify the employer; also the second part of this sub-clause refers to expense, etc, which the employer may incur. The last two points support the statement that the only undertaking by the contractor is to arrange the insurance. The reasons submitted for this stipulation for joint names are that it is a protection for the employer and a satisfaction to the insurer. This is because there is a contractual relationship between the contractor and the insurer involving direct responsibility for the premium and for the information disclosed on the proposal form which is incorporated into the policy. Both of these direct responsibilities of the contractor would not exist if he or she could only be regarded as an agent and not as a joint insured. Usually the contractor is well known to the insurer as the insurance is often placed with the contractor's public liability insurer. It is more satisfactory for the insurer to enter into a contract with a party whose financial standing and honesty are to some extent known than to contract only with the employer, who is usually unknown to the insurer.

Furthermore, if the insurer decides to stipulate for the work to be carried out in a certain way, he or she will have more control over the contractor who is a joint insured. However, the fact that the contractor cannot claim under the policy can cause misunderstandings in the handling of claims. The phrase "expense, liability, loss, claim or proceedings" is wide enough to include consequential loss, particularly as elsewhere in the contract (eg clause 22) the words "loss or damage" only are used where presumably only insurance cover for physical damage is required.

Further details of this aspect and of this clause generally is given in the author's book *Insurance Under The JCT Forms* with supplement published by Collins (now by Blackwell Scientific Publications).

The clause continues:

> by reason of injury or damage to any property other than the Works and Site Materials caused by collapse, subsidence, heave, vibration, weakening or removal of support or lowering of ground water arising out of or in the course of or by reason of the carrying out of the Works.

As the works are excluded, the property concerned can only belong to third parties or to the employer, which is extraneous to the works, but it does not have to adjoin the works, although it usually does.

"Heave" has now been added to the list of causes of the damage and it may occur in clay soil if the moisture content is increased; this can arise as a result of removal of tree roots or vegetation which have previously been taking water from the soil. Heave could give rise to claims under the 21.2.1 type of policy on, say, a housing estate where houses have been sold or handed over and are thus no longer part of the works.

The perils of collapse, subsidence, heave, vibration, weakening or removal of support are all risks which insurers catering for the building trade are prepared to cover. In *David Allen & Sons (Bill Posting) Ltd v Drysdale* (1939) Lewis J decided that

> Subsidence means sinking, that is to say movement in a vertical direction as opposed to a settlement which means movement in a lateral direction . . . but I am of the opinion that the word subsidence in this policy covers subsidence in the sense in which I have defined it, and also settlement.

In the same case it was said "Collapse denotes falling, shrinking together, breaking down or giving way through external pressure, or loss of rigidity or support". Unless a policy excludes "settlement" it is probably inadvisable to attempt to do so by a definition which comes from outside the policy.

The lowering of ground water levels is not a circumstance so familiar to the average insurer in that it is not a wording normally used in a subsidence exclusion. However, it can obviously have the same effect on property as vibration or the removal or weakening of support.

Below the surface of the ground, at varying depths, is a large sheet of water termed the ground water. Should the level of the ground water be rather high, work in the ground may involve a permanent or temporary lowering of the ground water by drainage of the sub-soil. The lowering of ground water can occur as a result of the following activities, among others:

(a) The construction of sub-soil drains which provide a remedy for dampness caused by waterlogged soil.

(b) Certain types of piling involving the removal of ground water.

(c) When constructing below the ground water table by pumping from open sumps, or by well points, until such construction is completed.

The removal of ground water, if substantial or over a long period, can cause subsidence. If mud or soil in suspension appears in the water being extracted or diverted, the builder should take steps to hold back the soil being carried with the water, because this is erosion which is a first step to subsidence.

At law every landowner *as distinct from the owner of a building* has a natural right of support, which means a right not to have that support removed by his or her neighbour. However, there is no natural right at law to support for buildings. "The owner of the adjacent soil may with perfect legality dig that soil away, and allow his neighbour's house, if supported by it to fall in ruins to the ground." See *Dalton v Angus & Co* (1881). However, if in these circumstances, the land on which the buildings stood would have fallen whether built upon or not, then an action is allowed in respect of damage to the buildings. Assuming damage to the land would have been negligible if no building had been there, the building owner's only right of action is to sue in negligence, ie he or she has no automatic right of action which the pure landowner (without buildings) has.

This absence of a natural right in the case of the building owner applies similarly to the support provided by one building to another. Nevertheless, the right to have buildings supported by land or by other buildings can be acquired as an easement, which does not automatically accompany ownership but must be acquired by grant, either express, implied or presumed.

(a) By express grant or reservation. Here the deed creating the grant will specify its exact nature. On the sale of a building, for example, the owner may expressly grant an easement of support in favour of the grantee over the land or building retained, or he may expressly reserve for himself a right of support over the building sold.

(b) By implied grant or reservation. In these cases there is a mutual easement of support between two adjacent buildings where the construction is such that each building must give some support to the other, eg semi-detached houses and terraced houses.

(c) By presumed grant. Where a right to support has been enjoyed for a long time, it is the law that it shall not be defeated merely because the person exercising the right cannot produce the grant concerned. In these cases the law presumes that a valid grant was made. The acquisition of easements in this way is known as "prescription" and is governed mainly by the Prescription Act, 1832. As a generalisation this provides that where a building has benefited from the support of another for the period stated (normally twenty years) without interruption, then the building will acquire a right to continued support.

Consequently in *Dalton v Angus & Co* (1881), where one of two adjoining houses was converted into a coach factory which caused more pressure upon the other house and was so used for over 20 years, the House of

Lords held that an action lay for demolishing the other house and so causing a part of the factory to collapse.

A natural right which exists automatically is protected by the law of tort. Thus the removal of support to land (as distinct from buildings) constitutes a nuisance which is actionable. Generally speaking, in these cases there is no necessity to consider the circumstances leading to the removal of the support, as is essential in the case of negligence, because the liability arises from the neighbour's decision to carry out work which creates a risk of removing support from the adjoining property. However, there is an exception because if, by drainage on his or her own land of water percolating from beneath neighbouring lands, an occupier draws off all such underground water, he or she becomes the owner of it and will not be held liable to neighbours though the effect may be to dry up the neighbouring land and remove support. Statute may, however, affect this exception.

In *Langbrook Properties Ltd v Surrey CC and Others* (1969) an example occurred of an occupier draining on his own land water percolating beneath neighbouring land without liability to the neighbour for the resultant dewatering and subsequent settlement of buildings. The plaintiff company, owners of a site which it was developing, claimed damages for nuisance and negligence against the defendants, alleging that by pumping out excavations on land adjacent to the plaintiff's land during the first six months of 1968, the defendants had abstracted water percolating beneath the plaintiff's land, causing dewatering, with the result that differential settlement of land and buildings took place. The defendants maintained, *inter alia,* that the statement of claim disclosed no cause of action. A preliminary issue was ordered to be tried to determine whether the plaintiff had any cause of action against the defendants or some one or more of them by reason of withdrawal of water by means of pumping from beneath the surface of the first defendant's land.

Plowman J said that the question is whether a man whose land has subsided as a result of the abstraction by his neighbour of water percolating under that land can in law maintain an action for consequential damage either in nuisance or in negligence. The action was not about water flowing in a defined channel, nor was it concerned with easements, either of support or of any other nature; nor did any question of derogation from any grant arise. The authorities established that a person might abstract water under his or her land which percolated in undefined channels to whatever extent he or she pleased, notwithstanding that that might result in the abstraction of water percolating under the land of a neighbour and thereby cause him or her injury. In such circumstances there was damage but no violation of legal right, and thus no legal remedy. There was, then, no room for the law of nuisance or negligence to operate. If there had been, it was highly probable that the courts would have already said so. In *Chasemore v Richards* (1859) the opportunity was there, since the water authority concerned was found to have had reasonable means of knowing the natural and probable consequences of their excavations, but there was no suggestion in the House of Lords that this was a relevant matter. Moreover, since it was not actionable to cause damage by the abstraction of underground water, even where that was done maliciously, as in *Bradford Corporation v Pickles* (1895), it would seem illogical that it should be actionable if it were done carelessly. A claim in nuisance could fare no better. Nuisance involved an unlawful interference with a man's enjoyment of land, and the interference, as the authorities showed, was not unlawful. The question posed in the order had to be answered in the negative.

It was stated earlier that if mud or soil in suspension appears in the water being extracted or diverted, the builder should take steps to hold back the soil being carried with the water because this is erosion, which is a first step to subsidence. Now the important question in the light of the *Bradford Corporation* and *Langbrook Properties* cases is whether the defendants would still be free from liability for such *erosion* and resultant subsidence by abstracting percolating water. The law report in the *Langbrook Properties* case gives no indication whether erosion took place or not. Undoubtedly, as stated, there was dewatering causing subsidence. If, for example, the percolating of the water beneath the plaintiff's land had been speeded up due to the pumping out of the excavations on the land adjacent to the plaintiff's land to such an extent that erosion took place, would there be any liability? The basic principle of law is that no interest in percolating water exists until appropriation, therefore no interest or right can be infringed. However, if soil as well as water is extracted, it is clearly arguable that a right to support of land is affected by more than the removal of percolating water. The court could therefore come to a different decision. The difficulty would be proving the extraction of soil and that it caused the subsidence or at least contributed to it as much as the dewatering. The expense of experts in these cases is discouraging to insurers who would wish to know the law, but sooner or later a case will arise which economically justifies the expense.

The House of Lords in *Redland Bricks Ltd v Morris and Another* (1969) considered the remedies available where excavators had removed support to neighbouring land. See Appendix 4.

It will be seen that the exceptions of clause 21.2.1 which now follow from the basis of exception 1 of the clause 21.2.1 policy which is considered later in this chapter.

Continuing the clause:

excepting injury or damage:
.1.1   for which the Contractor is liable under clause 20.2;

The purpose of this exclusion is to ensure that the negligence, etc of the contractor, etc is not covered by this insurance, as clause 21 (requiring insurances to cover the liability imposed by clause 20) deals with this situation. Incidentally, if the public liability policy of the contractor were arranged in the joint names of the contractor and employer, the latter would be covered and possibly (if the policy was wide enough) a 21.2.1 cover would not be necessary. However, such a public liability policy would not in any circumstances cover property belonging to the insured, whereas the 21.2.1 policy does cover property belonging to the employer other than the works.

The clause continues:

excepting injury or damage:
.1.2   attributable to errors or omissions in the designing of the Works;

This exception is quite wide as it does not state that the errors or omissions in the designing of the works have to be the responsibility of a certain party. Consequently, whether the damage is attributable to the errors or omissions of the architect, employer through his or her servants or agents, or even the contractor (although in the last case exception 1.1 would probably apply), it is excluded. It would be quite wrong to use this sub-clause to give a professional negligence cover to the architect, but this was probably never intended by any of the parties concerned. However, claims against the employer himself or herself are also excluded and his or her only redress would be against the architect.

The exclusion of damage to property attributable to errors or omissions in the designing of the works should be interpreted in its literal sense to mean the design of the works which if defective *would affect the works* not merely adjacent property. To suggest the insurer could or would use this exclusion to repudiate a claim of the *Gold v Patman* type on the grounds, for example, that the piles were designed or planned to be inserted too near adjacent property is interpreting the exclusion more widely than most insurers would do. If, on the other hand, the piles, for example, were not sunk sufficiently deeply (although in accordance with the plans or specification) to prevent the collapse of the building (the works) which fell on to adjacent property, then this would be circumstances where the design exclusion operates, as this is an error or omission which affected the works themselves.

Another category of work or damage also excepted by the clause is:

.1.3   which can reasonably be foreseen to be inevitable having regard to the nature of the work to be executed or the manner of its execution;

What is inevitable damage? If it could be said that it is non-accidental damage, then this exclusion is another way of bringing in the accidental element which both insurers and reinsurers are reluctant to omit from the operative clause of the public liability policy, but the words "inevitable" and "non-accidental" are not necessarily synonymous taken by themselves.

For example, damage by a deliberate trespass to land is not accidentally caused and therefore is outside the cover provided by the normal public liability policy, but it is not inevitable assuming it could have been avoided by adopting a different method of executing the work.

However, before it can be said that such deliberate damage is outside exception 3 and within the cover required by sub-clause 21.2.1, the wording of the exception *as a whole* must be considered. It is clear from the wording that if by the method of execution decided upon or the nature of the work to be executed the damage can reasonably be foreseen to be inevitable, the exclusion operates. Applying this to the example of deliberate damage it would seem that even although a different method of executing the work which avoids the damage is possible, the test of inevitability is applied to the method decided upon, and if this method is foreseeably certain to cause damage, the exclusion applies. If this is correct, then it is possible to equate this exclusion with the "accidental" stipulation of the normal public liability policy subject to the following paragraphs on this subject. Incidentally, by using the wording concerned, the drafters are ensuring that the exception operates only when the insured could be presumed to intend the natural consequences of the acts done.

The digging of a trench so close to a garden wall that it was bound to collapse (in circumstances not involving the operation of exception 1), even though the trench could have been planned to take a course avoiding such damage, is an example. The resultant claim would not be covered, either under the normal public liability policy with its "accident" cover or under the wording of sub-clause 21.2.1 because of exception 3.

There is another aspect of this exception to be considered. It limits the inevitable damage to that which *can reasonably be foreseen*. Consequently the test is not whether with hindsight, or on the opinion of experts after the damage is done, it was inevitable, but whether a reasonable person should have realised the inevitability of the damage before it occurred knowing the nature of the work to be done and the method of doing it. In these circumstances, it is possible that damage which it is decided was inevitable (after due consideration by experts following investigation and tests) after the damage has been done, but not clearly so to a reasonable person before the incident, will be covered by the insurance required by this sub-clause. In this respect, the exception cannot be matched with the accidental stipulation of the normal public liability policy, which would exclude all inevitable damage even if only ultimately found to be inevitable.

The law reports do not state whether the inevitability of the damage should have been realised by a reasonable person before it occurred in the case of *Gold v Patman*, bearing in mind the nature of the work and the method of execution. If so, it is apparent that this sub-clause would still not protect the employer, but probably it is not right that it should do so in those circumstances.

There is still another type of inevitable damage which is clearly outside exception 3, and it is that which is caused by extraneous, collateral or casual acts not connected with or necessitated by the nature of the work or the manner of the execution but which would not have occurred if the contractor had not been carrying out the work. In the majority of cases, exception 1 would exclude such acts, but not if committed by third parties. Bearing in mind the limitation of the sub-clause to the collapse, etc type of peril, it is difficult to envisage circumstances in which this could arise. Nevertheless, it should be mentioned, as experienced underwriters will know that circumstances not envisaged at the time of drafting a policy do arise. However, the standard public liability policy would cover these circumstances because they are "accidental" as far as the insured is concerned.

The most obvious example is that of the supplier's lorry driver who dumps a load of paving stones and heavy wet sand against some under-pinning of the first floor of the works, which inevitably causes a collapse affecting third party property that has an implied or presumed right of support. Assuming the wrongdoer is uninsured and a man of straw, the employer will invoke his or her 21.2.1 cover because sub-clause 20.2 and the complementary insurance sub-clause 21.1.1 will not help as there is no negligence of the contractor or of those for whom he or she is responsible.

The only possible exception to sub-clause 21.2.1 which could apply is exception 3. However, this type of inevitability clearly is not reasonably foreseeable having regard to the nature of the work to be executed or the manner of its execution, ie it does not arise from performance of the work but from an extraneous or casual act.

There are further exceptions to injury or damage:

.1.4 which is the responsibility of the Employer to insure under clause 22.C.1 (if applicable);

In the 1986 amendment the drafters have at last appreciated that this exclusion in the 1980 edition, which read "which is at the sole risk of the Employer under clause 22B or 22C (if applicable)", was largely unnecessary as the works are already excluded and clause 22 is generally speaking limited to the works (using this term as including site materials) although it has to be admitted that existing structures in clause 22C justify the exclusion of existing structures. This is now made clear by confining the exclusion to 22.C.1, which concerns existing structures and the contents thereof owned by the employer or for which he or she is responsible. Furthermore the basic sub-clause 21.2.1 now excludes "Works and Site Materials".

excepting injury or damage:
.1.5 arising from war risks or the Excepted Risks.

War risks have been considered in the previous chapter. Excepted risks are defined in clause 1.3 as:

ionising radiations or contamination by radioactivity from any nuclear fuel or from any nuclear waste from the combustion of nuclear fuel, radioactive toxic explosive or other hazardous properties of any explosive nuclear assembly or nuclear component thereof, pressure waves caused by aircraft or other aerial devices travelling at sonic or supersonic speeds.

Nuclear risks and sonic waves were also dealt with in the previous chapter.

The position of the employer under sub-clause 21.2.1

(a) All individual firms and companies having building work done, whether under the JCT Standard Form of Contract or not, should ensure that their own insurances cover their liability for building work and in particular that any risks or liabilities for which they are not obtaining an indemnity from the contractor are covered as far as possible, even if it leads to dual insurance. Unfortunately Lord Justice Hodson in *Gold v Patman* gave the impression that the contractor should be the agent in effecting any additional insurances required by the employer, when he stated that "It is plain from the nature of the contract that there would be no objection to a provision for the insuring of the building owner by the contractors being included in the bill of quantities as an obligation of the contractors . . .". Thus the tendency is for the employer to turn to the contractor instead of making his or her own arrangements. Worse still is the tendency for those seeking such insurance to attempt to widen sub-clause 21.2.1 to provide an employers' liability and public liability cover for the building activities, which should be arranged directly for the employer without involving the contractor. For example, a biscuit manufacturer which is about to have another factory built will have both an employers' and a public liability policy but probably not covering building work. Those policies will have to be extended to cover this work, but this can be done without involving the contractor. From the insurer's viewpoint the overlapping of the 21.2.1 policy with other policies which might be giving the employer cover is inadvisable, especially when the insurers are different.

(b) In practice, 21.2.1 cover is often arranged by the employer whose occupation is that of a property developer. He or she sometimes stipulates that a certain insurer will provide the cover and the employer's quantity surveyor or architect deals directly with the insurer. Possibly the contractor is glad to leave the employer's agent to arrange an insurance which does not benefit him or her and only saddles him or her with the job of an insurance agent.

(c) The 21.2.1 policy, it has been said already, is a hybrid in that it gives liability, material damage and consequential loss insurance cover within the same operative clause. All property which is adjacent to the site is vulnerable as a result of the building activities. No doubt the employer's adjacent property will be covered by a fire (and maybe special perils) policy which would not include the subsidence risks mentioned in sub-clause 21.2.1. However, the

employer's property may suffer from other perils not covered by a
21.2.1 policy or a fire and special perils policy. An illustration is
dust, which does not have to be excessive when arising from
building work to cause serious damage to delicate machinery and
electronic equipment such as computers (even though well protected) in neighbouring buildings. Thus there may be no liability
on the contractor because in negligence the vital question is, "Did
the defendant contractor take reasonable care?" If he or she did,
there can be no liability upon him or her.

(d) Whereas consequential loss following damage to the contract
     works is excluded, because the wording specifically excludes the
     works, consequential loss sustained by the employer following
     damage to third party property, to the employers' property or that
     for which he or she is responsible would be covered. This can result
     in a number of claims which may not be foreseen. For example,
     delay in completion of the works resulting from damage to
     adjacent property in the *Gold v Patman* situation can arise from the
     blocking of entrances to the site. It is difficult to argue that this is
     not an expense which the employer has incurred by reason of dam-
     age to property within the meaning of the sub-clause, because it
     does not arise out of damage to the works, which is excluded. Delay
     in completion of the works due to interference with the contrac-
     tor's work schedule by reason of damage to property (accepting
     the latter to be a valid 21.2.1 claim) is not so clearly an expense
     under the sub-clause as it could be due as much to the inability to
     find the necessary labour or other factors as due to the damage to
     adjacent property. Here it is a matter of what is the proximate cause
     of the delay. If the damage is the proximate cause of the delay, it is
     covered by the policy. This situation should not be confused with
     the position where adjacent property collapses (say a legitimate
     21.2.1 claim) on to the works, damaging them (the damage being
     specifically excluded under the 21.2.1 policy) and resulting in a
     delay-in-completion claim. This may arise because workmen
     otherwise used to progress the works have to clear debris or carry
     out repairs and the contract works schedule suffers, or they have
     to be paid overtime at the employer's expense in order to maintain
     the time schedule. In these circumstances the answer seems to lie
     in the basic fact that an expense which the employer may incur by
     reason of *damage to the works* is specifically excluded, and thus is
     not a valid claim. It is a consequential loss following damage to the

contract works. The fact that indirectly it is due to damage to adjoining property is irrelevant in the face of the specific exclusion. An advance profits policy may provide some cover for the employer. See Chapter 5 and Appendix 6.

The clause 21.2.1. policy

The decision by the employer to take out this insurance will depend upon the kind of work the contract requires. For example, piling, the removal of support to existing buildings or excavating near their foundations are clearly relevant, as is the type and condition of property adjacent to the site of the works. The greater the hazard the greater the requirement for this type of cover, ie there is a natural selection against the insurer. Thus a single-storey school to be erected in the middle of a large field involves little or no 21.2.1 risk. However, work on old property in the middle of a city, involving work near the foundations of third party buildings, carries a very high risk.

The amount of the required indemnity entered in the Appendix to the JCT contract can apply either to any one occurrence (or series of occurrences arising out of one event) or in the aggregate, ie the figure applies overall to the period of insurance. In any event the choice of amount bears no relation to the amount of the contract price. It is the value of adjoining property that has to be considered, not forgetting the contents thereof. Insurers catering for this risk can accept high limits, eg up to £10 million. Where higher sums are called for, co-insured or "layered" policies would be arranged with other insurers or reinsurers.

The policy wording

Section 4 of the policy set out in Appendix 1 will be taken as an example. The operative or insuring clause reads as follows:

> In the event of the Insured entering into any contract or agreement by which the Insured is required to effect insurance under the terms of Clause 21.2.1 of the Joint Contracts Tribunal Standard Form of Building Contract (or any subsequent revision or substitution thereof) or under the terms of any other contract requiring insurance of like kind the Company will indemnify the Insured and the Employer in respect of any expense liability loss claim or

proceedings which the Employer may incur or sustain by reason of Damage to
any property other than the Contract Works occurring during the Period of
Insurance within the Territorial Limits and caused by

    a)   collapse
    b)   subsidence
    c)   heave
    d)   vibration
    e)   weakening or removal of support
    f)   lowering of ground water

arising out of and in the course of or by reason of the carrying out of the contract
works

Provided that
1. the Company shall not be liable for any amount exceeding the Limit of
    Indemnity

2. the Insured shall notify the Company within 21 days of entering into or
    commencing work under such contract or agreement whichever is the
    sooner together with full details of the contract

3. once notified the Company may give 14 days notice to cancel the cover
    granted by this Section in respect of such contract or agreement or
    alternatively provide a quotation which may vary the terms of this Section

4. the indemnity provided by this Section in respect of such contract or agree-
    ment shall terminate 14 days from the date of issue of the quotation if the
    quotation has not by then been accepted by the Insured or the Employer.

The operative or insuring clause

This specimen policy adopts the practice of the majority of insurers and
follows the wording of clause 21.2.1. Whether it is correct to state that the
"Company will indemnify the Insured and the Employer" depends on
whether one looks at the schedule which may follow the clause requirement for a joint names policy, or the intention behind the clause which is
to protect the employer only*. It is a fact that the clause does not intend to
protect the insured contractor, therefore he or she will get no indemnity,
although the policy under discussion arguably takes the contrary view,
but it has to be pointed out that this cover is still qualified by the words

---

* It is understood that the insurer is removing the words "indemnify the insured" from this
operative clause.

"in respect of any expense liability loss claim or proceedings which the Employer may incur or sustain". "Employer" is defined later. The policy then continues with the words:

by reason of Damage to any property other than the Contract Works occurring during the Period of Insurance within the Territorial Limits.

So the policy covers damage to any property other than the works. The words "damage" and "contract works" are defined in the policy under the "definitions" section, as mentioned early in the previous chapter. The former includes "loss" and the latter includes "materials supplies" and "materials for use" by reason of or in connection with the contract. The "period of insurance" is given in the policy schedule and, as mentioned in the previous chapter, "territorial limits" are defined in the "definitions" section of the policy.

The policy then sets out the perils covered which are taken from the clause 21.2.1. These have already been considered in detail earlier in this chapter.

Proviso 1 together with the policy schedule indicate that the limit of indemnity applies in respect of any one occurrence or series of occurrences arising out of one cause.

Proviso 2 requires notification to the insurer "within 21 days of entering into or commencing work under such contract or agreement whichever is the sooner together with full details of the contract ". This is necessary as in the case of an annual policy the insurer must have details of every contract where this cover is required, as a survey may be required before cover can be considered and this may result in the operation of the next proviso.

Proviso 3 clearly gives the insurer the right to come off cover or impose underwriting terms.

Proviso 4 clearly gives the insured contractor or the employer the right to refuse to accept the underwriting terms just mentioned and failure to accept such terms will be taken as a refusal, the time limit being 14 days from the date of issue of the quotation. While this cover is for the protection of the employer the contractor can be involved if, for example, the insurer requires the work to be carried out in a certain way such as the shoring of third party property or the use of a certain type of shoring.

Employer

This section of the policy has a definition of "employer". It reads:

For the purpose of this Section Employer shall mean any person firm company ministry or authority named as the Employer in the contract or agreement entered into by the Insured.

Presumably the purpose of this definition is to indicate that any person or organisation who commissions work of construction can be the employer in this insurance contract.

Exceptions

Exception 1 follows the exceptions listed in clause 21.2.1 but the wording is slightly different and this calls for comment. Paragraph (a) reads:

> caused by the negligence omission or default of the Insured or any agent or Employee of the Insured or of any sub-contractor or his employees or agents.

Clause 21.2.1 merely refers to the contractor's liability under clause 20.2, and since the amendment in 1986 this clause uses the phrase "negligence, breach of statutory duty, omission or default of the Contractor etc " so the policy strictly speaking does not cover the requirements of clause 21.2.1 as breach of statutory duty should be excluded as well as negligence, omission or default.

Paragraph (b) reads:

> which is attributable to errors or omissions in the planning or the designing of the Contract Works.

While the word "planning" is additional to those in the contract clause, this would not make any difference to the operation of the exclusion.

Paragraph (c) reads:

> which can reasonably be foreseen to be inevitable having regard to the nature of the work to be executed or the manner of its execution.

This exception follows the wording of the clause.

Paragraph (d) reads:

> arising from Damage to property which is at the risk of the Employer under the terms of the contract or agreement.

While the wording is different from that in the clause the interpretation must be the same.

Paragraph (e) reads:

arising from Contractual Liability.

Now contractual liability is defined in the "definitions" of the policy as meaning liability which attaches by virtue of a contract or agreement but which would not have attached in the absence of such contract or agreement. This would not apply to the construction contract between the employer and the contractor, but would avoid liability under other contracts which the employer may have entered into which increase his common law liability to the owners or tenants of adjacent property. Such risks might be insurable, but the insurer wants the opportunity to assess this risk if he or she is asked to insure it. Most insurers will also exclude the liability risk arising from ownership, possession or use by or on behalf of the insured of any mechanically propelled vehicle in circumstances necessitating compulsory third party insurance under statute.

Paragraph (f) reads:

arising from Damage occasioned by pressure waves caused by aircraft or other aerial devices travelling at sonic or supersonic speeds.

This exception is self explanatory and in accordance with the fifth exception in clause 21.2.1 war risks and nuclear risks are excluded under the general exceptions of the policy.

Exception 2 reads:

if the contract or agreement specifies that shoring of any building or structure is required and such shoring is necessary within 35 days of commencement of the contract or agreement.

Presumably the insurer requires time to investigate the risk, hence this exception.

Exception 3 reads:

against any expense liability loss claim or proceedings arising from
a)   demolition or partial demolition of any building or structure
b)   the use of explosives
c)   tunnelling or piling work
d)   underpinning
e)   deliberate dewatering of the site.

This exception clearly lists underwriting terms enabling the insurer to avoid or at least consider these hazardous risks before accepting them, and reinforces the common law duty of disclosure of material facts (the principle of the utmost good faith), see Chapter 1.

Exception 4 reads:

> in respect of any sum payable under any penalty clause or by reason of breach of contract.

This exception is self explanatory.

Exception 5 reads:

> the excess specified in the Schedule.

This exception is also self explanatory. Incidentally the excess can be very large.

General exceptions and conditions

The terms set out in Chapter 2 and Appendix 1 under these headings apply, where stated, to this clause 21.2.1 of the policy.

CHAPTER 5

JCT Standard Form of Building Contract 1986

Loss or damage to the works and site materials

Article 1 of the 1980 Edition, all versions, provides that "the Contractor will upon and subject to the Contract Documents carry out and complete the Works shown upon, described by or referred to in those Documents". Clause 2.1 repeats this requirement and identifies the contract documents mentioned in Article 1. Unless the contract documents provide otherwise, eg the 1980 edition clauses 22B or 22C (see later), the contractor in spite of loss or damage to the works for whatever reason must carry out and complete the works and pay for the expense involved. This follows the basic rule set out in *Charon (Finchley) Ltd v Singer Sewing Machine Co Ltd* (1968), which did not concern the JCT contract but where the court quoted *Hudson's Building and Engineering Contracts*, 9th edition, page 223 as follows:

> Indeed, by virtue of the express undertaking to complete (and, in many contracts, maintain for a fixed period after completion) the contractor would be liable to carry out work again free of charge in the event of some accidental damage occurring before completion even in the absence of any express provision for protection of the risk.

Therefore the prudent contractor would wish to arrange the widest possible insurance cover for the "works".

Except in the 1980 clause 22B (local authorities versions) the JCT form has always provided that insurance cover be taken out to deal with loss or damage to the works from fire and special perils, as the insurance world calls this cover; ie fire, lightning, explosion, riot and civil commotion, earthquake, aircraft or other aerial devices or articles dropped therefrom, storm, tempest and flood, and bursting or overflowing of water tanks, apparatus or pipes. These are now defined in the 1986 amendment in clause 1.3 as specified perils. There are alternatives for the erection of a new building but no choice for the alteration of or extension to an existing building under clause 22, as follows:

A: the erection of a new building where the contractor must insure the works against loss or damage by all risks;

B: the erection of a new building where the employer must insure the works against loss or damage by all risks;

C: the alteration of or extension to an existing building where the employer must insure:

(a) the works against all risks

(b) existing structures and contents owned by him, or for which he is responsible against specified perils.

(The capital letters used above are used in the printed form to denote the sub-clause concerned.)

Clause 22. Insurance of the Works [m]

22.1   Clause 22A or clause 22B or clause 22C shall apply whichever clause is stated to apply in the Appendix.

22.2   In clause 22A, 22B, 22C and, so far as relevant, in other clauses of the Conditions the following phrases shall have the meanings given below:

All Risks   insurance which provides cover against any physical
Insurance: [n]   loss or damage to work executed and Site Materials but
                 excluding the cost necessary to repair, replace or rectify

1   property which is defective due to

.1   wear and tear,

.2   obsolescence,

.3   deterioration, rust or mildew;

[m1]   **2**   any work executed or any Site Materials lost or damaged as a result of its own defect in design, plan, specification, material or workmanship or any other work executed which is lost or damaged in consequence thereof where such work relied for its support or stability on such work which was defective;

3   loss or damage caused by or arising from

.1   any consequence of war, invasion, act of foreign enemy, hostilities (whether war be declared or not), civil war, rebellion, revolution, insurrection, military or usurped power, confiscation, commandeering, nationalisation or requisition or loss or destruction of or damage to any property by or under the order of any government *de jure* or *de facto* or public, municipal or local authority;

.2   disappearance or shortage if such disappearance or shortage is only revealed when an inventory is made or is not traceable to an identifiable event;

.3   an Excepted Risk (as defined in clause 1.3);

and if the Contract is carried out in Northern Ireland

.4   civil commotion;

.5   any unlawful, wanton or malicious act committed maliciously by a person or persons acting on behalf of or in connection with an unlawful association; "unlawful association" shall mean any organisation which is engaged in terrorism and includes an organisation which at any relevant time is a proscribed organisation within the meaning of the Northern Ireland (Emergency Provisions) Act 1973; "terrorism" means the use of violence for political ends and includes any use of violence for the purpose of putting the public or any section of the public in fear.

Site Materials: all unfixed materials and goods delivered to, placed on
                       or adjacent to the Works and intended for incorporation
                       therein.

Clauses 22.1 to 22.3 have been added to the 1980 edition by the 1986
Amendment.

Clause 22.1 is self-explanatory and by a footnote [m] the circumstances
under which clauses 22A, 22B and 22C are to be used are the same as in
JCT 80. See above.

Clause 22.2 defines the meaning of all risks insurance. The words
"physical loss" in the insuring clause make it clear that consequential loss
is not covered, see Chapter 2. While the footnote (m.1) seems to disallow
limitations on the design exclusion (see an explanation of this in chapter
2), the intention seems to be to disallow any additional exclusions as
clauses 22.A.1, 22.B.1 and 22.C.2 (all of which concern all risks insurance),
when referring to the cover to be provided, use the phrase "no less than
that defined in clause 22.2 (n) (o.l.)". However, this cannot disallow
exclusions setting out risks which are covered by other policies, eg motor,
marine and engineering risks. Footnote (n) makes the point that all risks
policies vary in their wording and footnote (o.l.) states that it may not be
possible for insurance to be taken out against certain of the risks covered
by the definition of "all risks insurance". It says this matter should be
arranged between the parties prior to entering into the contract, and either
the definition of "all risks insurance" given in clause 22.2 should be
amended or the risks actually covered should replace this definition. In
the latter case, clause 22.A.1, 22.A.3 or 22.B.1 (whichever is applicable) and
other relevant clauses in which the definition "all risks insurance" is used
should be amended to include the words used to replace this definition,
eg riot and civil commotion is unobtainable in Northern Ireland.

The extent of this insurance now required is not unreasonable but it
means that there will be many insured who will have annual blanket or
floater policies which do not conform with the revised contract conditions.
This is particularly so regarding the extension of design, etc cover now
required. While it should be simple to extend the cover, whether insurers
will be prepared to provide the JCT cover for all contracts, whether subject
to JCT conditions or not, and whether insureds will wish to pay for a cover
on non-JCT contracts which they do not consider necessary, remains to be
seen.

Contractors' all risks policies issued by insurers are not standardised
and there is some variation in the way these policies, and particularly the
exclusions, are expressed.

The all risks insurance exclusions listed in sub-clause 22.2 have been explained in Chapter 2, bearing in mind the Excepted Risks in clause 1.3 include nuclear risks and sonic waves.

22.3 .1   The Contractor where clause 22A applies, and the Employer where either clause 22B or clause 22C applies shall ensure that the Joint Names Policy referred to in clause 22A.1 or clause 22A.3 or the Joint Names Policies referred to in clause 22B.1 or in clause 22C.1 and 22C.2 shall

either   provide for recognition of each Sub-Contractor nominated by the Architect as an insured under the relevant Joint Names Policy

or   include a waiver by the relevant insurers of any right of subrogation which they may have against any such Nominated Sub-Contractor

in respect of loss or damage by the Specified Perils to the Works and Site Materials where clause 22A or clause 22B or clause 22C.2 applies and, where clause 22C.1 applies, in respect of loss or damage by the Specified Perils to the existing structures (which shall include from the relevant date any relevant part to which clause 18.1.3 refers) together with the contents thereof owned by the Employer or for which he is responsible; and that this recognition or waiver shall continue up to and including the date of issue of the certificate of practical completion of the Sub-Contract Works (as referred to in clause 14.2 of the Sub-Contract NSC/4 or NSC/4a) or the date of determination of the employment of the Contractor (whether or not the validity of that determination is contested) under clause 27 or clause 28, or, where clause 22C applies, under clause 27 or clause 28 or clause 22C.4.3. whichever is the earlier. The provisions of clause 22.3.1 shall apply also in respect of any Joint Names Policy taken out by the Employer under clause 22A.2 or by the Contractor under clause 22B.2 or under clause 22C.3 in respect of a default by the Employer under clause 22C.2.

22.3 .2   Except in respect of the Joint Names Policy referred to in clause 22C.1 (or the Joint Names Policy referred to in clause 22C.3 in respect of a default by the Employer under clause 22C.1) the provisions of clause 22.3.1 in regard to recognition or waiver shall apply to Domestic Sub-Contractors. Such recognition or waiver for Domestic Sub-Contractors shall continue up to and including the date of issue of any certificate or other document which states that the Domestic Sub-Contract Works are practically complete or the date of determination of the employment of the Contractor as referred to in clause 22.3.1 whichever is the earlier.

This new clause 22.3 should be read carefully and particular notice taken of the following points as frequently subcontractors damage the works and the question of recovery arises.

(a) The contractor, where clause 22A applies, and the employer, where either 22B or 22C applies, have to ensure that the joint names policies mentioned in those clauses either provide for recognition of each subcontractor nominated by the architect as an insured under those policies, *or* include a waiver by the relevant insurers of any right of subrogation which they may have against any such nominated subcontractor *but only in respect of loss or damage by the specified perils* to the works and site materials or the existing structures as the case may be. Specified perils are the same as the old "clause 22 perils". See the fire and special perils listed earlier.

(b) This means that even when all risks insurance is required by contract, ie in clause 22A or 22B or 22C.2, only the specified perils cover of the all risks insurance is to operate so far as nominated subcontractors are concerned. Apparently it was not considered possible to get insurers generally to extend the all risks insurance of the works to provide the all risks cover to nominated subcontractors. However, with the agreement of insurers the 1986 version of NSC/4 and 4a (the nominated subcontract see later) provides for the nominated subcontractors to obtain the benefit of the major part of the cover given to the employer and contractor jointly under the main contract 1986 joint names policy. This is the explanation given in the *Guide to the Amendments to the Insurance and Related Liability Provisions* 1986 issued with Practice Note 22.

(c) As regards existing structures to which clause 22C.1 applies, the application of clause 18.1.3 concerning partial possession by the employer means that the part of the works of which the employer is to take possession (the relevant part) from the relevant date is in effect no longer regarded as "the Works" but as an "existing structure" and therefore subject to the joint names policy taken out by the employer under clause 22.C.1. The contents of the existing structures owned by the employer, or for which he or she is responsible, are also included in the joint names policy cover.

(d) This recognition of each nominated subcontractor under the policy or waiver of the right of subrogation is to continue up to and including the date of issue of the certificate of practical completion of the *subcontract works* (as referred to in clause 14.2 of subcontract NSC/4 or NSC/4a) or the date of determination of the employment of the contractor (whether or not the validity of that determination is contested) under the earliest of the clauses listed.

(e) Except in respect of the joint names policy referred to in clause 22C.1 (or that referred to in clause 22C.3 in respect of a default by the employer under clause 22C.1) the provisions of clause 22.3.1 regarding recognition or waiver shall apply to domestic subcontractors up to and including the date of issue of any certificate or other document which states the domestic subcontract works are practically complete, or the date of determination of the employment of the contractor as referred to in clause 22.3.1, whichever is the earlier.

To summarise the position under clause 22.3, the two sub-clauses 22.3.1 (concerning nominated subcontractors) and 22.3.2 (concerning domestic subcontractors) protect subcontractors against specified perils either as an insured person or by waiver of subrogation rights by insurers, but domestic subcontractors do not get this benefit under sub-clause 22C.1 for existing structures and contents. The cases of *Welsh Health Technical Services Organisation v Hayden Young* (1986) and *Norwich City Council v Harvey and Briggs Amasco* (1988) on JCT terms operating before 1986 amendment indicate that the duty of care otherwise owed by the subcontractor defendant to the plaintiff employer can be qualified by the terms of the contract between the parties (although the employer never intended privity of contract between himself and the subcontractor imposing liability for fire and other special perils). By the terms concerned in those cases the plaintiff employer accepted the risk of fire and other special perils to its property under clauses 20B and 20C (now 22B and 22C). However, the position under the 1986 amendment is clearer, but it leaves all subcontractors responsible for losses, other than by specified perils, against which there is no contractual requirement to insure, and domestic subcontractors carry the risk of all loss or damage to existing structures and their contents. Incidentally, insurers refuse to give subcontractors all risks cover under the main contractor's or employer's CAR policy, particularly under annual open cover policies, as the materials they use are often attractive to thieves and the care taken in storage on site can vary. Furthermore, if the theft and malicious damage risks will not affect the subcontractor's record it may influence his or her security attitude. Also, the subcontractor's claims record will directly affect the main

contractor's insurance record if they were included within his or her
insurance cover.

Clause 22A. Erection of new buildings — all risks insurance of the works by the contractors [m]

22A.1   The Contractor shall take out and maintain a Joint Names Policy for
         All Risks Insurance for cover no less than that defined in clause 22.2
         [n] [o1] for the full reinstatement value of the works (plus the
         percentage, if any, to cover professional fees stated in the Appendix)
         and shall (subject to clause 18.1.3) maintain such Joint Names Policy
         up to and including the date of issue of the certificate of Practical
         Completion or up to and including the date of determination of the
         employment of the Contractor under clause 27 or clause 28 (whether
         or not the validity of that determination is contested) whichever is
         the earlier.

Clause 22A.1 now requires the contractor to take out and maintain a joint
names policy for all risks insurance for work executed and site materials
as it states "no less than that defined in clause 22.2 above" and it should
be noted that clause 22.2 includes a definition of site materials as well as
a draft policy. The cover has to be for the full reinstatement value of the
works (plus the percentage, if any, to cover professional fees). If the
insurance money is not adequate to cover the "full reinstatement value"
the shortfall would be the responsibility of the contractor as he or she has
a liability to complete the works (see the beginning of this chapter).

Consideration should be given to obtaining a policy which automatically provides for an uplift in the sum insured by a percentage which will
adequately reflect the increase in costs arising from inflation in respect of
building costs and professional fees. The contract price is rarely, if ever,
sufficient, so a type of escalation clause just described is important.

The liability to insure continues up to the date of issue of the certificate
of practical completion (including that date) or up to and including the
date of determination of the employment of the contractor under clause
27 or 28, whichever is the earlier. However, this is subject to clause 18.1.3
which indicates that the sum insured is reduced by the full value of any
part possession taken over by the employer as from the date on which the
employer takes possession.

22A.2   The Joint Names Policy referred to in clause 22A.1 shall be taken out with insurers approved by the Employer and the Contractor shall send to the Architect for deposit with the Employer that Policy and the premium receipt therefor and also any relevant endorsement or endorsements thereof as may be required to comply with the obligation to maintain that Policy set out in clause 22A.1 and the premium receipts therefor. If the Contractor defaults in taking out or in maintaining the Joint Names Policy as required by clauses 22A.1 and 22A.2 the Employer may himself take out and maintain a Joint Names Policy against any risk in respect of which the default shall have occurred and a sum or sums equivalent to the amount paid or payable by him in respect of premiums therefor may be deducted by him from any monies due or to become due to the Contractor under this Contract or such amount may be recoverable by the Employer from the Contractor as a debt.

It is important to note that a side heading to this sub-clause reads "Single policy — insurers approved by Employer — failure by Contractor to insure". Consequently, in the event of the completion date being extended, then it is essential to extend this single policy accordingly.

This is the usual sub-clause which appears in most construction contracts requiring insurers to be approved by the employer and the policy, premium receipt and relevant endorsement(s) have to be sent to the employer via the architect. Thus any statutorily authorised insurer could be approved.

The employer's authority to insure if the contractor fails to do so is self-explanatory. Now that there is a specimen all risks policy in the JCT contract, as far as the insuring clause and exclusions are concerned, there is clearly a test to be applied, whereas in the past the matter was usually left to an insurance broker specialising in construction work to arrange appropriate cover.

22A.3.1   If the Contractor independently of his obligations under this Contract maintains a policy of insurance which provides (*inter alia*) All Risks Insurance for cover no less than that defined in clause 22.2 for the full reinstatement value of the Works (plus the percentage, if any, to cover professional fees stated in the Appendix) then the maintenance by the Contractor of such policy shall, if the policy is a Joint Names Policy in respect of the aforesaid Works, be a discharge of the Contractor's obligation to take out and maintain a Joint Names Policy under clause 22A.1. If and so long as the Contractor is able to send to the Architect for inspection by the Employer as and when he is reasonable required to do so by the Employer documentary evidence that such a policy is being maintained then the Contractor shall be

discharged from his obligation under clause 22A.2 to deposit the
policy and the premium receipt with the Employer but on any
occasion the Employer may (but not unreasonably or vexatiously)
require to have sent to the Architect for inspection by the Employer
the policy to which clause 22A.3.1 refers and the premium receipts
therefor. The annual renewal date, as supplied by the Contractor, of
the insurance referred to in clause 22A.3.1 is stated in the Appendix.

The side heading to this sub-clause reads "Use of annual policy maintained by Contractor — alternative to use of clause 22A.2".

Where the contractor's annual policy is used, the last sentence of this
clause provides for the contractor to supply the employer with the annual
renewal date which is inserted in the appendix so that the employer is
aware of the date the policy has to be renewed. The purpose of this
sub-clause is to use the contractor's annual all risks policy endorsed in the
joint names of the employer as well as the contractor in respect of the
works concerned and so discharge the contractor's obligation under
clause 22A.1. By sending documentary evidence of the maintenance of the
policy to the architect for inspection by the employer the contractor
complies with his or her obligation under clause 22A.2.

22A.3.2   The provisions of 22A.2 shall apply in regard to any default in taking
out or in maintaining insurance under clause 22A.3.1.

Under this sub-clause the same provisions apply in respect of the
employer's rights to insure, should the contractor default in respect of his
or her existing annual insurance mentioned in sub-clause 22A.3.1.

22A.4.1   If any loss or damage affecting work executed or any part thereof or
any Site Materials is occasioned by any one or more of the risks
covered by the Joint Names Policy referred to in clause 22A.1 or
clause 22A.2 or clause 22A.3 then, upon discovering the said loss or
damage, the Contractor shall forthwith give notice in writing both to
the Architect and to the Employer of the extent, nature and location
thereof.

22A.4.2   The occurrence of such loss or damage shall be disregarded in
computing any amounts payable to the Contractor under or by virtue
of this Contract.

22A.4.3   After inspection required by the insurers in respect of a claim under
the Joint Names Policy referred to in clause 22A.1 or clause 22A.2 or
clause 22A.3 has been completed the Contractor with due diligence

shall restore such work damaged, replace or repair any such Site Materials which have been lost or damaged, remove and dispose of any debris and proceed with the carrying out and completion of the Works.

22A.4.4   The Contractor, for himself and for all Nominated and Domestic Sub-Contractors who are, pursuant to clause 22.3, recognised as an insured under the Joint Names Policy referred to in clause 22A.1 or clause 22A.2 or clause 22A.3, shall authorise the insurers to pay all monies from such insurance in respect of the loss or damage referred to in clause 22A.4.1 to the Employer. The Employer shall pay all such monies (less only the percentage, if any, to cover professional fees stated in the Appendix) to the Contractor by instalments under certificates of the Architect issued at the Period of Interim Certificates.

22A.4.5   The Contractor shall not be entitled to any payment in respect of the restoration, replacement or repair of such loss or damage and (when required) the removal and disposal of debris other than the monies received under the aforesaid insurance.

These remaining sub-clauses deal with insurance claims for loss or damage to the works, etc.

Sub-clause 22A.4.1 concerns the requirement of the contractor to notify and give details to the architect and the employer if such loss or damage occurs which is covered by the joint names policy. Otherwise the architect and employer may know nothing about it.

Sub-clause 22A.4.2 provides that the occurrence of loss or damage is to be disregarded in computing amounts payable to the contractor. Thus the contractor must be paid for all such work as though no loss or damage had occurred. This means the contractor is entitled to payment for the reinstatement work from the insurance money received under the joint names policy as well as for the work he or she had originally done in accordance with the contract but which had been subsequently lost or damaged.

Sub-clause 22A.4.3 emphasises the fact that the contractor has to restore damaged work or replace or repair damaged or lost site materials in respect of a claim under the joint names policy, but only after the insurers have carried out any inspection they may require.

Sub-clauses 22A.4.4 and 22A.4.5 indicate that adequate policy cover and sum insured are vital since only insurance monies (less the percentage, if any, to cover professional fees stated in the appendix) shall be available for payments to the employer, and then by certificates (usually monthly) of the architect, to the contractor in respect of restoration of the damage, ie by instalments. Note that in sub-clause 22A.4.4 subcontractors can be considered joint insureds or subrogation rights waived by insurers but only in respect of the specified perils as stated in clause 22.3.

Clause 22B. Erection of new buildings — all risks insurance of the works by the employer

22B.1   The Employer shall take out and maintain a Joint Names Policy for All Risks Insurance for cover no less than that defined in clause 22.2 [n] [o.1] for the full reinstatement value of the Works (plus the percentage, if any to cover professional fees stated in the Appendix) and shall (subject to clause 18.1.3) maintain such Joint Names Policy up to and including the date of issue of the certificate of Practical Completion or up to and including the date of determination of the employment of the Contractor under clause 27 or clause 28 (whether or not the validity of that determination is contested) whichever is the earlier.

22B.2   The Employer shall, as and when reasonably required to do so by the Contractor, produce documentary evidence and receipts showing that the Joint Names Policy required under clause 22B.1 has been taken out and is being maintained. If the Employer defaults in taking out or in maintaining the Joint Names Policy required under clause 22B.1 then the Contractor may himself take out and maintain a Joint Names Policy against any risk in respect of which a default shall have occurred and a sum or sums equivalent to the amount paid or payable by him in respect of the premiums therefor shall be added to the Contract Sum.

22B.3   .1   If any loss or damage affecting work executed or any part thereof or any Site Materials is occasioned by any one or more of the risks covered by the Joint Names Policy referred to in clause 22B.1 or clause 22B.2 then, upon discovering the said loss or damage, the Contractor shall forthwith give notice in writing both to the Architect and to the Employer of the extent, nature and location thereof.

22B.3   .2   The occurrence of such loss or damage shall be disregarded in computing any amounts payable to the Contractor under or by virtue of this Contract.

22B.3 .3 After any inspection required by the insurers in respect of a claim under the Joint Names Policy referred to in clause 22B.1 or clause 22B.2 has been completed the Contractor with due diligence shall restore such work damaged, replace or repair any such Site Materials which have been lost or damaged, remove and dispose of any debris and proceed with the carrying out and completion of the Works.

22B.3 .4 The Contractor, for himself and for all Nominated and Domestic Sub-Contractors who are, pursuant to clause 22.3, recognised as an insured under the Joint Names Policy referred to in clause 22B.1 or clause 22B.2, shall authorise the insurers to pay all monies from such insurance in respect of the loss or damage referred to in clause 22B.3.1 to the Employer.

22B.3 .5 The restoration, replacement or repair of such loss or damage and (when required) the removal and disposal of debris shall be treated as if they were a Variation required by an instruction of the Architect under clause 13.2.'

This clause 22B has been redrafted in similar terms to the 1986 clause 22A, but of course with the employer not the contractor taking out the joint names policy for all risks insurance.

In sub-clause 22B.1 there is no longer provision for the employer to take the "sole risk" of loss or damage. Instead there is an obligation on the employer, in both the private and local authorities' editions, to take out the insurance mentioned in the previous paragraph. This was not previously required in the local authorities' edition. The insurance has to conform with the requirements of clause 22.2. Because of the joint names policy the necessity for both parties to insure their interest is now avoided as the rights of subrogation by the insurer against the contractor cannot exist under this type of policy. Prior to the 1986 amendment the contractor would have to insure the works, etc against the non-listed perils as the cover required from the employer only applied to fire and specific perils.

The omitted "sole risk" clause was one of the reasons which led to the employer being held liable for damage caused by negligence of the contractor in the case of *Archdale and Co Ltd v Comservices Ltd* (1954) and *Scottish Special Housing Association v Wimpey* (1986) but more details of these cases will be given in the commentary on clause 22C later.

In the 1986 private version of clause 22B.2 the contractor is entitled to proof from the employer that the joint names policy exists and if the employer defaults in his or her obligation, the contractor may take out and maintain this policy. In the local authorities' version the contractor has no such right and clause 22B.2 is marked "Number not used".

Clause 22B.3 contains five sub-clauses dealing with insurance claims for loss or damage to the works, etc requiring notice and details by the contractor as in sub-clause 22A.4.1, payment to the contractor as in sub-clause 22A.4.2, restoration of work after insurers' inspection as in sub-clause 22A.4.3, payment of insurance monies to the contractor via the employer and architect and limited to the insurance as in sub-clause 22A.4.4 and 22A.4.5.

No change has been made to the principle in the 1980 clause 22B that the employer pays for the restoration, etc of loss or damage to the works as if it were a variation. Thus any shortfall in insurance payment in meeting the cost of paying for the variation is borne by the employer. In clause 22A the shortfall is borne by the contractor.

Clause 22C. Insurance of existing structures — insurance of works in or extensions to existing structures [m]

22C.1   The Employer shall take out and maintain a Joint Names Policy in respect of the existing structures (which shall include from the relevant date any relevant part to which clause 18.1.3 refers) together with the contents thereof owned by him or for which he is responsible, for the full cost of reinstatement, repair or replacement of loss or damage due to one or more of the Specified Perils [o.2] up to and including the date of issue of the certificate of Practical Completion or up to and including the date of determination of the employment of the Contractor under clause 22C.4.3 or clause 27 or clause 28 (whether or not the validity of that determination is contested) whichever is the earlier. The Contractor, for himself and for all Nominated Sub-contractors who are, pursuant to clause 22.3.1, recognised as insured under the Joint Names Policy referred to in clause 22C.1 or clause 22C.3 shall authorise the insurers to pay all monies from such insurance in respect of loss or damage to the Employer.

22C.2   The Employer shall take out and maintain a Joint Names Policy for All Risks Insurance for cover no less than that defined in clause 22.2 [n] [o 2] for the full reinstatement value of the Works (plus the percentage, if any, to cover professional fees stated in the Appendix) and shall (subject to clause 18.1.3) maintain such Joint Names Policy up to and including the date of issue of the certificate of Practical

Completion or up to and including the date of determination of the employment of the Contractor under clause 22C.4.3 or clause 27 or clause 28 (whether or not the validity of that determination is contested) whichever is the earlier.

The drafters of the 1986 Amendment appreciated that the insurance market may not give full all risks insurance on the existing structure and contents since they were not part of the works, and it was decided to confine the insurance obligation concerning them to the old clause 22 perils, now called specified perils. Generally speaking, while the contractor may be in a better position to insure the works, the existing structure is usually already insured by the employer but not for all risks, so it is appropriate to put the onus of insurance on the employer. In fact a footnote (0.2) to both 22C.1 and 22C.2 draws attention to the fact that in some cases it may not be possible for insurance to be taken out against certain of the specified perils or the risks covered by the definition of "all risks insurance". In this event the definitions concerned in clauses 1.3 and 22.2 must be amended accordingly.

There are two reasons for this footnote. In the first place with certain buildings, eg historical ones, insurance for particular risks is not available, and in some areas insurance against certain perils, eg flood, riot and civil commotion, may not be obtainable.

The first two sub-clauses of clause 22C treat separately the following two situations:

Sub-clause 22C.1 deals with loss or damage *to the existing structures and the contents owned by the employer or for which he is responsible* where the insurance is against the *specified perils* (see definition in clause 1.3).

Sub-clause 22C.2 deals with loss or damage *to the works carried out in the existing structures or for extensions thereto where the insurance is against* the risk covered by the 1986 clause 22.2 definition of *all risks insurance.*

In the Practice Note 22 issued by the JCT and *Guide to the Amendments to the Insurance and Related Liability Provisions:* 1986, it is stated that the works insurance taken out by the employer has to be in the joint names of the employer and contractor. So there is no need for the contractor to take out insurance in respect of the works and site materials for loss or damage due to any of the risks covered by the 1986 definition of "all risks insurance" and the previous reference to "sole risk" in the 1980 clause 22C.1 has been omitted. Any shortfall in the insurance monies not sufficient to cover the cost of reinstatement (whether due to inadequacy of cover or to any excesses provision — uninsured amounts — in the insurance policy) is borne by the employer. However, a further question

concerning the omission of the words "shall be at the sole risk of the
Employer" is whether it will have any effect on the decision in *Scottish
Special Housing Association v Wimpey* (1986), confirming *Archdale and Co
Ltd v Comservices Ltd* (1954), if that situation arises under the new wording.
Thus if the contractor negligently destroys the building by one of the
insured risks, who is legally liable when clause 22C applies (or 22B for that
matter)? The answer must be that the insurance arranged by the employer
will operate without any subrogation rights against the contractor. Also
in the case of clause 22C.1, by virtue of the last sentence, as the nominated
subcontractor is a joint insured, any subrogation rights against him or her
are also waived. In effect, this House of Lords' decision in the *Wimpey* case
will be followed. This leaves open the position where there is a large excess
under the all risks policy and prima facie the employer is liable for this
amount because he or she has undertaken to provide insurance without
excess as there is no mention of an excess in the draft policy in clause 22.2.
However, there is a model in Appendix D of the Practice Note 22 and
Guide to the 1986 Amendment published by the JCT, to change the
liability for payment of excesses under the all risks insurance which the
employer is required to take out under clause 22C.2.

The employer might well consider adopting this new clause, which will
be numbered clause 22C.4.4.3. It provides for the contractor to bear the
cost of rectifying loss or damage which is uninsured because of excess
provisions in the joint names policy to be taken out by the employer and
where the loss or damage is due to the negligence, etc of the contractor or
any subcontractor. The employer has to inform the contractor at the tender
stage of the amount of the excesses in the joint names and if they are for
large amounts the employer should remember that the contractor and
subcontractor would themselves have to take out (or consider doing so)
insurance for any liability for the potential uninsured loss or damage
arising from the excess and this could add considerably to the cost of the
works as well as making administration more involved.

In the case of joint named policies the contractor as one of the insured
must authorise the insurer to pay all monies to the employer as the other
insured, and this authorisation must also be given on behalf of all nominated subcontractors where they are joint insureds. See the last sentence
in clause 22C.1 and 1986 clause 22.3.1.

22C.3   The Employer shall, as and when reasonably required to do so by the
         Contractor, produce documentary evidence and receipts showing
         that the Joint Names Policy required under clause 22C.1 or clause
         22C.2 has been taken out and is being maintained. If the Employer

defaults in taking our or in maintaining the Joint Names Policy required under clause 22C.1 the Contractor may himself take out and maintain a Joint Names Policy against any risk in respect of which the default shall have occurred and for that purpose shall have such right of entry and inspection as may be required to make a survey and inventory of the existing structures and the relevant contents. If the Employer defaults in taking out or in maintaining the Joint Names Policy required under clause 22C.2 the Contractor may take out and maintain a Joint Names Policy against any risk in respect of which the default shall have occurred. A sum or sums equivalent to the premiums paid or payable by the Contractor pursuant to clause 22C.3 shall be added to the Contract Sum.

In the 1986 clause 22C.3 the requirements regarding proof of insurance and procedure in case of default in taking out insurance are the same as in the 1980 clause 22C.1.2 in the private edition. However, it should be remembered that the insurances are different for the existing structures and contents on the one hand and the works and site materials on the other; consequently in the former case, where there is default, the contractor is given a right of entry and inspection to make a survey and inventory of the existing structures and relevant contents in the subject matter of the insurance, in order to get the sum insured correct.

In the local authorities' edition the contractor is not entitled to proof of insurance or right to insure in case of default and thus 1986 clause 22C.3 is marked "Number not used".

22C.4   If any loss or damage affecting work executed or any part thereof or any Site Materials is occasioned by any one or more of the risks covered by the Joint Names Policy referred to in clause 22C.2 or clause 22C.3 then, upon discovering the said loss or damage, the Contrac- tor shall forthwith give notice in writing both to the Architect and to the Employer of the extent, nature and location thereof and

22C.4   .1   the occurrence of such loss or damage shall be disregarded in computing any amounts payable to the Contractor under or by virtue of this Contract;

22C.4   .2   the Contractor, for himself and for all Nominated and Domestic Sub-Contractors who are, pursuant to clause 22.3, recognised as an insured under the Joint Names Policy referred to in clause 22C.2 or clause 22C.3, shall authorise the insurers to pay all monies from such insurance in respect of the loss or damage referred to in clause 22C.4 to the Employer;

22C.4   .3   .1   If it is just and equitable so to do the employment of the Contractor under this Contract may within 28 days of the occurrence of such loss or damage be determined at the option of either party by notice by registered post or recorded delivery from either party to the other. Within 7 days of receiving such a notice (but not thereafter) either party may give to the other a written request to concur in the appointment of an Arbitrator under article 5 in order that it may be determined whether such determination will be just and equitable;

22C.4   .3   .2   upon the giving or receiving by the Employer of such a notice of determination or, where a reference to arbitration is made as aforesaid, upon the Arbitrator upholding the notice of determination, the provisions of clause 28.2 (except clause 28.2.2.6) shall apply.

22C.4   .4   If no notice of determination is served under clause 22C4.3.1, or, where a reference to arbitration is made as aforesaid, if the Arbitrator decides against the notice of determination, then

22C.4   .4   .1   after any inspection required by the insurers in respect of a claim under the Joint Names Policy referred to in clause 22C.2 or clause 22C.3 has been completed, the Contractor with due diligence shall restore such work damaged, replace or repair any such Site Materials which have been lost or damaged, remove and dispose of any debris and proceed with the carrying out and completion of the Works; and

.4   .2   the restoration, replacement or repair of such loss or damage and (when required) the removal and disposal of debris shall be treated as if they were a Variation required by an instruction of the Architect under clause 13.2.

As in the case of clauses 22A and 22B the last sub-clauses in clause 22C deal with insurance claims. Sub-clause 22C.4 requires the same notice in writing of loss or damage to the works, etc by the contractor to the architect and the employer as was required in sub-clause 22B.3.1, otherwise neither the architect nor the employer would know of it. Sub-clauses 22C.4.1 and 22C.4.2 are the same as sub-clauses 22B.3.2 and 22B.3.4 respectively.

Because of the wider effect of any loss or damage (it includes the existing structures and their contents) in addition to the works, all the 22C sub-clauses are more involved than those in 22B. This is particularly so under the option of determination in sub-clause 22C.4.3.1, partly because it only applies where there is loss or damage to the works. Where equitable (within 28 days of such loss or damage) the contract may be determined by either party by registered post or recorded delivery. If objected to within seven days, written notice of reference to arbitration may be given. The words "(but not thereafter)" emphasise that the party objecting must act *at once*. Incidentally, Article 5.2.2 has been altered so that reference to an arbitrator, to decide whether a determination of the contractor's employment under clause 22C.4.3.1 is just and equitable, can be made before practical completion.

Upon determination of the contract by the contractor clause 28.2 applies, except sub-clause 28.2.2.6, which states that the employer must pay the contractor any direct loss and/or damage caused to the contractor by the determination. Clause 28.2 states that the contractor must with reasonable despatch remove all his or her temporary buildings, plant, tools, equipment, goods and materials, and sets out the terms under which the contractor is to be paid. If the contract is not determined, the contractor must proceed with the work of making good as a variation required by the architect/supervising officer. See sub-clause 22C.4.3.2.

The "just and equitable" right to determine the contract by either party, with no right of the contractor to direct loss or damage caused by the determination, apparently in this context means in the main no right to loss of profit (see *Hudson's Building and Engineering Contracts*, ninth edition, pages 450-2). The exclusion of sub-clause 28.3.3.6 contrasts rather oddly with the comparatively severe remedy of the contractor solely to determine (and be paid such consequential loss) in clauses 22A and B which is given by sub-clause 28.1.3.1 if the works are suspended for the stipulated period due to the risks insured under those two clauses. It is beyond the scope of this book to take this matter any further but in any event there seems to be no obvious explanation why the contracts for new buildings to which clauses 22A and B apply should favour the contractor in this way.

Incidentally, it may seem strange to the insurance official to find loss of profit considered as a direct loss, but the explanation lies in the decisions of the line of cases from *Millar's Machinery Co v David Way & Son* (1934), *Saint Line Ltd v Richardson, Westgarth & Co Ltd* (1940), *Wraight Ltd v PH and T (Holdings) Ltd* (1968) to *Croudace Construction Ltd v Cawoods Concrete Products Ltd* (1978). Further details of the *Saint Line* case as a good example of the legal meaning of "direct" on the one hand and "indirect and consequential" on the other, will be found in Appendix 4.

If the reinstatement of the structure other than the works is considerable or involves work of which he or she has no experience, the contractor or employer may wish to determine the contract. The employer may even not want to proceed with the works if the main structure is largely destroyed. Assuming there is some damage to the works, he or she could carry out his or her wishes in accordance with this clause.

Sub-clause 22C.4.4 deals with the situation where no notice of determination is made or the arbitrator decides against the notice of determination. In this event, after any inspection required by the insurers under the joint names policy the contractor must proceed with the work of making good as a variation required by the architect as mentioned above.

22D. Insurance for Employer's loss of liquidated damages — clause 25.4.3

22D.1 Where it is stated in the Appendix that the insurance to which clause 22D refers may be required by the Employer then forthwith after the Contract has been entered into the Architect shall either inform the Contractor that no such insurance is required or shall instruct the Contractor to obtain a quotation for such insurance. This quotation shall be for an insurance on an agreed value basis [o.3] to be taken out and maintained by the Contractor until the date of Practical Completion and which will provide for payment to the Employer of a sum calculated by reference to clause 22D.3 in the event of loss or damage to the Works, work executed, Site Materials, temporary buildings, plant and equipment for use in connection with and on or adjacent to the Works by any one or more of the Specified Perils and which loss or damage results in the Architect giving an extension of time under clause 25.3 in respect of the Relevant Event in clause 25.4.3 The Architect shall obtain from the Employer any information which the Contractor reasonably requires to obtain such quotation. The Contractor shall send to the Architect as soon as practicable the quotation which he has obtained and the Architect shall thereafter instruct the Contractor whether or not the Employer wishes the Contractor to accept that quotation and such instruction shall not be unreasonably withheld or delayed. If the Contractor is instructed to accept the quotation the Contractor shall forthwith take out and maintain the relevant policy and send it to the Architect for deposit with the Employer, together with the premium receipt therefor and also any relevant endorsement or endorsements thereof and the premiums receipts therefor.

22D.2 The sum insured by the relevant policy shall be a sum calculated at the rate stated in the Appendix as liquidated and ascertained damages for the period of time stated in the Appendix.

22D.3 Payment in respect of this insurance shall be calculated at the rate referred to in clause 22D.2 (or any revised rate produced by the application of clause 18.1.4) for the period of any extension of time finally given by the Architect as referred to in clause 22D.1 or for the period of time stated in the Appendix, whichever is the less.

22D.4 The amounts expended by the Contractor to take out and maintain the insurance referred to in clause 22D.1 shall be added to the Contract Sum. If the Contractor defaults in taking out or in maintaining the insurance referred to in clause 22D.1 the Employer may himself insure against any risk in respect of which the default shall have occurred.

If the occurrence of the risks referred to in 1986 clause 25.4.2 (specified perils) give rise to an extension of time and the fixing of a later completion date, the employer is unable to benefit from clause 24 (damages for non-completion) and consequently has no right to receive liquidated damages for the weeks or other period by which the completion date has been extended. This 1986 clause 22D is designed to give the employer the opportunity to require the contractor to arrange insurance to compensate the employer for the damages which he or she cannot recover under clause 24, and thus overcomes an unsatisfactory situation for the employer particularly if delay was due to the contractor. Before the introduction of clause 22D employers with some experience of insurance, and the aid of a broker versed in the insurances required by the construction industry, would often take out an advance profits cover to protect them against financial losses, which they might incur if damage to the works during construction caused a delay in their ability to obtain rent or sell the completed building on time. It was from this situation that the Joint Contracts Tribunal decided that it was necessary to put an optional requirement into the Standard Form for the eventuality described above.

This is a completely new clause, and although insurers may be reluctant to give this cover (as they were with the original 19(2)(a) clause), one insurer has provided it for some years and like the 19(2)(a) clause (now 21.2.1) it may prove to be profitable to insurers. Some insurers do not like "agreed value" sums insured but really the figure concerned can work to either party's disadvantage. Nevertheless the adoption of an agreed value does avoid any dispute over the amount of the payment due under the insurance once the policy is issued. (A copy of the Trinity Insurance Company's policy for Clause 22D appears in Appendix 3.)

A footnote in the contract appreciates this and makes the legal point that the insurers will normally reserve the right to be satisfied that the sum referred to in clause 22D.2 is not more than a genuine pre-estimate of the damage which the employer considers, at the time he or she enters into the contract, he or she will suffer as a result of any delay. This genuine pre-estimate distinguishes the sum from a penalty clause which legally is disregarded for all purposes.

Clause 22D.1 provides for an insurance to be arranged by the contractor for the employer's loss of liquidated damages. It provides that where the Appendix states that this insurance may be required, the architect makes the decision to inform the contractor either that no insurance is required or that he or she should obtain a quotation for such insurance. It is on an agreed value basis and operates until practical completion. It should be appreciated that this insurance stems from the extension of time allowed by clause 25.3, in particular arising from delay caused by loss or damage from the specified perils to the works, work executed, site materials, temporary buildings, plant or equipment ie the works, etc specified. The insurance is in respect of specified perils only and the sum insured is the rate of liquidated damages times the period selected.

Payment is based on the rate of liquidated damages times the period of extension finally granted arising out of the delay caused by the specified perils: see clause 22D.3. This claims payment is subject to a qualification reading "or any revised rate produced by the application of clause 18.1.4". Clause 18 deals with partial possession by the employer. Clause 18.1.4 states that if part of the works is taken over by the employer, the value insured by the material damage insurance, arranged by the contractor, is reduced by the value of that part. This formula is carried through to the liquidated damages by clause 22D.3.

It is interesting to note that clause 22D includes cover for the consequences of loss or damage to temporary buildings, plant or equipment as these items are not specifically required to be insured elsewhere in the contract. Also elsewhere the works are required to be insured against all risks. Evidently the reluctance of insurers to offer the cover required by this clause forced this compromise.

Under clause 22D.4 the premiums paid by the contractor are to be added to the contract sum, and if the contractor defaults in providing the insurance, the employer may insure against any risks in respect of which the default shall have occurred.

Advance profits insurance

Clause 22D was provided to cope with a particular situation. Some members of the Joint Contracts Tribunal thought it was wrong that the contractor should be given an extension of time when the "Clause 22 perils" (in the 1980 edition) were caused by his or her negligence. However, the contractors' representatives, on the JCT, would not agree to exclude an extension of time when the contractor was negligent, so clause 22D became the resultant compromise.

Now the clause 22D insurance may not provide a real measure of the employer's probable loss, and it is possibly better for the employer to take out advance profits insurance, or at least to consider that option. The latter insurance can provide all risks cover, which is wider than the specific perils under clause 22D, and the employer is more likely to correctly assess the amount of his or her annual earnings and the effect an accident would have on them. For example, he or she should consider loss of rent, loss of other income, increased bank charges, and increased cost of working, if the completion date is delayed because of damage caused by an accident. In fact the Trinity Insurance Company Ltd compares the clause 22D insurance with advance profits insurance in the following form. Incidentally, in this form reference is made to "Advanced Profits" insurance although, as the term relates to an interruption insurance arranged in advance of the insured's business commencing, it is arguable that "Advance Profits" is the more correct term. Finally, in reading the following form it should be appreciated that the employer will have to come to a decision, concerning advance profits insurance, before instructing the contractor to obtain a quotation in accordance with sub-clause 22D.1, as these insurances are alternatives.

Employers loss of liquidated damages — Clause 22D

The case for...	But, on the other hand...
1. Payments are for an "Agreed Amount" per week (usually based on the *anticipated rental* or *profit* to be derived from the project) therefore the principal can budget for the amount to be received in the event of delay.	1. The "Agreed Amount" is fixed at the outset. During a long project changes in interest rates or higher rents could make the agreed amount inadequate. (Sums insured can be amended at any time under an "advanced profits" insurance. Also, as the policy is not "agreed value" the premium is usually lower.)

<table>
<tr><td>

2. Straightforward policy wording — tied in exactly with the contract conditions.

</td><td>

2. Cover is restricted to "Clause 22" perils, as stated in the contract. (A wider range of perils cover is available under an advanced profits policy.)

</td></tr>
<tr><td>

3. Separate policy is issued for each project.

</td><td>

3. (A single "open declaration" policy can be issued for advanced profits, with charge notes for each project. "One-off" policies are, of course, available.)

</td></tr>
<tr><td>

4. Quotations are obtained and cover is arranged by the contractor.

</td><td>

4. A contractor's poor loss record could adversely affect the premium. (Under advanced profits, control of the principal's insurance arrangements remains with the principal.)

</td></tr>
<tr><td>

5. For contracts subject to "sectional" completion, amounts of cover are agreed for each section at the outset.

</td><td>

5. The "22D" policy will only pay for damages relating to an affected section. If damage occurs to a section to be occupied by a *key tenant* such as Sainsbury's or Marks & Spencer, other potential tenants may be reluctant to take possession, thereby causing loss to the principal. (Advanced profits could cater for this possibility by providing cover for the development as a whole.)

</td></tr>
<tr><td>

6. The "22D" policy is normally subject to a *two* week "excess".

</td><td>

6. (A lower "excess" can normally be negotiated under an advanced profits policy.)

</td></tr>
</table>

Generally the decision regarding advance profits will need to be:

(a) whether the cover can be limited to fire and other normal additional perils; or

(b) whether the cover should follow the CAR insurance of the contractor, assuming that cover applies to the premises in course of erection.

The protection to be arranged depends on the type of loss likely to be incurred, which in turn depends on the intended use of the new building. If it is to be let it will be loss of rent. If it is to be used in an existing business it will be loss of profit or income.

In Appendix 6 an example is given, of a specification of an advance profits policy arranged for a property developer as used by the Trinity Insurance Company. This covers loss of rent after damage covered by a CAR policy. The insured employer will have to decide how long he or she wishes the protection to apply, which is called the indemnity period. This period starts to run on the date on which, but for the damage to the works, the building would have been ready for occupation. The cover then follows the pattern of the normal business interruption policy.

Clause 23. Date of possession, completion and postponement — use by employer

Sub-clauses 23.1 and 23.2 merely refer to the date the contractor is given possession of the site when he or she is expected to proceed with the works and complete them before the completion date, and also give the architect a right to postpone work. The 1986 amendment adds three new paragraphs as follows:

23.3.1 For the purposes of the Works insurances the Contractor shall retain possession of the site and the Works up to and including the date of issue of the certificate of Practical Completion, and, subject to clause 18 the Employer shall not be entitled to take possession of any part or parts of the Works until that date.

23.3.2 Notwithstanding the provisions of clause 23.3.1 the Employer may, with the consent in writing of the Contractor, use or occupy the site or the Works or part thereof whether for the purposes of storage of his goods or otherwise before the date of issue of the certificate of Practical Completion by the Architect. Before the Contractor shall give his consent to such use or occupation the Contractor or the Employer shall notify the insurers under clause 22A or clause 22B or clause 22C.2 to .4 whichever may be applicable and obtain confirmation that such use or occupation will not prejudice the insurance. Subject to such confirmation the consent of the Contractor shall not be unreasonably withheld.

23.3.3 Where clause 22A.2 or clause 22A.3 applies and the insurers in giving the confirmation referred to in clause 23.3.2 have made it a condition of such confirmation that an additional premium is required the Contractor shall notify the Employer of the amount of the additional premium. If the Employer continues to require use or occupation under clause 23.3.2 the additional premium required shall be added to the contract Sum and the Contractor shall provide the Employer, if so requested, with the additional premium receipt therefor.

Clause 23.3.1 refers to the operation of clause 18 (partial possession by the employer) as an exception to the contractor's right to remain in possession of the site. While it may be that the certificate of practical completion will certify such completion at a date prior to the date of issue of the certificate, nevertheless for the purposes of the contractor giving up possession and the cessation of the works insurance cover, the date of issue of the certificate is the only operative date.

Clause 23.3.2 caters for the employer who wishes to use or occupy the works for storage or otherwise before the date of issue of the certificate of practical completion, subject to the consent of the contractor (which cannot be unreasonably withheld), and confirmation that the insurance will not be prejudiced by such use or occupation. This occupation will be a change of risk and notification is to do with a disclosure of material fact. This operates whether clause 22A, clause 22B, or clause 22C.2 to 4 applies.

If the insurer requires an additional premium for this facility, clause 23.3.3 provides that the employer, if he or she still wishes to so use or occupy the works, reimburse the contractor for the additional premium if clause 22A applies.

As most all risks policies contain an exclusion making cover void from date of breach, if the employer has use or occupation of the works, observance of the above clause is imperative to avoid a breach of this exclusion.

Acknowledgements are made to Collins (now Blackwell Scientific Publications) for permission to use parts of the author's book *Insurance under the JCT Forms with supplement* in writing this chapter.

CHAPTER 6

JCT Nominated Subcontract NSC/4 and 4a 1986, and other JCT contracts

JCT Nominated Subcontract NSC/4 and 4a

NSC/4 and 4a by the 1986 amendment provides for the nominated subcontractor to obtain much of the benefit of the insurance cover given to the employer and the contractor jointly under the main contract joint names policy. It is important to appreciate how this benefit is obtained, its limitations, the risks of loss or damage which are not covered and the period of this benefit. The main difference between NSC/4 and 4a is in the tendering and not in the wording of the clauses which follow. Clause 8 reads as follows:

8 **Loss or damage to the Main Contract Works and to the Sub-Contract Works**

8.1 Clause 8A shall apply where it is stated in the Sub-Contract Documents that clause 22A shall apply to the Main Contract; clause 8B shall apply where it is stated in those Documents that clause 22B shall apply to the Main Contract; clause 8C shall apply where it is stated in those Documents that clause 22C shall apply to the Main Contract.

8.2 The exception set out in clause 8A.2.1 or clause 8B.2.1 or clause 8C.2.1 whichever is applicable shall extend to any loss or damage for which either the Employer or the Contractor as Joint Insured under the Joint Names Policy referred to in clause 22A or clause 22B or clause 22C.2 of the Main Contract Conditions does not make a claim under that Policy or to the extent that no claim under that Policy can be made because of a condition therein that the insured shall bear the first part of any claim for loss or damage.

8.3   Nothing in clause 8A or clause 8B or clause 8C whichever is applicable shall in any way modify the Sub-Contractor's obligations in regard to defects in the Sub-Contract Works as set out in clauses 14.3 and 14.4.

8.4   Where the Sub-Contractor is, pursuant to clause 22.3 of the Main Contract Conditions, recognised as an insured under Joint Names Policy referred to in clause 22A or clause 22B or clause 22C of the Main Contract Conditions, whichever is applicable to the Main Contract, the Sub-Contractor shall not object to the payment by the insurers under such Joint Names Policy to the Employer of any relevant insurance monies.

8.5   The occurrence of loss or damage affecting the Sub-Contract Works occasioned by one or more of the Specified Perils shall be disregarded in computing any amounts payable to the Sub-Contractor under or by virtue of this Sub-Contract.

NSC/4 follows the three main contract optional works insurance clauses 22A, 22B and 22C.2 (see Chapter 5) by providing in clause 8.1 that NSC/4 optional clause 8A or 8B or 8C applies according to which of the three optional clauses is included in the main contract. In view of the considerable length and complexity of clauses 8A, 8B and 8C (they are also repetitious) they are not set out in this chapter but they can be found in Appendix 8. These clauses only concern subcontract works but they are related to clauses 22A, B and C which concern all the works.

How the subcontractor benefits from the joint names policy of the main contract

Sub-clauses 8A.1, 8B.1 and 8C.1 indicate that the subcontractor is either recognised as an insured under the joint names policy of the main contract or the insurers waive any rights of subrogation they may have against the subcontractor. This follows the wording of clause 22.3.1 of the main contract. See Chapter 5. However the joint names policy only covers the subcontractor for specified perils. The subcontractor must consider whether to insure for non-specified perils, eg impact by vehicles, subsidence, theft and vandalism.

The limitation of the subcontractor's benefit to specified perils cover where causing loss or damage to the subcontract works

Clause 8.2 indicates the exceptions in the three sub-clauses 8A.2.1, 8B.2.1 and 8C.2.1. The point of these three sub-clauses is to indicate that the subcontractor is responsible for loss or damage to the subcontract works and site materials, except where this is due to the specified perils, as the main contract insurance would then come into operation. In this connection the subcontractor is not even responsible for his or her negligence, breach of statutory duty or default. Similarly the subcontractor is not responsible where the employer or contractor has been guilty of these civil wrongs, and this also applies where any local authority or statutory undertaker, executing work solely in pursuance of its statutory obligations, negligently causes loss or damage to the subcontract works and site materials.

Clause 8.2 also states that, even where a policy excess operates under the main contract insurance, the responsibilities set out in the sub-clauses 8A.2.1, 8B.2.1 or 8C.2.1 still apply.

Clause 8.3 makes clear that 8A, 8B and 8C do not modify the subcontractor's obligations to remedy defects in the subcontract works as set out in clauses 14.3 and 14.4, which includes the benefit of the architect's instructions as to the cost of making good such defects. These defects include those due to materials and workmanship not in accordance with the subcontract.

Clause 8.4 follows clause 22.3 of the main contract; thus where the subcontractor is an insured under a joint names policy, he or she must agree to payment by the insurers to the employer of any relevant insurance monies.

Clause 8.5 makes clear that the loss or damage affecting the subcontract works occasioned by the specified perils shall be disregarded in computing amounts payable to the subcontractor.

The limitation of the subcontractor's responsibility for non-specified perils causing loss or damage to the subcontract works

In sub-clauses 8A.2.2, 8B.2.2 and 8C.2.2 it is stated that where, during the progress of the subcontract works, subcontract materials or goods have been fully, finally and properly incorporated into the works (see next heading) before practical completion of the subcontract works, the subcontractor shall be responsible, in respect of loss or damage to subcontract works comprising the materials or goods so incorporated caused by the occurrence of a peril other than a specified peril. However, this responsibility is only for the cost of restoration of such works lost or damaged and removal and disposal of any debris arising therefrom in accordance with clause 8A.3 (or 8B.3 or 8C.3 as the case may be) *but only to the extent that such loss or damage is caused by the negligence, breach of statutory duty, omission or default of the subcontractor or any person for whom the subcontractor is responsible.*

The duration of the benefit of the subcontractor under the joint names policy

This benefit is for the period up to and including the date of issue of the certificate of practical completion of the subcontract works (clause 14.2) or the date of any determination of the contractor's employment under the main contract, whichever occurs first. These dates are known as "terminal dates" (see clause 6.1.2). "Fully, finally and properly incorporated into the Works" is not defined in the contract but most contractors consider that the whole unit in, for example, the case of a roof or wall must be completed before the tiles or bricks involved can be considered as fully, finally and properly incorporated. In the case of electrical, gas and heating installations, the complete installation must be connected up and tested, and the service operating before this phrase applies. However, it is advisable for the parties concerned to agree the interpretation before a claim arises, ie when the contract is negotiated.

A summary of the position

(a) *Loss or damage by the specified perils:*

Up to the earlier of the terminal dates the nominated subcontractor is not liable for loss or damage, whether to the subcontract works and site materials, or to the main contract works and site materials (other than the subcontract works, etc), or to existing structures, etc under clause 8C even if caused by the subcontractor's negligence, etc. The contractor and employer are always liable for their own negligence so far as the nominated subcontractor is concerned.

(b) *Loss or damage caused by risks other than specified perils up to the earlier of the terminal dates:*

(i) To the nominated subcontract works and site materials. The nominated subcontractor is responsible for repair or replacement unless the loss or damage was due to the main contractor's negligence, etc or that of the employer or any local authority, etc; but if the subcontract materials or goods have been fully, finally and properly incorporated into the works before practical completion the nominated subcontractor is only responsible if the loss or damage is due to the negligence, etc of the nominated subcontractor, etc.

(ii) To the main contract works and site materials other than the nominated subcontract works, etc.
       The nominated subcontractor is only responsible if the loss or damage is due to the negligence, etc of the subcontractor, etc.

(ii) To the existing structures and contents where clause 8C applies. The nominated subcontractor is responsible if the loss or damage is due to his or her negligence, etc.

(c) *After the earlier of the terminal dates the nominated subcontractor is only liable* for any loss or damage to the main contract works and site materials (including the practically completed nominated subcontract works) and, where clause 8C applies, to the existing structures and contents, if the loss or damage is due to the nominated subcontractor's negligence, etc.

Clause 9. Policies of insurance — production — payment of premiums

The first two sub-clauses of this clause do not concern the subcontract works, or the works at all.

Clause 9.3 gives a right to the nominated subcontractor to have documentary evidence provided by the main contractor in order to check that the benefits of the relevant joint names policies under the main contract have been provided as in clause 8A or (except where the 1986 local authorities version is applicable to the main contract) clause 8B or clause 8C. The exception in brackets occurs because the local authorities' versions do not give the contractor a right to documentary evidence showing that joint names policies in the main contract clauses 22B and 22C have been taken out and maintained. If the main contractor does not produce this evidence, the nominated subcontractor can take out insurance against any loss or damage which he or she may suffer arising from such default by the contractor which would not have taken place had the contractor complied with clauses 8A or 8B or 8C. The premium for the latter insurance (the result of the default just mentioned) is recoverable from the contractor. This right of recovery is given by sub-clause 9.4.

Clause 10. Subcontractor's plant, etc — responsibility of contractor

The Contractor shall only be responsible for any loss or damage to the plant, tools, equipment or other property belonging to or provided by the Sub-Contractor, his servants or agents and to any materials or goods of the Sub-Contractor which are not Sub-Contract Site Materials to the extent that such loss or damage is due to any negligence, breach of statutory duty, omission or default of the Contractor or of any person for whom the Contractor is responsible.

Basically the subcontractor is responsible for his or her own plant, tools and equipment, etc; and shall insure them accordingly. The contractor is only responsible for this property where loss or damage is caused by his or her negligence, etc.

It should be noted that the insurances to be arranged under clauses 8A, 8B or 8C concern only the contract works and site materials and not plant, tools and equipment which the subcontractor owns or uses or to materials or goods not forming part of the subcontract works or site materials.

Domestic subcontractors

Domestic subcontractors are defined in JCT 80 and the 1986 revision to main contract clauses 1.3 and 19.2 as follows:

The Contractor shall not without the written consent of the Architect (which consent shall not be unreasonably withheld) sub-let any portion of the Works. A person to whom the Contractor sub-lets any portion of the Works other than a Nominated Sub-Contractor is in this Contract referred to as a "Domestic Sub-Contractor".

Consequently whereas nominated subcontractors are those whose final selection and approval are reserved to the architect, domestic subcontractors are defined in the JCT Practice Note 9 as any other subcontractor whose selection remains with the contractor alone. A form of subcontract for domestic subcontractors has been published under the reference DOM/1 by agreement with the various specialist subcontractor organisations. In accordance with main contract clause 19.4 the DOM/1 contract is automatically determined in the event of the main contractor's contract being determined. The DOM/1 conditions are almost identical in their wording with the Nominated Subcontract NSC/4. Thus the remarks made above under the heading "JCT Nominated Subcontract NSC/4 and

4a'' apply equally to the clauses in DOM/1 which carry the same numbers. Under the new 1986 main contract clause 22.3.2 the employer and contractor, under clauses 22A and 22B and 22C.2 to 22C.4, must give similar benefits to domestic subcontractors under the joint names policies to those given to nominated subcontractors. The only exception occurs in clause 22C.1 where loss or damage by the specified perils occurs to the existing structures and contents owned by the employer or for which he or she is responsible. The joint names policy does not protect the domestic subcontractor from such loss or damage. See clause 22.3.2 in Chapter 5.

Some main JCT contracts other than JCT 1980

At this stage it is appropriate to look briefly at some other main JCT contracts and indicate when they are used and how they bear a close relationship with those insurance clauses calling for cover for the works under the Standard Form of Building Contract 1980 (JCT 80), dealt with in Chapter 5.

It will assist reference to these additional contracts to use an abbreviated form, thus The Intermediate Form of Building Contract 1984 will be referred to as IFC84 and The Agreement for Minor Building Works 1980 as MW80. JCT80 as amended in 1986 is indicated by JCT86.

The Agreement For Minor Building Works (MW80)

Practice Note 20 (revised July 1988) issued by the JCT explains the requirement for MW80. The endorsement on the back of the Minor Works Agreement mentions that Practice Note M2 has been issued which indicates the appropriate use of the form as follows:

1   The Form of Agreement and Conditions is designed for use where minor building works are to be carried out for an agreed lump sum and where an Architect or Contract Administrator has been appointed on behalf of the Employer.

2   The form is for use for Works for which a lump sum offer has been obtained based on drawings and/or specifications and/or schedules but without detailed measurements. It follows that those documents should be sufficient to enable the Contractor accurately to identify the Works to be done without the provision of bills of quantities by the Employer. Where the

Works are of a complex nature a bill of quantities would ordinarily be necessary.

3   The form is for use where the period required for the execution of the Works is such that full labour and materials fluctuations provisions are not required.

4   Subject to the above, the form is generally suitable for contracts up to the value of £70,000 (1987 prices).

5   In some contracts for which the form is used the Employer may wish to seek to control the selection of sub-contractors for specialist work. While this may be done by naming a person or company in the tender documents or in instructions on the expenditure of a provisional sum, there are no provisions in the form which deal with the consequences of what is, in effect, the nomination of a sub-contractor; nor is there any standard form of sub-contract which would be applicable to such selected sub-contractors. Such control of selection could also be achieved by the Employer entering into a direct contract with the specialist.

6   For Works where the criteria mentioned above do not apply reference would be made to Practice Note 20 for guidance as to the appropriate form to be used.

The Minor Works Form may be acceptable when the value of the contract does not exceed £70,000. Generally where the value of the works exceeds £70,000 or where, irrespective of the value of the contract, it is considered that more detailed conditions are required then either the Standard Form Without Quantities (JCT 80) or the Intermediate Form (IFC 84), without bills of quantities, should be used.

The responsibility for the works under MW80 is generally similar to JCT80 and IFC84, but it is less detailed and the differences are mainly omissions. There are only two alternatives which are, firstly, insurance of new works by the contractor under sub-clause 6.3A (compare it with clause 22A of JCT80), and secondly, insurance of existing structures by the employer under sub-clause 6.3B (compare with 22C of JCT80). The perils to be insured are exactly the same as the specified perils in JCT80. MW80 does not make reference to the excepted risks described in JCT86, which strictly speaking means that the contractor is responsible for loss or damage by nuclear risks and sonic waves. However, as stated elsewhere, as there is an insurance pool covering the nuclear reactor operator who is made liable for nuclear risks from such reactor, and the Government takes responsibility thereafter, this omission is probably not as onerous as it sounds. Nevertheless, it should be noted that the CAR policy would not cover such risks.

There is no provision for determination of the contract after loss or damage if just and equitable under sub-clause 6.3B as there is under clause 22C4.3.1 of JCT86. Thus the parties must make their own arrangements for determination. Sub-clause 6.3B does not place any obligation on the contractor to give notice to the employer of any loss or damage that has occurred. Even so a contractor would be expected to notify the architect and thereafter work with him or her.

The party responsible for insuring is required to produce evidence of insurance under sub-clause 6.4, to the other party on request, but there is no provision for either the contractor or employer to insure if the other defaults or to recover the premiums. Presumably the party not in default after giving the other notice might take out the insurance and then by arbitration claim recovery of the premium in damages by breach of contract.

The Practice Note 22 and Guide to the Amendments to the Insurance and Related Liability Provisions: 1986 has the following to say about the Agreement for Minor Building Works 1980 edition (revised 1985):

> The 1986 amendments to the Agreement for Minor Building Works do *not* provide for the inclusion in clause 6.3.A (insurance of Works — new buildings) or clause 6.3B (insurance of Works to existing structures) of the obligation in the 1986 Amendment 2 to the Standard Form 1980 Edition to insure the Works for the risks referred to in the new 1986 definition in that Amendment 2 of "All Risks Insurance".... It was considered that the provisions in the 1980 Edition of the Agreement for Minor Building Works for insurance of the Works against loss and damage by fire, etc (the same list of perils as those in the definition of "Clause 22 Perils" in the Standard Form 1980 and "Specified Perils" in the Standard Form 1986) was satisfactory for the kind of work for which the Minor Works Agreement is considered suitable. As the majority of such work is likely to be extensions or alterations or repair to existing buildings (for which clause 6.3B requires the Employer to take out the Works insurance) but on which the Employer would not normally have cover for the risks referred to in the new 1986 definition of "All Risks Insurance" it was considered that a change to a requirement to take out cover for "All Risks Insurance" would cause unwarranted complications.

The Intermediate Form of Building Contract (IFC84)

IFC84 was introduced to fill the gap between JCT80 and MW80. Practice

Note 20 issued by the JCT makes the following suggestions concerning the use of IFC84:

On the kind of work for which the Intermediate Form is intended to be used the endorsement on its back cover reads:

This Intermediate Form is issued for contracts in the range between those for which the JCT Standard Form of Building Contract (1980 Edition) and the JCT Agreement for Minor Building Works are issued.

The Form is suitable where the proposed building works are:

1   of a simple content involving the normally recognised basic trades and skills of the industry;

2   without any building service installations of a complex nature, or other specialist work of a complex nature:

3   adequately specified, or specified and billed, as appropriate prior to the invitation of tenders.

'Guidance on the intended use of the Form including the length of time and contract value above which the Form should not normally be used is set out in [this] Practice Note 20 (revised July 1988) and in Practice Note IN/1 (revised January 1987).'

The further guidance referred to in that endorsement is as follows. The Intermediate Form has been prepared so as to be suitable for contracts for which the more detailed provisions of the Standard Form (1980 Edition) are considered by the Employer or by his professional consultants to be unnecessary in the light of the foregoing criteria. The Form would normally be the most suitable form for use, subject to these criteria, where the contract period is not more than twelve months and the value of works is not more than £280,000 (1987 prices), but this must be read together with paragraph 14 on the money limits within which the use of a Minor Works Form may be appropriate.

The Intermediate Form may however be suitable for somewhat larger or longer contracts, provided the three criteria referred to in the endorsement are met, but Employers and their professional consultants should bear in mind that the provisions of the Intermediate Form are less detailed than in the Standard Form (1980 Edition) and that circumstances may arise, if it is used for unsuitable works, which could prejudice the equitable treatment of the parties.

Like MW80 the insurance clauses in IFC84 all come within clause 6 but whereas the insurance of the works in MW80 only consists of two alternatives, IFC follows the JCT80 in giving three choices (see below). IFC84 clause 6.3.3 is equivalent to clause 22.3 of JCT80 as amended in 1986 (Nominated and domestic subcontractors — benefit of joint names policies — specified perils).

Clauses 6.3A, 6.3B and 6.3C of IFC84 follow the wording of clauses 22A, 22B and 22C of JCT86 (see earlier). However there are minor exceptions as follows. Clause 6.3B.2 is equivalent to clause 22B.2 of JCT86 (Failure of employer to insure — rights of contractor) with the addition of the words "Except where the Employer is a local authority" as an introductory statement to clause 6.3B.2.

Similarly clause 6.3C.2 is equivalent to clause 22C.2 of JCT86 (Works in or extension to existing structures — all risks insurance — employer to take out joint names policy) with the addition of the introductory statement mentioned in clause 6.3B.2. This is because the equivalent clause 22B.2 and 22C.2 are not used in the local authorities' version of JCT80.

The new clause 22D (JCT86) regarding liquidated damages appears as 6.3D in IFC84.

JCT Fixed Fee Form of Prime Cost Contract (October 1976 revision)

This contract, which was first published in March 1967, provides for the remuneration of a contractor by repaying his or her costs and in addition a fixed fee for his or her services. The contract is issued under the sanction of the same associated bodies under which the Standard Form of Building Contract is issued. Presumably a post-1980 contract in line with JCT 86 will eventually appear. According to the RIBA such a contract is under consideration. Clauses 15 and 16 (the insurance clauses) among others were revised in July 1972 to bring them into line with the July 1972 wording of the standard form. The intention is to use this form when the exact nature of the work is not known, to a greater or lesser degree, at the time the contract is executed. Fortunately the wording follows closely that of the standard 1980 form, and this enables the commentary to be kept short.

It must be appreciated that, as this contract follows the JCT 1972 contract, the wording does not include the 1986 amendment as given in the wording set out in Chapter 5. Thus, for example, the requirement for insurance cover for the works in the fixed fee contract is for fire and special perils (defined as "specified perils" in the 1986 amendment) and not for a contractors' all risks policy.

Clause 16. Insurance of the works against fire, etc

Clauses 16(A) and 16(B) are alternatives, thus one must be struck out.

Clause 16(A).
Clause (A) is applicable to the erection of a new building when the employer is responsible for and is required to insure against the listed perils, and the wording follows clause 22B of the standard form but not the wording under the local authorities' edition where there is no provision for insurance. There is no provision in the fixed fee form for *the contractor* to insure (see Chapter 5) as in the standard form, for a new building. See clause 22A, JCT 86. However, a footnote suggests that this can be done by using the wording of the pre-1980 clause 20(A) of the standard form, which is equivalent to 22A of JCT 1980. It is strange that the present fixed fee form does not allow for this by printing such a clause.

If the contractor does have to arrange insurance in accordance with clause 16(A) upon the employer's default, he or she can recover his outlay under section C of the first schedule. There is thus no need for the provision for repayment by adding the figure to the contract sum as in JCT 80.

Clause 16(B).
Clause (B) is applicable to alterations to an existing building when the employer is at risk (including the contents owned by him or her and for which he or she is responsible) and required to insure against the specific perils. The wording follows clause 22C of the standard form. The remarks made under clause 16(A), concerning recovery of any premium outlay by the contractor on the employer's default in insuring, apply.

Insurance requirements for the Fixed Fee Form of Prime Cost Contract

While the insurance requirements to cover the works do not call for a CAR policy but a fire and special perils policy (the same perils as mentioned in Chapter 5 as "specified perils"), it is prudent for the employer to use a CAR policy under clauses 16A and B. Although the contractor must complete the contract (clause 2) and thus is responsible for the non-specified perils (as clauses 16A and B do not apply to these perils) the employer should not assume that the contractor will arrange such a limited insurance cover for the non-specified perils, which he or she should do. If the contractor has an annual CAR policy this will be sufficient. However, nothing is said about joint names cover or for the contractor to insure at all, unless the footnote mentioned under the "clause 16A" heading above is followed. Considering the wording of clauses 16(A) and (B), how is the works sum insured to be calculated? Clause 26 states that the fixed fee given in the second schedule covers all items of cost, charge, expense, insurance and profit which are not included in the definition of prime cost contained in the first schedule, which refers to labour, materials and goods, plant consumable stores and services and work subcontracted. It therefore seems that the correct sum is the estimated prime cost amount (less that for plant consumable stores and services) plus the fixed fee.

CHAPTER 7

The ICE Conditions, fifth edition (June 1973, revised January 1979)

This contract gave rise to the contractors' all risks policy as this contract form has always required all risks cover for the works, unlike the JCT contract, which only came around to calling for all risks cover in November 1986.

In the ICE contract the clauses concerned are clauses 20 and 21. Clause 20 reads as follows:

Care of the Works.
20. (1) The Contractor shall take full responsibility for the care of the Works from the date of the commencement thereof until 14 days after the Engineer shall have issued a Certificate of Completion for the whole of the Works pursuant to Clause 48. Provided that if the Engineer shall issue a Certificate of Completion in respect of any Section or part of the Permanent Works before he shall issue a Certificate of Completion in respect of the whole of the Works the Contractor shall cease to be responsible for the care of that Section or part of the Permanent Works 14 days after the Engineer shall have issued the Certificate of Completion in respect of that Section or part and the responsibility for the care thereof shall thereupon pass to the Employer. Provided further that the Contractor shall take full responsibility for the care of any outstanding work which he shall have undertaken to finish during the Period of Maintenance until such outstanding work is complete.

Responsibility for Reinstatement.
(2) In the case of any damage loss or injury from any cause whatsoever (save and except the Excepted Risks as defined in sub-clause (3) of this Clause) shall happen to the Works or any part thereof while the Contractor shall be responsible for the care thereof the Contractor shall at his own cost repair and make good the same so that at completion the Permanent Works shall be in good order and condition and in conformity in every respect with the

requirements of the Contract and the Engineer's instructions. To the extent that any such damage loss or injury arises from any of the Excepted Risks the Contractor shall if required by the Engineer repair and make good the same as aforesaid at the expense of the Employer. The Contractor shall also be liable for any damage to the Works occasioned by him in the course of any operations carried out by him for the purpose of completing any outstanding work or of complying with his obligations under Clauses 49 and 50.

Excepted Risks.
    (3) The "Excepted Risks" are riot war invasion act of foreign enemies hostilities (whether was be declared or not) civil war rebellion revolution insurrection of military or usurped power ionising radiations or contamination by radio-activity from any nuclear fuel or from any nuclear waste from the combustion of nuclear fuel radioactive toxic explosive or other hazardous properties of any explosive nuclear assembly or nuclear component thereof pressure waves caused by aircraft or other aerial devices travelling at sonic or supersonic speeds or a cause due to use or occupation by the Employer his agents servants or other contractors (not being employed by the Contractor) of any part of the Permanent Works or to fault defect error or omission in the design of the Works (other than a design provided by the Contractor pursuant to his obligations under the Contract).

These three sub-clauses apportion responsibility for loss or damage to the works between the contractor and employer and the following definitions from the contract should be noted.
    "Permanent works" means the permanent works to be constructed, completed and maintained in accordance with the contract.
    "Temporary works" means all temporary works of every kind required in or about the construction, completion and maintenance of the works.
    "Works" means the permanent works together with the temporary works.

Care of the works

Apart from the fact that clause 8 of the contract states that the contractor shall construct, complete and maintain the works, clause 20(1) makes the contractor fully responsible for the care of the works until 14 days after the issue of the completion certificate. The 14 days start from the date of issue of the certificate. This extension gives the employer time to arrange insurance cover. The CAR policy must cover the 14 days. If the engineer issues a certificate of completion in respect of any section or part of the permanent works before he or she issues a certificate for the whole works, the contractor shall cease to be responsible for that section or part 14 days after the issue date of the certificate of that section or part.

Thereafter the employer becomes responsible for the section or part concerned, but the contractor is still responsible for the remainder of the works, and even for any outstanding work which he or she has agreed to undertake during the period of maintenance.

Responsibility for reinstatement

Damage, loss or injury from any cause whatsoever (except the excepted risks in sub-clause 20.3) to the works, while the contractor is responsible for them, shall be put right at the contractor's expense. There is a doubt whether the phrase "any cause whatsoever" includes negligence by the employer. In this respect *AE Farr Ltd v The Admiralty* (1953) and *Smith v South Wales Switchgear* (1978) clash and the Unfair Contract Terms Act 1977 is also involved. The *Smith's* decision was that a phrase like "any cause whatsoever" does not include negligence in that it requires that the word "negligence" should be used or a synonym for it (evidently it did not consider the phrase concerned to be a synonym for negligence). On the other hand in *Farr's* case in the Government contract, known as CCC/Works/1 Edition 5, which had a similar clause to clause 20.2 of the ICE conditions, the phrase "any cause whatsoever" was given a wide meaning and included the employer's negligence. Incidentally, the current Government form GC/Works/1 has no such problem as the Government accepts liability for its own negligence. As *Farr's* case was heard in 1953 and there have been two editions of this contract issued since, it can be argued that it is the drafter's intention that the contractor should not be able to sue the employer for the employer's negligence in these circumstances. The next question is whether clause 20.2, in so far as it makes the contractor responsible for loss or damage to the work caused by the employer's negligence, satisfies the requirement of reasonableness under the 1977 Act. Possibly it does, as the intention of the drafters representing the parties may well prevail in deciding reasonableness, and the intention of the drafters has just been suggested from *Farr's* decision. Incidentally, the intention of clause 21 (considered later) is to provide a CAR policy for the joint benefit of the contractor and the employer, so that whoever is responsible will be protected by the insurance.

Excepted risks

The phrase "any cause whatsoever" in clause 20.2 is qualified by the exclusion of "excepted risks" from the contractor's responsibility and these excepted risks listed in clause 22.3 were considered in detail in Chapter 2 with the exception of riot and the last two exceptions (use or occupation by the employer and defect in design of the works). The excepted risks form the basis of the exclusions in the CAR policy, except for riot in the United Kingdom.

(a) "Riot" is defined in s. 1 of the Public Order Act 1986 as follows:

1.— (1)   Where 12 or more persons who are present together use or threaten unlawful violence for a common purpose and the conduct of them (taken together) is such as would cause a person of reasonable firmness present at the scene to fear for his personal safety, each of the persons using unlawful violence for the common purpose is guilty of riot.

(2)   It is immaterial whether or not the 12 or more use or threaten unlawful violence simultaneously.

(3)   The common purpose may be inferred from conduct.

(4)   No person of reasonable firmness need actually be, or be likely to be, present at the scene.

(5)   Riot may be committed in private as well as in public places.

(6)   A person guilty of riot is liable on conviction on indictment to imprisonment for a term not exceeding ten years or a fine or both.

This section creates a new offence of riot, replacing the common law offence which is abolished in s. 9(1)

The principal differences between the new offence and the common law are as follows:

(a)   twelve or more persons rather than three are required;
(b)   there is no specific need to show an intention to resist any opposition by force;
(c)   no person need actually feel alarmed by the display of violence;
(d)   action falling short of the use of violence will not render a person guilty.

In *J W Dwyer Ltd v Receiver of Metropolitan Police District* (1967) it was indicated that an essential element of a riot enabling a claim to be made under the Riot (Damages) Act 1886 was "tumult". A comment on the recovery aspect under this Act appears in the next paragraph.

While this definition indicated that a more organised clash with authority was required than that, for example, displayed by hooligans leaving a football ground after their club's defeat, on the other hand in *Munday v Metropolitan Police District Receiver* (1949) a similar situation did arise when a private property was damaged after invasion by a football crowd endeavouring to see a match when the ground was full. It was clear from the uncontradicted evidence of the plaintiff's gardener, who had met with violence when he tried to recover his ladder from those who had climbed on to a garage, that there was a riot. This case is of interest to insurers who occasionally find it necessary to claim under the Riot (Damages) Act 1886 if property insured by them is damaged in a riot. Incidentally, those claiming have only 14 days from the occurrence in which to record an application for recovery against the appropriate authority.

It is a short step from *Munday's* case to visualise a similar situation where a new uncompleted football stand is being built and unauthorised entry in defiance of authority could result in damage to the erection by rioters. Now while the ICE Conditions do not require the contractor under his or her all risks policy to insure against riot it is the practice of insurers not to exclude this risk in England, Scotland and Wales and as the policy provides cover in the joint names of the employer and contractor the employer's responsibility under the contract for riot may be covered by this policy. Some policies exclude risks which are the responsibility of the principal under conditions of contract. As already stated, all the other "excepted risks" are excluded from the policy and strictly speaking insurers would normally require notification of damage, within seven days in the case of riot in order to get their recovery claim made within 14 days against the police authority.

Exception (b), and the next one, are the most important in the list of excepted risks from a practical point of view.

a cause due to use or occupation by the Employer his agents servants or other contractors (not being employed by the Contractor) of any part of the Permanent Works.

This exception has been considered, when discussing the employer's responsibility for the works after completion, as an additional liability of the employer for the works used or occupied by the employer, etc irrespective of completion. Furthermore, the exception quoted above does not exactly fit in with the equivalent part of the exclusion under the usual contractors' all risks policy which often merely excludes damage to parts taken into use or occupancy. Thus the policy exclusion is wider in that it is not concerned with cause but narrower in that it only excludes the parts taken into use. See further discussion in Chapter 2.

A case concerning this exception (although involving the JCT Form) was *English Industrial Estates Corporation v George Wimpey & Co Ltd* (1973) and details will be found earlier in Chapter 2.

The words " or other contractors (not being employed by the contractor)" mean that the risk attaches to the employer once subcontractors employed directly by the employer use or occupy the site and cause loss or damage arising from that use or occupancy. Thus the loss or damage is not limited to the part occupied; it can happen to any part of the works as long as the loss or damage was caused by the use or occupancy "of any part of the permanent works" by the employer, etc. However, it is more likely that subcontractors directly employed by the employer will cause such loss or damage than the employer or his or her servants or agents, particularly before substantial completion, for two reasons. In the first place there are usually more subcontractors than employers, servants or agents and secondly they are usually longer in occupation than the employer, his or her servant or agents, whose visits to the site tend to be transient, although this is not applicable if the latter are in permanent occupation.

The period of 14 days after the issue of the completion certificate stipulated in sub-clause 20(1), which can mean 35 days after actual completion because of the additional period for the issue of the completion certificate in clause 48, does mean that for 35 days this excepted risk might be invoked. In this period it is more likely that the employer, his or her servants or agents might use or occupy the works, although specialist contractors might be employed to install special equipment, or the employer's tenant may use or occupy part of the works.

The final excepted risk reads:

> *to fault defect error or omission in the design of the Works (other than a design provided by the Contractor pursuant to this obligations under the Contract).*

Presumably the introductory words to the previous risk, "a cause due", apply to this risk as they are connected by the conjunction "or ".

In the first place the limitation in brackets should be noted, the point being that if the contractor submits a design for part of the works or is requested to do so by the engineer and the contract does not allow for this the employer is still responsible for that design under this clause. The limitation mentioned in brackets is important as it saddles the contractor with responsibility for his or her own design work and this type of cover is normally only available in a limited form under the contractors' all risks policy, although a few insurers will not exclude the consequences of design but the actual defective design work itself is always excluded. It is normally a matter for the professional indemnity policy to cover but usually this policy is only issued to proposers who are qualified in their profession. The point to remember is that many contractors' all risks insurers exclude *all* claims arising from defective design. When it is essential for the contractor to obtain some cover for his or her liability for design work he or she should approach an insurance broker specialising in the construction industry, but the contractor should be prepared for the type of cover which leaves him or her responsible for a financial proportion of any claim, either in the shape of an excess (deductible) or a direct percentage of the loss. Cover might be offered on an excess of loss basis, ie the insurer only covering claims which exceed a fairly substantial sum, eg £50,000.

The legal and insurance aspects are discussed in some detail in Chapter 2 when considering the policy exclusion based on this contractual exception. The word "design" in construction contracts will include any requirement which may regulate or control the suitability of the completed work for its intended purpose (not only structural designs, calculations and dimensions but also the choice of materials and control of work processes). See *Hudson on Building and Civil Engineering Contracts*, tenth edition, page 274. It appears that the excepted risk applies either to a design defect of the permanent works or of the temporary works.

Because the words "solely due to the engineer's design of the works", included in the fourth edition of the ICE Contract, have been dropped from the fifth edition the defective design can now be wholly or partly the fault of any person (subject to the limitation in brackets at the end of clause 20(3)). There seems little doubt that this excepted risk has been widened by the removal of the words "solely due to the engineer's design" and this allows the contractor to invoke the excepted risk in many cases of serious damage to the works. Consequently, contractors' insurers and those of the engineer, and possibly the insurers of the employer as well, have found themselves involved in lengthy disputes, if not litigation.

In the case of *Norman Hughes & Co Ltd v Ruthin Borough Council* (1971) counsel for the employer conceded that if the arbitrator concluded that settlement of a sewer was not due to bad workmanship on the part of the contractor, it followed by a simple process of elimination that the engineer's design was the sole cause of the settlement that had taken place, in that the ground had rendered that design unsuitable.

The relevance of this case is arguably that the removal of the words "solely due to the engineer's design" from the fifth edition makes it easier for a court to come to the conclusion reached in *Norman Hughes'* case, decided before the fifth edition was published, because the excepted risk has been widened to include wholly or in part any person's design other than that of the contractor. Thus, if the contractor is eliminated as the designer and the fault is not due to his or her bad workmanship then the excepted risk must apply to any other faulty design.

In the fifth edition of the ICE contract, as compared with the fourth edition, there is also in this excepted risk a limitation to "fault defect error or omission" in design but whether this has the effect of confining the exception to negligent design was discussed in the chapter on the "contractors' all risks policy" when considering the case of *Queensland Government Railways and Another v Manufacturers' Mutual Insurance Ltd* (1969). In the case of *CJ Pearce & Co Ltd v Hereford Corporation* (1968) the word "design" was said to mean:

> that documents of the nature of the plans, and so forth, are handed to the contractor, showing the precise detail of the work the contractor is to carry out. In other words the word "design" deals with how the work is to be carried out and not which work is to be carried out.

For further discussion of the design exclusion in the contractors' all risk policy see Chapter 2 on that policy and the case of *Pentagon Construction (1969) Co Ltd v United States Fidelity and Guarantee Co* (1978) which is unsatisfactory on the meaning of "design" because two judges disagreed and the third judge abstained.

Insurance of the works, etc

21 Without limiting his obligations and responsibilities under Clause 20 the Contractor shall insure in the joint names of the Employer and the Contractor:

(a) the Permanent Works and the Temporary Works (including for the purposes of this Clause any unfixed materials or other things delivered to the Site for incorporation therein) to their full value;

(b) the Constructional Plant to its full value;

against all loss or damage from whatever cause arising (other than the Excepted Risks) for which he is responsible under the terms of the Contract and in such manner that the Employer and Contractor are covered for the period stipulated in Clause 20(1) and are also covered for loss or damage arising during the Period of Maintenance from such cause occurring prior to the commencement of the Period of Maintenance and for any loss or damage occasioned by the Contractor in the course of any operation carried out by him for the purpose of complying with his obligations under Clauses 49 and 50.

Provided that without limiting his obligations and responsibilities as aforesaid nothing contained in this Clause shall render the Contractor liable to insure against the necessity for the repair or reconstruction of any work constructed with materials and workmanship not in accordance with the requirements of the Contract unless the Bill of Quantities shall provide a special item for this insurance.

Such insurances shall be effected with an insurer and in terms approved by the Employer (which approval shall not be unreasonably withheld) and the Contractor shall whenever required produce to the Employer the policy or policies of insurance and the receipts for payment of the current premiums.

This insurance clause is complementary to clause 20.

Probably the most important sentence in clause 20, it will be recollected, is the first one in sub-clause 20(1) making the contractor responsible for loss or damage to the works until they are officially completed plus 14 days. If there is any loss or damage to the works other than by the excepted risks the contractor must pay for the repair or replacement himself or herself.

Obviously the employer wishes to be satisfied that the contractor has sufficient money to carry out those responsibilities under the clause expeditiously, otherwise any delay will result in loss to the employer. This is the reason for the insurance clause 21. It does not alter in any way the effect of clause 20 as it opens with the following statement: "Without limiting his . . . responsibilities under clause 20 . . .".

The CAR policy called for by this clause is a material damage policy and thus it does not cover any form of consequential loss, and it should be understood that the phrase "loss or damage" is so limited.

The contractor is required:

(1) to insure in the joint names of the employer and the contractor (which means that both benefit); **The insured**

(2) the permanent and temporary works (including unfixed materials and other things on site for incorporation therein) to their full value; **The subjectmatter of the insurance and the sum insured**

(3) the constructional plant to its full value;

(4)   against all loss or damage from whatever
      cause arising (other than the excepted risks)   The perils insured
      for which he is responsible under the terms   against
      of the contract;

(5)   both during the construction period and the
      maintenance period arising from a cause oc-
      curring during the construction period or   The period of in-
      through damage caused by the contractor   surance
      during operations carried out in accordance
      with the maintenance clause plus 14 days in
      each case.

The clause is considered in the following stages, which do not follow
exactly the item numbers above.

1. Insurance in the joint names of the employer and contractor

From the employer's point of view insurance in the joint names may
seem necessary to prevent the contractor's insurers recovering from the
employer after paying a claim in cases where the contract indicates that
the employer is responsible (the excepted risks). See *MacGillivray and
Partington on Insurance Law*, seventh edition, 1981 where it states in
section 1213: "The fact that the policy is in joint names will almost
invariably man that both parties are intended to benefit and that there
is no scope for subrogation." This is verified in *Petrofina (UK) Ltd and
Others v Magnaload Ltd and Others* (1983). See Appendix 4. However,
when it is appreciated that the contractors' all risks policy excludes the
excepted risks, other than riot in England and Wales, this argument
becomes almost irrelevant. Nevertheless, it does give the employer the
right to claim directly against the contractor's insurers under the policy
in respect of damage by any risk which is covered and there may be a
good reason for taking this shorter route to recovery rather than
claiming against the contractor under the contract.

2. The subject matter of the insurance

"Permanent works" is defined in clause 1 as meaning "the permanent
works to be constructed, completed and maintained in accordance with
the contract".
      "Temporary works" is defined in the same clause as meaning "all
temporary works of every kind required in or about the construction,
completion and maintenance of the works". On to these definitions is
grafted "any unfixed materials or other things delivered to the site for
incorporation therein", which is more precise than the fourth edition

of this contract which reads "materials and other things brought on to the site". It is now clear that the temporary works do not include temporary buildings on construction sites. See also the drafting discrepancy between clauses 20 and 21 mentioned under heading (5) below. In any event it will be seen from the Schedule in the policy in Appendix 1 that all the items mentioned under this and the next headings are covered.

3. The construction plant

This is defined in clause 1 as meaning:

all appliances or things of whatsoever nature required in or about the construction, completion and maintenance of the Works but does not include materials or other things intended to form or forming part of the Permanent Works.

This definition is wide enough to include the temporary buildings on construction sites. It is a fact that a high proportion of fires on construction sites start in the temporary buildings. This type of fire usually means that several structures are destroyed, including offices containing important drawings and stores with key components.

4. The sum insured

An important aspect is choosing an adequate sum insured, bearing in mind the words used in clause 21 are "to their full value" or "to its full value" as the case may be, which, ignoring such matters as debris removal costs and professional fees, must cover the reinstatement cost of the works, so that the insured has to make a calculation:

(a)   of the increases in cost of materials, goods and labour charges during the period of the contract, ie price fluctuations, and

(b)   following damage during the construction period, of the effect of inflation on those costs incurred:

(i)   in the reinstatement of the damaged works, and

(ii) in completion of those parts of the works that have not been started at the time of damage and which are delayed as a consequence, although this cover is not required by the contract wording.

Thus it would be incorrect simply to insure for the original contract

value. It is the usual practice for contractors' all risks policies to provide
for an automatic increase in the sum insured (indemnity limit in the
policy schedule) for contract works by an amount not exceeding 20%
subject always to an adjustment of premium but this type of clause can
only cater for (a) and (b)(i) above.

In the event of it being impossible to envisage a total loss then (subject
to clause 21 being altered accordingly) it is permissible for the insurance
to be arranged on a "first loss" basis and not on a "full value" basis.
This means that the contractor decides what the maximum loss will
probably be and insures for that sum. This could happen when the
works are to be built in sections, which often occurs in civil engineering
when the work covers a large area and it is not possible to envisage a
total loss of all the sections.

5. The perils insured against

The words "all loss or damage from whatever cause other than the
excepted risks for which he is responsible under the contract" are clear
enough in themselves. However, in this clause the words apply to
permanent and temporary works plus unfixed materials and constructional plant, while in clause 20 reference is only made to the works, ie
no reference is made to unfixed materials or constructional plant.
Furthermore "works" is defined in clause 1(1) as meaning "the permanent works together with the temporary works", and neither of the
definitions of permanent or temporary works includes unfixed materials, etc. Nevertheless, there seems little doubt that, while the contract
requirement for insurance cover concerns a wider field than the works,
it does not include the excepted risks.

6. The period of insurance

The cover is stated to be for the period stipulated in clause 20(1) which
is the construction period starting with the commencement of the
works until 14 days after the engineer shall have issued a certificate of
completion for the whole of the works pursuant to clause 48. Cover is
also to be provided during the maintenance period for any delayed loss
or damage arising from an insured cause or event occurring prior to
the period of maintenance and loss or damage actually caused by the
contractor while working on the site (that is, in carrying out his or her
maintenance obligations under clauses 49 and 50). Incidentally, 14 days
after the issue of the certificate of completion of partial completion may
in fact result in the cover continuing for 35 days after actual completion,
because under clause 48 the engineer has 21 days, after notice from the
contractor of actual completion, to issue the certificate.

7. The proviso (concerning no insurance for the repair or reconstruction of any work . . . not in accordance with the contract)

Assuming "materials and work not in accordance with the requirements of the contract" means defective materials or work, the proviso is limited to the actual repair or reconstruction of the defective work itself. Defective work resulting in structural or other failure causing considerable destruction or damage to other parts of the works, not themselves defective, is not within the proviso. Such consequential loss must be insured and in fact the contractors' all risks policy only excludes the cost of repairing the defective work or materials. It has been suggested that the words "workmanship not in accordance with the requirements of the contract" might include failure by the contractor to comply with any express provisions in the bills or specifications requiring the contractor to take certain measures to protect the works during construction such as shoring or pumping for drainage.

However, if the policy exclusion is worded as mentioned above, ie excluding defective work or materials and not in the specific wording of the contract it would not be possible for the insurers to use the wording of the policy exclusion to repudiate liability in the event of the failure just explained but it might be argued by insurers that a reasonable precautions condition had been violated. Such a condition is usually worded as follows:

The Insured shall take reasonable precautions to prevent loss . . . and to safeguard the property insured.

Presumably the purpose of this proviso in not asking for insurance is that it was thought by the drafters that difficulty might be experienced in obtaining such cover.

8. Approval of insurer

The contractor is required to see that the insurance is effected with an insurer and in terms approved by the employer (which approval must not be unreasonably withheld).

The only satisfactory way for the contractor to comply with this stipulation is to submit the proposed policy of the proposed insurer to the employer so that he or she may satisfy himself or herself on the matter. This is suggested in spite of the fact that the final paragraph of clause 21 goes on to require the contractor to produce the policy or policies and receipts for the premiums whenever required.

Whether in practice employers adopt any procedure to ensure this approval is carried out formally is doubtful. Presumably they will regard members of the Association of British Insurers as acceptable, which does not mean non-members are not acceptable. However, it does give the employer a veto if it should ever be needed. In many cases this duty is carried out by the engineer on behalf of the employer. It is a heavy responsibility to saddle a member of one profession with the knowledge of another, and the consulting engineers would be well advised to seek the assistance of professionals from the insurance industry unless they have their own insurance experts on the staff. Otherwise if they approve a policy which ultimately turns out to be inadequate, causing a loss to the employer, they (the engineers) could be sued for professional negligence.

Clause 21 makes no provision for the operation of an annual contractors' all risks policy (as distinct from a policy issued for the specific contract) but normally if such a policy provides the cover required by clause 21 it would be accepted.

The engineer will inform the employer of the certified completion of the works (and usually prior to the estimated date thereof) in order that the employer may make suitable arrangements for insurances in his or her own name from the date the contractor's policy ceases to provide the cover the employer requires.

The FIDIC contract fourth edition 1987

While this contract is not included in the Chartered Institute of Loss Adjusters examination syllabus, it has been included in the 1992 Examination Scheme of the Chartered Insurance Institute (approved by Council 1989) in the syllabus of the new subject "Construction Insurance". Furthermore, those contractors concerned in contracts overseas will inevitably become involved with this contract sooner or later if not already involved.

This contract in its wording no longer closely follows the current edition of the English ICE Conditions of Contract, nevertheless the basic requirements are so similar to each clause of the ICE Conditions already considered that it lends itself to a commentary in this chapter.

The first five paragraphs in the Foreword to these Conditions (explaining their purpose and form) are quoted below, and only the relevant clauses from Part 1 (General Conditions) will be considered in this commentary.

The terms of the fourth edition of the Conditions of Contract for Works of Civil Engineering Construction have been prepared by the Fédération Internationale des Ingénieurs Conseils (FIDIC) and are recommended for general use for the purpose of construction of such works where tenders are invited on an international basis. The Conditions are equally suitable for use on domestic contracts.

The version in English of the Conditions is considered by FIDIC as the official and authentic text for the purpose of translation.

In the preparation of the Conditions it was recognised that while there are numerous clauses which will be generally applicable there are some clauses which must necessarily vary to take account of the circumstances and locality of the works. The clauses of general application have been grouped together in this document and are referred to as Part I — General Conditions. They have been printed in a form which will facilitate their inclusion as printed in the contract documents normally prepared.

The General Conditions are linked with the Conditions of Particular Application, referred to as Part II, by the corresponding numbering of the clauses, so that Parts I and II together comprise the Conditions governing the rights and obligations of the parties.

Part II must be specially drafted to suit each individual contract.

While the differences in wording between this contract and the ICE Conditions will be commented upon as each clause is considered the general pattern is given below in comparison with that of the ICE Conditions.

ICE Conditions	*FIDIC Contract*
Clause 20 Three sub-clauses: (1) Care of the works. (2) Responsibility for reinstatement. (3) Excepted risks.	Four sub-clauses: .1 Care of works. .2 Responsibility to rectify loss or damage. .3 Loss or damage due to employer's risks. .4 Employer's risks (same as ICE Excepted Risks plus any operation of the forces of nature). *Note:* .2 and .3 include the same requirements as the ICE responsibility for reinstatement.

Clause 21	Insurance of works, etc, including a proviso exonerating contractor from insuring additionally to that required by the contract, subject to any relevant requirement in the bill of quantities.	Four sub-clauses: .1 Insurance of works and contractor's equipment. .2 Scope of cover. .3 Responsibility for amounts not recovered. .4 Exclusions. *Note:* all four sub-clauses basically include the same requirements as clause 21 in the ICE Conditions.
Clause 25	Remedy on contractor's failure to insure.	Four sub-clauses: .1 Evidence and terms of insurances. .2 Adequacy of insurances. .3 Remedy on contractor's failure to insure. .4 Compliance with policy conditions. *Note:* the first two sub-clauses basically cover the same ground as clause 21 of the ICE Conditions. See comment on the fourth sub-clause later.

Care of Works

20.1 The Contractor shall take full responsibility for the care of the Works and materials and Plant for incorporation therein from the Commencement Date until the date of issue of the Taking-Over Certificate for the whole of the Works, when the responsibility for the said care shall pass to the Employer. Provided that:

(a) if the Engineer issues a Taking-Over Certificate for any Section or part of the Permanent Works the Contractor shall cease to be liable for the care of that Section or part from the date of issue of the Taking-Over Certificate, when the responsibility for the care of that Section or part shall pass to the Employer, and

(b) the Contractor shall take full responsibility for the care of any outstanding Works and materials and Plant for incorporation therein which he undertakes to finish during the Defects Liability Period until such outstanding Works have been completed pursuant to Clause 49.

Responsibility to Rectify Loss or Damage

20.2 If any loss or damage happens to the Works, or any part thereof, or materials or Plant for incorporation therein, during the period for which the Contractor is responsible for the care thereof, from any cause whatsoever, other than the risks defined in Sub-Clause 20.4, the Contractor shall, at his own cost, rectify such loss or damage so that the Permanent Works conform in every respect with the provisions of the Contract to the satisfaction of the Engineer. The Contractor shall also be liable for any loss or damage to the Works occasioned by him in the course of any operations carried out by him for the purpose of complying with his obligations under Clauses 49 and 50.

Loss or Damage Due to Employer's Risks

20.3 In the event of any such loss or damage happening from any of the risks defined in Sub-Clause 20.4, or in combination with other risks, the Contractor shall, if and to the extent required by the Engineer, rectify the loss or damage and the Engineer shall determine an addition to the Contract Price in accordance with Clause 52 and shall notify the Contractor accordingly, with a copy to the Employer. In the case of a combination of risks causing loss or damage any such determination shall take into account the proportional responsibility of the Contractor and the Employer.

Employer's Risks

20.4 The Employer's risks are:

(a)   war, hostilities (whether war be declared or not), invasion, act of foreign enemies,

(b)   rebellion, revolution, insurrection, or military or usurped power, or civil war,

(c)   ionising radiations, or contamination by radio-activity from any nuclear fuel, or from any nuclear waste from the combustion of nuclear fuel, radio-active toxic explosive, or other hazardous properties of any explosive nuclear assembly or nuclear component thereof,

(d)   pressure waves caused by aircraft or other aerial devices travelling at sonic or supersonic speeds,

(e)   riot, commotion or disorder, unless solely restricted to employees of the Contractor or of his Subcontractors and arising from the conduct of the Works,

(f) loss or damage due to the use or occupation by the Employer of any
     Section or part of the Permanent Works, except as may be provided
     for in the Contract,

(g) loss or damage to the extent that it is due to the design of the Works,
     other than any part of the design provided by the Contractor or for
     which the Contractor is responsible,

(h) any operation of the forces of nature against which an experienced
     contractor could not reasonably have been expected to take precau-
     tions.

A comparison between this clause and clause 20 of the fifth edition of the
ICE Conditions of Contract discloses the following differences.

(a) The contractor's full responsibility for the care of the works dates
     in both contracts from the commencement of the works but where-
     as the ICE Conditions add 14 days to the date of the issue of the
     certificate of completion, the FIDIC Contract uses the date of issue
     in the certificate of taking over as the date the contractor's respon-
     sibility ceases. Similarly, the 14-day period applies to any part of
     the works issued with a certificate of completion in the case of the
     ICE Conditions but not in respect of the FIDIC Contract.

(b) Both contracts make it clear that in the event of damage from any
     of the excepted risks (or employer's risks as the case may be) the
     contractor need only make it good to the extent required by the
     engineer and then only at the cost of the employer.

(c) The employer's risk reading "any operation of the forces of nature
     against which an experienced contractor could not reasonably
     have been expected to take precautions" is additional to the ex-
     cepted risks in the ICE Conditions.
         It is clear that the reason for the discrepancy is that the possibility
     of this risk occurring abroad is greater, therefore the employer is
     probably forced to accept it as his or her responsibility. It has been
     said that the vagueness of the expression just quoted seems to
     confer a discretion on the arbitrator, in which the borderline
     between interpretation and sympathy is likely to be confused. It
     has already been stated in the Preface that the excepted risks (with
     the possible exception of riot) form the basis of the exceptions to
     the contractors' all risks policy but contrary to popular belief, "act

of God" or "forces of nature" are not exclusions normally used in insurance policies.

They certainly do not appear in the policies discussed in this book. Nevertheless, one must agree that the expression is very vague although the general intention is clearly to saddle the employer with unforeseeable risks and those which a reasonable contractor cannot provide for or insure against. Inevitably there must be borderline cases, and contractors may be encouraged to take chances with a view to increasing their profits always hoping to invoke the exception should damage occur. Incidentally, this "forces of nature" excepted risk as such is not required to be insured against but it could include risks such as storm and flood which are covered by the contractors' all risks policy. On the other hand, hurricanes, earthquakes, tidal waves and volcanic eruptions and the like are risks to be taken into account when fixing terms for overseas contracts. Thus they are often only partially insurable.

Insurance of Works and Contractor's Equipment

21.1 The Contractor shall, without limiting his or the Employer's obligations and responsibilities under clause 20, insure:

(a)   the Works, together with materials and Plant for incorporation therein, to the full replacement cost

(b)   an additional sum of 15 per cent of such replacement cost, or as may be specified in Part II of these Conditions, to cover any additional costs of and incidental to the rectification of loss or damage including professional fees and the cost of demolishing and removing any part of the Works and of removing debris of whatsoever nature.

(c)   the Contractor's Equipment and other things brought onto the Site by the Contractor, for a sum sufficient to provide for their replacement at the Site.

Scope of Cover

21.2 The insurance in paragraphs (a) and (b) of Sub-Clause 21.1 shall be in the joint names of the Contractor and the Employer and shall cover:

(a)   the Employer and the Contractor against all loss or damage from whatsoever cause arising, other than as provided in Sub-Clause 21.4, from the start of work at the Site until the date of issue of the relevant Taking-Over Certificate in respect of the Works or any Section or part thereof as the case may be, and

(b) the Contractor for his liability:
      (i) during the Defects Liability Period for loss or damage arising
           from a cause occurring prior to the commencement of the Defects
           Liability Period, and

      (ii) for loss or damage occasioned by the Contractor in the course of
            any operations carried out by him for the purpose of complying
            with his obligations under Clauses 49 and 50.

Responsibility for Amounts not Recovered
21.3 Any amounts not insured or not recovered from the insurers shall be borne
by the Employer or the Contractor in accordance with their responsibilities
under Clause 20.

Exclusions
21.4 There shall be no obligation for the insurances in Sub-Clause 21.1 to include
loss or damage caused by

(a) war, hostilities (where war be declared or not), invasion, act of foreign
     enemies,

(b) rebellion, revolution, insurrection, or military or usurped power, or
     civil war,

(c) ionising radiations, or contamination by radio-activity from any
     nuclear fuel, or from any nuclear waste from the combustion of
     nuclear fuel, radio-active toxic explosive, or other hazardous proper-
     ties of any explosive nuclear assembly or nuclear component thereof,

(d) pressure waves caused by aircraft or other aerial devices travelling
     at sonic or supersonic speeds.

The differences between the FIDIC Contract in clause 21 and the same
clause in the ICE Conditions are set out below.

(a) The part of this clause dealing with the care of the works in both
     these contracts is the same in its objective except that the term
     "temporary works" has been dropped by FIDIC as the word
     "works" has been defined as including both temporary and per-
     manent works (see clause 1(1)(f)(i)). Furthermore, the FIDIC Con-
     tract adds 15% to the replacement value to cover professional fees
     and the cost of removing demolished works and debris, and also a
     sum for the contractor's equipment.

(b) In sub-clause 21.2 concerning the scope of the insurance cover the allowable exclusions are those listed in sub-clause 21.4, whereas in the ICE Conditions the excepted risks are excluded, which is a longer list. The difference between these two lists is that the ICE includes loss or damage due to the use or occupation by the employer and due to the contractor's design, but as these two risks are those of the employer under the contract in FIDIC the contractor would not wish to cover them anyway. In any event there would have to be a special arrangement as these two risks are standard exclusions under the CAR policy.

(c) The ICE Conditions contain a proviso paragraph which does not appear in the FIDIC Contract. This paragraph provides that it is for the contractor to decide whether to insure or not against the necessity to repair or reconstruct work due to defective materials or workmanship, unless the bill of quantities provides a special item for this insurance. In view of the exception in the contractors' all risks policy this cover, if requested by the bill of quantities, is normally only available to a limited extent, ie the exception applies to the cost of repairing, replacing or rectifying the actual property which is defective in material or workmanship which means that only loss or damage to the property protected by the policy which is caused by such defective material or workmanship, is covered. See Chapter 2 for further details concerning this exclusion. Reference should also be made to an earlier part of this chapter where this whole proviso is considered in more detail.

Evidence and Terms of Insurances

25.1 The Contractor shall provide evidence to the Employer prior to the start of work at the Site that the insurances required under Contract have been effected and shall, within 84 days of the Commencement Date, provide the insurance policies to the Employer. When providing such evidence and such policies to the Employer, the Contractor shall notify the Engineer of so doing. Such insurance policies shall be consistent with the general terms agreed prior to the issue of the Letter of Acceptance. The Contractor shall effect all insurances for which he is responsible with an insurer and in terms approved by the Employer, which approval shall not be unreasonably withheld.

Adequacy of Insurances

25.2 The Contractor shall notify the insurers of changes in the nature, extent or programme for the execution of the Works and ensure the adequacy of the insurances at all times in accordance with the terms of the Contract and shall, when required, produce to the Employer the insurance policies in force and the receipts for payment of the current premiums.

Remedy on Contractor's Failure to Insure

25.3 If the Contractor fails to effect and keep in force any of the insurances required under the Contract, or fails to provide the policies to the Employer within the period required by Sub-Clause 25.1, then and in any such case the Employer may effect and keep in force any such insurances and pay any premium as may be necessary for that purpose and from time to time deduct the amount so paid from any monies due or to become due to the Contractor, or recover the same as a debt due from the Contractor.

Compliance with Policy Conditions

25.4 In the event that the Contractor or the Employer fails to comply with conditions imposed by the insurance policies effected pursuant to the Contract, each shall indemnify the other against all losses and claims arising from such failure.

The evidence and approval of terms of the insurance, and remedy on the contractor's failure to insure are more or less the same in both contracts. The exceptions to note are that the provision of the policy to the employer in FIDIC must take place within 84 days of the commencement date of the contract (there is no such requirement in ICE), and the remedy on failure to insure in ICE appears in clause 25 whereas the other requirements in ICE appear in clause 21.

This leaves sub-clause 25.4 in FIDIC as an additional requirement not appearing in ICE. Thus if either the contractor or the employer fails to comply with the terms of the insurance policy which results in a loss to the other party, the guilty party must indemnify the other party to the contract. This is not unreasonable and will presumably override any attempt by the guilty party to use another tem of the contract to avoid liability, eg the mere requirement to insure on the part of the contractor if the insurance fails due to the non-compliance with the policy terms by the employer will not interfere with the application of this clause 25.4.

Acknowledgements are made to George Godwin (Longman Group) for permission to use parts of the author's book *Insurance under the ICE Contract* in writing this chapter.

CHAPTER 8

Form of subcontract designed for use with the ICE General Conditions of Contract

This form of subcontract is published by the Federation of Civil Engineering Contractors, which is one of the three bodies sponsoring the ICE Conditions of Contract. Apparently it is appropriate whether or not the subcontractor has been nominated by the employer under the principal contract. This form includes five schedules for completion by the parties. The fifth schedule concerns "insurances". This form also includes "Notes for the guidance of contractors on the completion of the schedules" and these notes concerning the fifth schedule read as follows:

> Reference should be made to Clause 14 (Insurances) of the Sub-Contract. In completing the two parts of the Schedule the parties should take care to ensure that all insurances required by the Main Contract are effected by one or other of them and that there is no unnecessary duplication of insurance.
> Part 1 should specify insurances to be effected by the Sub-Contractor.
> Part 2 should specify the policy of insurance which the Contractor is effecting in pursuance of Clause 21 of the Main Contract Conditions, if it is intended that the Sub-Contractor shall have the benefit thereof. In such cases his interest should be noted either generally or specifically on the policy and this Part of the Schedule should so state. If the Sub-Contractor is not to have any benefit under the policy of the Contractor, then that Part should be marked "not applicable".

The fifth schedule itself only contains two sub-headings after the main headings of "Fifth Schedule" and "Insurances" and they are:

> Part I Subcontractor's insurances;
> Part II Contractor's policy of insurance.

Appendix 5 gives examples of how this fifth schedule might be completed.

The relevant clauses of the subcontract form are clause 12: indemnities, and clause 14: insurances, which is dealt with below.

Insurances

14. (1)   The Sub-Contractor shall effect insurance against such risks as are specified in part I of the Fifth Schedule hereto and in such sums and for the benefit of such persons as are specified therein and unless the said Fifth Schedule otherwise provides, shall maintain such insurance from the time that the Sub-Contractor first enters upon the Site for the purpose of executing the Sub-Contract Works until he has finally performed his obligations under Clause 13 (Maintenance and Defects).

(2)   The Contractor shall maintain in force until such time as the Main Works have been completed or ceased to be at his risk under the Main Contract, the policy of insurance specified in Part II of the Fifth Schedule hereto. In the event of the Sub-Contract Works, or any Constructional Plant, Temporary Works, materials or other things belonging to the Sub-Contractor being destroyed or damaged during such period in such circumstances that a claim is established in respect thereof under the said policy, then the Sub-Contractor shall be paid the amount of such claim, or the amount of his loss, whichever is the less and shall apply such sum in replacing or repairing that which was destroyed or damaged. Save as aforesaid the Sub-Contract Works shall be at the risk of the Sub-Contractor until the Main Works have been completed under the Main Contract, or if the Main Works are to be completed by sections, until the last of the sections in which the Sub-Contract Works are comprised has been completed, and the Sub-Contractor shall make good all loss of or damage occurring to the Sub-Contract Works prior thereto at his own expense.

(3)   Where by virtue of this clause either party is required to effect and maintain insurance, then at any time until such obligation has fully been performed, he shall if so required by the other party produce for inspection satisfactory evidence of insurance and in the event of his failing to do so, the other party may himself effect such insurance and recover the cost of so doing from the party in default.

The first point which would probably occur to the insurance official is the assumption that the subcontractor will have several insurances but the contractor will apparently have only one policy. The various policies available appear in the Combined "Contractors Insurance Policy" in

Appendix 1 and as far as construction contracts are concerned they fall into two categories. The material damage policy covers the works, and the policy concerned in the ICE Conditions is the contractors' all risks policy. The other category is the legal liability policies of which there are two main policies: the employers' liability policy and the public liability policy.

It would therefore be logical to expect both Part I and Part II of the fifth schedule to refer to these policies of insurance. It is true that a contractors' combined policy, as explained in Chapter 2, covers in one document under three or four different sections risks which are normally covered by several policies, namely material damage and legal liabilities. Perhaps this is what the drafters of Part II had in mind in referring to the "Contractor's policy of insurance". The only other assumption is that clause 14 only applies to insurance of works. However, this is hardly likely as the preceeding clause 12 clearly envisages legal liabilities and, moreover, Part I of the fifth schedule refers to the subcontractor's insurances in the plural. Therefore, until the main contractor, in completing Part II has decided whether or not to allow the subcontractor to benefit from his or her CAR policy, Part I cannot be completed.

Sub-clause 14 (1)

As sub-clause 14 (1) only refers to Part I of the fifth schedule it only applies to those insurances required from the subcontractor and it is arguable that as the contractor under the main contract is responsible for insuring the works (including presumably the subcontract works) subject to the excepted risks in sub-clause 20(3) of the main contract, no insurance of the subcontract works is usually required from the subcontractor. However, even on this argument, he or she would be obliged to have the usual employers' and public liability policies because of the indemnity mentioned in clause 12 and also because of the statutory requirement of compulsory employers' liability insurance. If the subcontractor had a combined employers' and public liability policy it would be the subcontractor who had only one policy of insurance, not the contractor. Nevertheless, when one comes to consider Part II it is clear that the subcontractor under Part I may have to cover the subcontract works under his or her own contractors' all risks policy in addition to the usual liability policies just mentioned.

Apart from indicating that the insurances to be effected by the subcontractors are those specified in Part I of the fifth schedule, sub-clause

14(1) also specifies that Part I will detail the sums and persons to be insured. Presumably as this part, unlike Part II, is certainly dealing with liability policies the intention is to indicate a limit of indemnity for any one occurrence under the subcontractor's public liability policy, bearing in mind that the employers' liability policy is normally unlimited or if the statute concerned is followed a figure of two million pounds applies. Should it be decided that the subcontractor should also take out a contractors' all risks policy on the subcontract works then this must be indicated in Part I with the appropriate sum insured. However, unless the subcontractor is not to benefit from the main contractors' all risks policy it is difficult to envisage circumstances where it would be necessary for the subcontractor to take out such a policy on the subcontract works, as normally this would only result in the payment of a double premium for the subcontract works, and according to the guidance notes duplication of insurance is to be avoided.

If a separate policy is not required from the subcontractor(s) as just indicated, it is important, if it is intended that the subcontractor(s) should be indemnified in like manner to the main contractor under the latter's policy, that the subcontractor's name(s) should appear as joint insured for their respective contract works.

Sub-clause 14(1) concludes by indicating the period of the subcontractor's insurances, ie from the time the subcontractor first enters upon the site to execute the subcontract works until he or she has finally performed his or her obligations under clause 13 (maintenance and defects).

Finally, if subcontractors are uncertain about the position of their constructional plant, temporary works materials and other equipment on site belonging to them even though they are to have the benefit of the main contractor's CAR policy so far as the subcontract works are concerned, they should enquire the position from the main contractor and if they receive an unsatisfactory answer they should arrange their own insurance for these items, assuming they have no insurance already. Incidentally, in case there is any confusion between the subcontractor being given the benefit of the main contractor's CAR policy and the fact that the main contractor has an obligation to insure the contract works (including the subcontract works) under clause 21 of the main contract, it should be appreciated that the clause 21 insurance being in the joint names of the main contractor and the employer only covers the employer's and contractor's interest in the subcontract works. The subcontractors are not named parties under that policy, and their interest is not covered unless the main contractor so agrees. If their interest is covered then the subcontractors should ensure that their names are added to the main contractor's policy as named insureds and thus they become party to it and potential beneficiaries under it.

Sub-clause 14(2)

Sub-clause 14(2) deals with the insurance that is required to be maintained by the contractor and the statement reads:

The Contractor shall maintain in force until such time as the Main Works have been completed or ceased to be at his risk under the Main Contract, the policy of insurance specified in Part II of the Fifth Schedule hereto.

So again, the stipulation appears to be for *one* policy and the policy the drafters have in mind seems to be the contractors' all risks policy covering the works, etc (no thought is apparently given to the legal liability policies also required by the contractor), as the sub-clause continues as follows:

In the event of the Sub-Contract Works, or any Constructional Plant, Temporary works, materials or other things belonging to the Sub-Contractor being destroyed or damaged during such period in such circumstances that a claim is established in respect thereof under the said policy, then the Sub-Contractor shall be paid the amount of such claim or the amount of his loss, whichever is the less, and shall apply such sum in replacing or repairing that which was destroyed or damaged.

The statement here is not what happens in practice, as until the subcontractor becomes a party to the policy contract he or she cannot be paid directly by the insurer. Once he or she has the benefit of the policy he or she can be paid, usually via the main contractor.

Sub-clause 14(3)

Sub-clause 14(3) states that either party to the subcontract who is required to effect insurance shall if so required by the other party produce the appropriate policy, together with receipts for premiums payable thereunder. If he or she fails to do so the other party may effect such insurance and recover the cost of doing so from the party in default.

CHAPTER 9

GC/Works/1 edition 2 and proposed edition 3

The Property Services Agency (PSA) of the Department of the Environ-
ment is the Directorate of Contracts concerning contracts designed for use
by Government departments. The current edition of the General Conditions of Government Contracts for Building and Civil Engineering Works
is edition 2 of GC/Works/1 which has been in use since September 1977.
The following general points about these conditions should be noted:

(a) They are intended for both building and civil engineering works
and consequently they combine the purposes of the JCT form and
the ICE conditions.

(b) Unlike the JCT and ICE contracts they are not drafted by the
representative bodies of both parties to the contract and in that
sense this contract is a unilateral one. Thus "The Authority" (the
Government department concerned) is able to make decisions
which govern both parties. Also a number of matters are excluded
from arbitration. Arbitration is not permitted on any matter "as to
which the decision or report of the Authority or of any other person
is by the Contract expressed to be final and conclusive".

(c) The numbered paragraphs of this contract are called "Conditions"
not "Clauses".

(d) Until the proposed edition 3 there was no contractual obligation
on the contractor to take out insurances either in respect of loss or
damage to the works or any of the risks he or she is required to
take. Presumably it was felt that it was a matter of commercial
prudence for a contractor to insure, consequently there was no

necessity to make a contractual requirement to do so. As for the possibility of substantial claims being made against the authority because the indemnities from an insolvent contractor are worthless, presumably it was felt that the Government was capable of standing this.

(e) A shorter version of this contract exists for minor works known as form GC/Works/2 — edition 2 which was issued in January 1980. Many of the conditions follow the main form but there is no provision for bills of quantity.

GC/Works/1 edition 2

Conditions 25 and 26 deal with the contractors' responsibility for loss or damage to the works. Therefore they are broadly speaking the equivalent of clause 22 of the JCT form and clause 20 of the ICE conditions.

Condition 26

Condition 26 will be considered first as condition 25 is a qualification of condition 26, and it (condition 25) has been amended. Condition 26 reads as follows:

26 (1) All things not for incorporation which are on the Site and are provided by or on behalf of the Contractor for the construction of the Works shall stand at the risk and be in the sole charge of the Contractor, and the Contractor shall be responsible for, and with all possible speed make good, any loss or damage thereto arising from any cause whatsoever, including the accepted risks.

(2) (a) The Contractor shall (unless the Authority exercises his powers to determine the Contract) with all possible speed make good any loss or damage arising from any cause whatsoever occasioned to the Works or to any things for incorporation on the Site (including any things provided by the Authority) and shall notwithstanding such loss or damage proceed with the execution and completion of the Works in accordance with the Contract.

(b) The cost of making good such loss or damage shall be wholly borne by the Contractor, save that —

(i) where the loss or damage is wholly caused by the neglect or default of a servant of the Crown acting in the course of his employment as such, the Authority shall pay the Contractor for making good the loss or damage, and where it is partly caused by such neglect or default, the Authority shall pay the Contractor such sum as is proportionate to that servant's share in the responsibility for the loss or damage, and

(ii) where the loss or damage is wholly caused by any of the accepted risks the Authority shall pay the Contractor for making good the loss or damage and where it is partly so caused the Authority shall pay the Contractor such sum as is proportionate to the share of any of the accepted risks in causing the loss or damage.

(c) Any sum payable by the Authority under sub-paragraph (2)(b) of this Condition shall be ascertained in the same manner as a sum payable in respect of an alteration or addition under the Contract and shall be added to the Contract Sum.

Clearly by Condition 26(1) all things *not* for incorporation but which are provided, by the contractor, for the construction of the works are the contractors' responsibility, including loss or damage arising from the accepted risks. This will include site huts or plant owned or hired by the contractor and his or her subcontractors, whether nominated or domestic. Obviously it is for the contractor to ensure that, where appropriate, this risk is passed on to his or her other subcontractors.

The phrase "the accepted risks" needs some explanation. It refers to the risks which are accepted by the employing authority (rather like the "excepted risks" in clause 20(3) of the ICE conditions although only the nuclear, kindred war risks and sonic waves appear in both contracts as the employer's responsibilities) which are listed in condition 1 (2) and which read as follows:

(2) In the Contract the following expressions shall, unless the context otherwise requires, have the meanings hereby respectively assigned to them:—

'the accepted risks' means the risks of—

(a) fire or explosion,

(b) storm, lightning, tempest, flood or earthquake,

(c)   aircraft or other aerial devices or objects dropped therefrom, includ-
       ing pressure waves caused by aircraft or such devices whether travel-
       ling at sonic or supersonic speeds,

(d)   ionising radiations or contamination by radioactivity from any
       nuclear fuel or from any nuclear waste from the combustion of
       nuclear fuel,

(e)   the radioactive, toxic, explosive or other hazardous properties of any
       explosive nuclear assembly or nuclear component thereof,

(f)   riot, civil commotion, civil war, rebellion, revolution, insurrection,
       military or usurped power or Kings' enemy risks (within the defini-
       tion of that expression contained in section 15(1)(a) of the War Risks
       Insurance Act 1939 as for the time being in force);

It should be noted that in 1984 amendment no. 3 (incorporating amendment no. 2) to GC/Works/1 edition 2 was issued by the PSA, under which
condition 1 paragraph (2) replaces the above definition and it now reads:

(a)   ionising radiations or contamination by radioactivity from and nuclear
       waste from the combustion of nuclear fuel,

(b)   the radioactive, toxic, explosive or other hazardous properties of any
       explosive nuclear assembly or nuclear component thereof.

(c)   pressure waves caused by aircraft or other aerial devices whether travel-
       ling at sonic or supersonic speeds.

(d)   civil war, rebellion, revolution, insurrection, military or usurped power.

It will be appreciated that fire, explosion, storm, lightning, tempest, flood
or earthquake and even aircraft or other aerial devices (other than pressure waves caused by aircraft or other aerial devices) as well as riot and
civil commotion, are now *not* within the accepted risks. Although the
proposed GC/Works/1 edition 3 will be dealt with later it is relevant to
mention that in that edition the amendment no. 3 is followed with the
addition of the words "war, invasion, act of foreign enemy, hostilities
(whether or not war has been declared)" which have never been included
in the "accepted risks" although no doubt, taken for granted as the
Government in the past has accepted responsibility for such loss or
damage.
    It is also relevant to comment that in the past the Government authority

has taken great advantage of the qualification of reasonable precautions required from the contractor by condition 25(1) with the result that the perils not now accepted by the Government authority have never been the advantage they may appear to have been to the contractor; but more of this later.

Turning to condition 26 (2) (a) of GC/Works/1 edition 2 the contractor is required "(unless the Authority exercises his powers to determine the Contract)" to make good any loss or damage arising from any cause whatsoever occasioned to the works or to any things for incorporation on the site (including things provided by the employer).

Condition 26 (2) (b) deals with the exceptions to the contractors' responsibility mentioned in condition 26 (2) (a). There are two such exceptions. Condition 26 (2) (b) (1) excludes loss or damage caused wholly or partly by "the neglect or default of a servant of the Crown acting in the course of his employment as such" or in condition 26 (2) (b) (ii) if it is caused, wholly or partly, by "any of the accepted risks". In either of those exceptions the contractor will be paid for the work involved by the authority, but if there is some apportionment of "blame", only the appropriate portion of the sum equivalent to the servants' share of responsibility will be paid.

Condition 25

By condition 25(1) the contractor is also required to "take all reasonable precautions to prevent loss or damage from any of the accepted risks, and to minimise the amount of any such loss or damage or any loss or damage caused by a servant of the Crown," and to comply with any instructions given by the superintending officer (SO) designated in the Abstract of Particulars. As might be expected the PSA's idea of "reasonable" varies considerably from that of the contractor in the practical interpretation of condition 25(1), as it seems there is usually an argument as to whether the contractor has done something which the PSA can class as unreasonable. For example, on Merseyside some years ago steel erectors had reached the stage of erecting stanchions with cross connections of deep proportions. Each stanchion was bolted into the ground and supported by wire hawsers. An exceptional storm occurred (66 on the Beaufort scale was mentioned although there is some doubt about this) and this continued for nine days before the stanchions collapsed. There was no doubt about the violence of the wind as two pontoon piers in the estuary sank. However, the PSA refused to accept responsibility as one of the stanchions had only three hawsers whereas the other stanchions had four. Also, two or three of the holes in the metal bases through which the stanchions were bolted had been elongated to fix the bolts properly which the steel erectors claimed was a common practice. This shows that however excessive a peril may be it could not be assumed under the edition 2 wording of "accepted risks" before the amendment no 3 that there would not be something which the contractor had done which could be used to invoke condition 25(1). Possibly the current wording without the common perils is a fairer way of letting the contractor know the position.

The contractor is also required by condition 25(2) to "comply with any statutory regulations (whether or not binding the Crown) which govern the storage of explosives, petrol, or other things (whether or not for incorporation) which are brought on the site". As well as cutting down "the accepted risks", Amendment no. 3 also alters condition 25 as follows:

(a) In condition 25(1) there is a widening of the reasonable precautions to be taken by the contractor as it reads:

> The Contractor shall take all reasonable steps and precautions (including any steps and precautions expressly required under or by virtue of the Contract) to prevent and to minimise the extent of loss or damage to the Works and any things for incorporation on the Site (including things provided by the Authority) arising from any cause whatsoever (including any of the causes referred to in Condition 26(2) (b).

(b) In condition (25(2) there is a rewording which refers to statutory regulations which govern the storage *and use* of things, otherwise the general requirement is the same. Thus the regulations are to include those governing "use" as well as "storage".

The proposed GC/Works/1 edition 3

It cannot be emphasised too strongly that at the time of writing this edition 3 is only at the "proposed" stage.

Generally edition 3 bears little resemblance to the current edition 2.

The addition to the amendment 3 alteration to "accepted risks" has already been mentioned when considering those risks.

The most important change to any insurance officials is the insurance alternatives in condition 8. According to the PSA "Alternative A" is to be used for contracts up to £3 million whereas "Alternative B" is to be used for larger projects.

Condition 8 — Insurance

Insurance **(1)** The Contractor shall by such existing or new policies as he sees fit effect and maintain for the duration of the Contract and the longest maintenance period;

(a) employers' liability insurance in respect of persons in his employment;

(b) insurance against loss or damage to the Works and Things for which the Contractor is responsible under the terms of the Contract;

(c) insurance against personal injury to any persons and loss or damage to property arising from or in connection with the Works which is not covered by sub-paragraphs (a) and (b) above.

(2) Any insurance policy effected under paragraph (1)(b) shall be for the full reinstatement value (including the cost of transit and off-site risks).

Alternative A **(3)** The Authority shall have the right to receive, on request, a copy of insurances effected or held. The Contractor shall within 21 days from acceptance of the tender and also within 21 days of any subsequent renewal or expiry date of relevant insurances send to the Authority a certificate in the form attached to the Abstract of Particulars from his insurer or his broker attesting that appropriate insurance policies have been effected.

Paragraph (1) requires three policies "for the duration of the Contract and the longest maintenance period", ie:

(a) an employers' liability policy,

(b) a CAR policy,

(c) a public liability policy.

At least this seems to be the effect of this introductory paragraph.

Paragraph (2) expands the CAR policy requirements by referring to the sum insured as being "for the full reinstatement value (including the cost of transit and off-site risks)".

Alternative A

This is paragraph (3) and the Government authority who is the employer offering the contract for tender can request a copy of the insurances concerned. The contractor has 21 days from acceptance of the tender (and also within the same period of any subsequent renewal or expiry date of the insurances) send to the authority a certificate in the form attached to the Abstract of Particulars from his or her insurer or broker verifying that the appropriate policies have been effected. This form of certificate will be found in Appendix 9 which is entitled "Summary of Essential Insurance Requirements — to be read in conjunction with Condition 8 of the General Conditions of Contract".

Alternative B **(3)** In addition to employers' liability insurance the Contractor shall effect and maintain insurance in the joint names of the Authority, the Contractor and all subcontractors in accordance with the Summary of Essential Insurance Requirements attached to the Abstract of Particulars. Without prejudice to the Authority's right to receive, on request, a copy of insurances effected or held the Contractor shall within 21 days of acceptance of the tender send to the Authority a certificate in the form attached to the Abstract of Particulars provided by his insurer or broker attesting that a combined policy of insurance has been effected in accordance with the Contract.

(4) If without the approval of the Authority, the Contractor fails to effect and maintain insurance as described, or obtains a different policy of insurance, the Authority may effect appropriate insurance cover and deduct the cost of doing so from any advance payment due to the Contractor under the Contract. Where the Contractor effects the required insurance by annually renewable policy or policies then if the Works are not complete at the renewal date or dates the Contractor shall give notice to the Authority that the policy or policies have been renewed. Should the policy or policies no longer exist or are known to the Contractor to be ineffective the Contractor shall produce evidence to the Authority that alternative fully equivalent cover has been arranged.

(5) For the avoidance of doubt it is agreed that nothing in this Condition shall relieve the Contractor from any of his obligations and liabilities under the Contract.

Alternative B

This is the alternative paragraph (3) and the joint names insurance set out in the Summary of Essential Requirement referred to (apart from the employers' liability insurance) is a combined CAR and public liability policy. This paragraph (3) then follows the requirements of Alternative A in calling for a copy of the insurances effected when a request is made and a certificate within 21 days of the acceptance of the tender in the form attached to the Abstract of Particulars from the insurer or broker. However this certificate for Alternative B is different from that required in Alternative A. See Appendix 9. The Alternative B certificate certifies that the policy or policies effected by the contractor for CAR and public liability shall jointly indemnify for their respective rights and interests:

(a) the PSA or any client body for which it may work,

(b) the contractor,

(c) all subcontractors,

(d) professional consultants to (a) above.

The CAR section of the Summary of Essential Insurance Requirements

The main aspects requiring comment are as follows:
(a) *The insured and insured period*
Consists of the PSA or any client body for whom it acts, the contractor and/or subcontractor, and professional consultant to the PSA or any client body mentioned above. The total construction period plus the maintenance period comprises the insured period.

(b) *Risks insured*
All risks of physical loss or damage which emphasises that consequential loss is not covered.

(c) *Property insured*
(i) Permanent works and materials or equipment for incorporation therein including free supplied items.

(ii) Temporary works which by definition means those things constructed for the purpose of erecting the permanent works and which shall not pass to the ownership of the authority. These works do not include temporary buildings constructional plant and equipment. This also verified by the remarks made under the heading "Notes" (see below).

(d) *Amount insured*
The contract sum including an allowance for variations and free supplied items.

(e) *Territorial limits*
While on site or in transit thereto or therefrom (other than by sea or air), including loss or damage occurring during any deviation therein or storage in the course of transit, temporary off-site storage or temporary removal from the site, or held for any purpose of the project at the insured's premises or anywhere in the United Kingdom. This is wider cover than normally given in a CAR policy.

(f) *Retained liability (deductibles) for each and every occurrence*
   (i)   £2500 in respect of loss or damage caused by storm, tempest, flooding, water, subsidence or collapse.

   (ii) £1000 for other insured loss or damage.

   (iii) £50 in respect of employees' personal effects, tools or other property except when caused by fire or explosion when there shall be no retained liability.

   (iv) Loss or damage to temporary buildings, constructional plant and equipment, the first £500 including a series of occurrences constituting a single event.

(g) *Notes*
Two notes appear at the end of the Summary of Essential Insurance Requirements, firstly drawing specific attention to the fact that the insurance should indemnify the contractor and nominated and domestic subcontractors and secondly stating that if the policy does not provide cover in respect of loss of or damage to temporary buildings constructional plant and equipment and employees' personal effects and tools, the risk should be priced in respect of those items within the Bills of Quantities in the normal way.
   Paragraph (4) contains the usual requirement that if the contractor

fails to insure or insure as required, the Authority may effect appropriate insurance and deduct the cost from the payment due to the contractor. Annual policies are similarly catered for. *Paragraph (5)* is self-explanatory.

Condition 13. Protection of works

This conditions reads:

Protection of Works	**(1)**	The Contractor shall during the execution of the Works take measures and precautions needed to take care of the Site and the Works , and shall have custody of all Things on the site against loss or damage from fire and any other cause. The Contractor shall be solely responsible for and shall take all reasonable and proper steps for protecting, securing, lighting and watching all places on or about the Works and the Site which may be dangerous to his workpeople or to any other person.
	(2)	The Contractor shall comply with any statutory regulations (whether or not binding on the Crown) which govern the storage and use of all Things which are brought on to the Site in connection with the Works.

This condition bears some resemblance to condition 25 in edition 2 as amended and as the intention is clearly the same, the comments made earlier in the amendment number 3 version apply to both paragraphs. Particular attention is drawn to the requirement of the contractor to take precautions to take care not only of the works but also of all things on the site. This could be important as condition 19 does not make any specific reference to the contractors' responsibility for things for incorporation into the works, and apparently it is not arguable that "loss or damage" in condition 19 would include such things because the definition of this phrase in condition 19 is confined to the works and any thing *not* for incorporation which is on site.

Condition 19. Loss or damage

Loss or damage	**(1)**	This Condition applies to any loss or damage which arises out of or is in any way connected with the execution or purported execution of the Contract.

(2)   The Contractor shall without delay and at his own cost reinstate, replace or make good to the satisfaction of the Authority, or if the Authority agrees, compensate the Authority for, any loss or damage.

(3)   Where a claim is made, or proceedings are brought against the Authority in respect of any loss or damage, the Contractor shall reimburse the Authority any costs or expenses which the Authority may reasonably incur in dealing with, or in settling, that claim or those proceedings.

(4)   The Authority shall notify the Contractor as soon as possible of any claim made, or proceedings brought, against the Authority in respect of any loss or damage.

(5)   The Authority shall reimburse the Contractor for any costs or expenses which the Contractor incurs in accordance with paragraphs (2) and (3) to the extent that the loss or damage is caused by:

   (a) the neglect or default of the Authority or of any contractor or agent of the Authority,

   (b) any Accepted Risk or Unforeseeable Ground Conditions, or

   (c) any other circumstances which are outside the control of the Contractor or of any of his subcontractors or suppliers and which could not have been reasonably contemplated under the Contract.

(6)   In this Condition loss or damage includes:

   (a) loss or damage to property,

   (b) personal injury to or the sickness or death of any person,

   (c) loss or damage to the Works or to any Thing not for incorporation which is on the Site, and

   (d) loss of profits or loss of use suffered because of any loss or damage.

This condition is very different from the condition 26 of edition 2, which is confined to damage to the works. It can be seen from paragraph (6) that this condition 19 does not only apply to loss or damage to the works and anything not for incorporation which is on site, but also to third party injury or damage to property and loss of profits or loss of use suffered because of any loss or damage. However, the contractor is still basically responsible for loss or damage to the works and to any thing not for incorporation which is on site. (See particularly paragraphs (1) and (2) as (3) deals with third party proceedings.) The exceptions are mainly similar to those in condition 26 of edition 2 with two differences. Thus by paragraph (5) where loss or damage is caused by the following, the authority will reimburse the contractor for any costs or expenses:

(a) the neglect or default of the authority or of any contractor or agents of the authority;
(b) any accepted risk or unforeseeable ground conditions; or
(c) any other circumstances which are outside the control of the contractor or any of his subcontractors or suppliers and which could not have been reasonably contemplated under the contract.

The two differences in the exceptions are unforeseeable ground conditions and any other circumstances outside the contractors' (etc) control which could not have been reasonably contemplated under the contract.

The first difference (unforeseeable ground conditions) is a reasonable concession to the contractor and the phrase is defined in condition 1 (Definitions etc) as meaning "ground conditions certified by the PM in accordance with condition 7 (Conditions affecting Works)".

PM is defined in the same definitions condition as "the Project Manager appointed for the time being by the Authority to manage and superintend the Works on his behalf ". Paragraphs (3) to (5) of condition 7 deal with "Unforeseeable Ground Conditions" and read as follows:

(3) If, during the execution of the Works, the Contractor becomes aware of ground conditions (excluding those caused by weather but including artificial obstructions) which he did not know of, and which he could not reasonably have foreseen having regard to any information which he had or ought reasonably to have ascertained, he shall by notice immediately

(i) inform the PM of those conditions, and

(ii) state the measures which he proposes to take to deal with them.

(4) If the PM agrees that the ground conditions specified in a notice under paragraph (3) could not reasonably have been foreseen by the Contractor having regard to any information he should have had in accordance with that paragraph and paragraph (1), he shall certify those conditions to be Unforeseeable Ground Conditions. The PM shall notify the Contractor of his decision.

(5) If as a result of Unforeseeable Ground Conditions the Contractor in executing the Works properly carries out or omits any work which he would not otherwise have carried out or omitted, then, without prejudice to any instruction given by the PM the value of the work carried out or omitted shall be ascertained in accordance with Condition 42 (Valuation of Variation Instructions) and the Contract Sum shall be increased or decreased accordingly.

These paragraphs are self-explanatory but attention is drawn to the reference to paragraph (1) of condition 7 in paragraph (4). Paragraph (1) merely requires the contractor to satisfy himself or herself as to various aspects of the site. One of these aspects mentioned in sub-condition 1(d) reads "the nature of the soil and material (whether natural or otherwise) to be excavated". This might give the PM an opportunity to assert his or her position as judge and jury in favour of the authority.

The second difference, ie exception (c) of paragraph (5) of condition 19 concerning other circumstances outside the contractors' or his or her subcontractors' or suppliers' control (which could not have been reasonably contemplated) is probably more beneficial to the contractor than the "unforeseeable ground conditions" exception as the former is not stated in the contract to be subject to the PM's decision. In this connection it should be appreciated that paragraph (6) of condition 7 states "The Contractor shall not be released from any risks or obligations imposed on or undertaken by him . . . because he did not or could not foresee any matter which might affect or have affected the execution of the Works", which could reduce the effect of both these exceptions. However, possibly the *contra proferentum* rule, mentioned in Chapter 1 under the heading "The insurance contract", might assist the contractor here as ambiguity should be construed against the drawer of the document, ie the authority.

CHAPTER 10

Subcontract GW/S for use with GC/Works/1

A major difficulty for the construction industry until 1985 was the lack of a standard form of subcontract for use with contracts let under the Government Form GC/Works/1 and thus the publication in 1985 of Subcontract GW/S was of some significance.

This form was produced by the Building Employers Confederation and the Federation of Building Specialist Contractors and agreed with the specialist subcontractor organisations, FASS and CASEC.

This GW/S form is intended for use with GC/Works/1, edition 2 for building work only and not for civil engineering. It is designed for both nominated and domestic subcontractors.

It should be noted that the clauses which follow are only applicable where the main contract does not incorporate amendment no 3 to GC/Works/1, edition 2, which it will be seen in Chapter 9, among other things, replaces the definition of "accepted risks".

Clause 31. Loss or damage to subcontract works — subcontractor's obligations

This clause reads as follows:

> 31 (1) The Sub-Contractor shall (unless the Authority exercises his power to determine the Main Contract) with all possible speed make good any loss or damage arising from any cause whatsoever occasioned to the Sub-Contract Works or to things for incorporation in the sub-Contract Works which are on the site and shall notwithstanding such loss or damage proceed with the executing and completion of the Sub-Contract Works in accordance with the Sub-Contract[b].

(2) Without prejudice to the obligation in clause 31 (1) the Contractor shall pay to the Sub-Contractor the appropriate share of the insurance monies due in respect of such loss or damage upon receipt thereof from the insurers with whom the insurance referred to in clause 32 has been taken out. Any sum paid by the Contractor under clause 31(2) shall be ascertained in the same manner as a sum payable in respect of an alteration or addition under the Sub-Contract.

Sub-clause 31 (1) passes on to the subcontractor the main contractor's onerous obligation, under condition 26 (2) (a) of the main contract (see Chapter 9), to make good loss or damage to the works, as it includes the subcontract works, and things for incorporation in the subcontract works which are on the site. Footnote [b] refers to the limitation of insurance to the "Clause 32 Perils" (see below).

Sub-clause 31 (2) indicates the contractor's obligation to pay the sub-contractor the appropriate share of the insurance monies due in respect of the loss or damage to the subcontract works once the insurers have paid out in accordance with clause 32 which follows.

Clause 32. Loss or damage to the works and things for incorporation on the site — clause 32 perils.

This clause reads:

32 (1) The Contractor shall in the joint names of the Contractor and every sub-contractor insure against loss or damage by the Clause 32 Perils for the full reinstatement value thereof (together with the cost of any professional fees or services) all work executed and all things for incorporation on the site and shall keep such work and things for incorporation so insured until the Authority assumes responsibility for any loss or damage to the Works.

(2) If the Contractor shall independently of his obligations under this Sub-Contract maintain a policy of insurance which covers (inter alia) the aforesaid work and things for incorporation against the Clause 32 Perils to the full reinstatement value thereof (together with the cost of any professional fees or services) then the maintenance by the Contractor of such policy shall, if the interest of every sub-contractor is endorsed thereon as a joint insured, be a discharge of the Contractor's obligations to insure under clause 32(1) in the joint names of the Contractor and every sub-contractor.

(3)   The insurance policy referred to in clause 32(1) or clause 32(2) shall
       provide for payment of the costs incurred by the Contractor and
       Sub-Contractor in making good loss or damage in accordance with
       Condition 26(1) of the Main Contract and clause 31(1) respectively
       upon the acceptance of any claim thereunder and such payment shall
       not be conditional on any decision by the Authority in regard to
       payment or non-payment under Condition 26(2)(b) of the Main
       Contract.

This clause ensures that there is money available to meet the liability in
clause 31 by providing for insurance, by the contractor, of the whole
works. This policy must be in the joint names of the contractor and every
subcontractor and insure against the "clause 32 perils" (see below) for the
full reinstatement value (including professional fees or services) all work
executed and all things for incorporation on the site. The joint names
insurance will prevent any right of subrogation or indemnity between the
contractor and subcontractor and every other subcontractor named in the
policy. The insurance continues until the authority (the Government
department concerned) assumes responsibility for any loss or damage to
the works. However, there is no condition under GC/Works/1 edition 2
under which the authority specifically assumes such responsibility and,
where necessary, this should be cleared with the authority.

Sub-clause 32 (2) provides an alternative which, in effect, states that if
the contractor has a CAR policy, which provides similar joint names cover,
then a separate joint names policy would not need to be taken out.

"Clause 32 perils" are defined in clause 1 (3) in exactly the same terms
as the "specified perils" are defined in clause 1 (3) of JCT 80 (see Chapter
5). In view of the subcontractor's responsibility under sub-clause 31 (1) he
or she may wish to arrange his or her own insurance against risks other
than the "clause 32 perils", such as theft or malicious or accidental
damage. This is mentioned in footnote [b].

If joint names cover were not provided then the subcontractor would
need to take out insurance to cover any claim made by way of subrogation
by the contractor's insurers (see Chapter 1), but the joint names insurance
will prevent subrogation operating. A joint names insurance in this way
keeps the cost of insurance down. The contractor can claim reimburse-
ment under condition 26 (2) (b) (i) and (ii) (see Chapter 9 and below) and
the insurer for the joint names insurance under clause 32 would then,
through the contractor, obtain some recovery from the authority where
condition 26 (2) (b) (i) and (ii) applies.

Sub-clause 32 (3) is worded so as to avoid any delay in meeting claims under the joint names policy until any payment under condition 26 (2) (b) by the authority is made. Condition 26 (2) (b) of the main contract deals with the two exceptions to the contractor's responsibility to deal with loss or damage to the works, namely when caused by the neglect or default of a servant of the Crown acting in the course of his or her employment, and when caused by the "accepted risks" (unamended by amendment no 3).

Clause 34. Precautions against loss or damage from accepted risks

This clause states:

34 (1)   The Sub-Contractor shall take all reasonable precautions to prevent loss or damage from any of the Accepted Risks and to minimise the amount of any such loss or damage or any loss or damage caused by a servant of the Crown. The Sub-Contractor shall comply with such authorised directions to this end as may be given to him from time to time in writing by the Contractor.

(2)   The Sub-Contractor shall comply with any statutory regulations (whether or not binding on the Crown) which govern the storage of explosives, petrol or other things (whether or not for incorporation) which are brought on the site.

It follows condition 25 of GC/Works/1 in restricting the operation of condition 26 (2) (b) (see the previous heading) and is self explanatory.

Clause 37. Insurance — production of policies

37   As and when reasonably required to do so by the other the Contractor and Sub-Contractor shall produce (and shall cause any other person to produce) for inspection by the other documentary evidence that the insurance required by or referred to in clauses 32 and 36 are properly effected and maintained but on any occasion the Contractor or Sub-Contractor may (but not unreasonably or vexatiously) require to have produced for inspection the policy or policies and premium receipts in question.

This is the usual requirement to produce documentary evidence that the insurance required by clause 32 (clause 36 does not concern this book as it deals with liability to third parties) are properly effected and maintained.

Clause 38. Loss or damage not within clauses 31 and 32 responsibility

It reads:

38 (1) Subject to clauses 31 and 32 the Sub-Contractor shall be responsible for loss or damage to any things for incorporation which are on the Site for the Sub-Contractor's use until such things have been fully, finally and properly incorporated into the Works except for any loss or damage due to any negligence omission or default of the Contractor his servants or agents or any other sub-contractor of the Contractor engaged upon the Works or any part thereof his servants or agents or of the Authority or any person for whom the Authority is responsible.

(2) Where things for incorporation have been fully, finally and properly incorporated into the Works before completion of the Sub-Contract Works the Contractor shall be responsible for loss or damage to such things except for any loss or damage caused thereto by the Sub-Contractor his servants or agents or sub-contractors.

The terms of this clause are similar to those covering this subject in NSC/4 and DOM/1 (see Chapter 6). Consequently, for example, if the unfixed materials or goods of the subcontractor are damaged by fire, then the subcontractor would be obliged to replace them (clause 31 (1)) but would be entitled to be paid by the contractor the appropriate share of the insurance monies received by the contractor in that regard under the policies referred to in clauses 32 (1) or 32 (2) (clause 31 (2)). However, if the unfixed materials were stolen or damaged by vandals then (subject to the loss or damage not being due to the negligence, omission or default of the contractor, his or her servants, agents or other subcontractors) the subcontractor would again have to replace them but would have to bear the cost of replacement himself or herself (clause 38 (1)). Therefore, it would be prudent for the subcontractor to consider effecting his or her own insurance for loss or damage other than the "clause 32 perils".

Clause 38 (2) is clear in placing responsibility for loss or damage to the subcontract works, which have been fully, finally and properly incorporated into the works, before completion of the subcontract works, on the contractor. The exception to this statement arises when such loss or damage is caused by the subcontractor, his or her servants or agents or other subcontractors.

The phrase "fully, finally and properly incorporated into the Works" is considered in Chapter 6.

Clause 39. Subcontractor's responsibility for plant, etc

39   All things not for incorporation which are on the Site and are
        provided by or on behalf of the Sub-Contractor for the construction
        of the Sub- Contract Works shall stand at the risk and be in the sole
        charge of the Sub-Contractor and the Sub-Contractor shall (except for
        any loss or damage due to any negligence, omission or default of the
        Contractor, his servants or agents or sub-contractors other than the
        Sub-Contractor, his servants or agents or sub-contractors) be respon-
        sible for, and with all possible speed make good, any loss or damage
        thereto arising from any cause whatsoever including the Accepted
        Risks.

While this clause states that the subcontractor's own or hired-in property is his or her responsibility this does not prevent the subcontractor claiming if this property were damaged by the negligence of any other person whether the contractor, another subcontractor, the authority or other third parties (see the list of persons in parenthesis).

CHAPTER 11

Construction Plant Hire Association's Model Conditions for the Hiring of Plant

Plant lent and let on hire

At common law there are two features to consider under this heading:

(a) the liability of the lender or person hiring out; and

(b) the liability of the borrower or person hiring in.

The extent of the liability depends on whether the loan was gratuitous or for reward.

With a gratuitous loan, the lender is under an obligation to point out any defect in a chattel of which he or she has knowledge and which may make it unfit for the purpose for which it is lent. As a general rule the borrower is under an obligation to exercise common prudence in the care of the chattel while it is in his or her possession.

When the owners of plant let it out on hire for reward, they are under an implied obligation to see that it is reasonably fit for the purpose for which it is hired out. They give an implied warranty that it is as fit for that purpose as reasonable care and skill on their part can make it. If they knew or ought to have known of a defect they are liable for the immediate results and consequences reasonably within the contemplation of the parties. Under the Supply of Goods and Services Act 1982 s. 9 there are implied terms of merchantable quality and fitness of purpose, on the part of the supplier.

In turn, hirers must take reasonable care of the plant and they will be liable for its loss or damage due to their negligence. Apart from the terms of a special contract the hirers would be liable for:

(a) actual loss and/or the cost of reparation;

(b) loss caused by depreciation of the plant;

(c) loss of use,

as these items would be reasonably within the contemplation of the parties in view of the nature of the transaction.

Responsibility for operators of plant

The position where the owner's operator is transferred with the plant lent or hired out and the operator's negligence causes injury, loss or damage, raises the question as to whether the owner or hirer is vicariously responsible for the negligence. The test to decide the answer to this question is "whether or no, the hirer had authority to control the manner of the execution of the relevant acts of the servants". See *Mersey Docks and Harbour Board v Coggins and Griffith (Liverpool) Ltd* (1947). In that case it was decided that the owner of the plant retained sufficient control to be responsible. Unless detailed control as to how the work is to be done has passed to the hirer, the almost invariable result is going to be that the owner will remain liable. Usually the situation is that a special contract imposed by the owner of the plant applies, and this contract in the vast majority of cases is based on the contract named in the next heading.

Construction Plant Hire Association's Model Conditions for the Hiring of Plant

These conditions replace the CPA's previous "General Conditions for the Hiring of Plant" from September 1979. The abbreviation CPA Conditions is still used although the name Construction Plant Hire Association came into use in July 1981.

These revised general conditions are the result of several years' negotiations between the CPA representing the plant hire industry, the Federation of Civil Engineering Contractors, representing the main client industry of civil engineering and the Office of Fair Trading, and having regard to the provisions of the Restrictive Trade Practices Acts and latterly of the Unfair Contract Terms Act 1977.

Introductory notes state that the Department of Prices and Consumer Protection and the Office of Fair Trading have agreed for the purposes of s. 21 (2) of the Restrictive Trade Practices Act 1976 that the recommendation of these revised conditions is not to be regarded as warranting investigation by the Restrictive Practices Court.

These notes also state that if any amendments are made to these Model Conditions by the contracting parties, they will cease to be the Model Conditions and must not be referred to as such.

A number of amendments have been made to bring the offer and acceptance forms into line with current use. However it is *not* intended to comment on all the changes but only on those which are likely to affect insurers.

On the offer and acceptance forms there are two footnotes which concern insurers. The first one states that unless otherwise agreed the hirer is responsible for insuring against his or her liabilities under clauses 8 and 13. Further comments will be made later when discussing these two clauses in detail. The second footnote states that acceptance of the plant on site implies acceptance of all terms and conditions stated on this offer (see clause 3) unless otherwise agreed. Clause 3 of these conditions repeats this statement.

Turning to the clauses in the "Conditions", clause 1 (Definitions) contains no change from the previous conditions except that a "working week" covers the period from starting time on Monday to finishing time on Friday instead of Saturday and there is a new sub-clause defining the hire period as the time from which the plant leaves the owner's depot until the plant is received back at the owner's named depot or equal. The last two words here presumably cater for the plant which is passed on directly to the next hirer. Fortunately responsibility is now upon the plant owner while the plant is in transit between depot and site and vice versa, provided it is under the owner's control, and also between sites when driven by the owner's driver (see clause 13 (c) later). Thus there is usually no need to decide which hirer is responsible while the plant is travelling to a new hirer (but see a possible exception later when discussing clause 13(c)).

Clause 2 (Extent of Contract) gives a clearer definition of the extent of the contract terms; thus the offer and acceptance forms are incorporated into the contract conditions.

Clause 4. Unloading and loading

Clause 4 reads:

The Hirer shall be responsible for unloading and loading the plant at site, and any personnel supplied by the Owner shall be deemed to be under the Hirer's control and shall comply with all directions of the Hirer.

Clause 4, which in the previous conditions was clause 5, has been amended to state that *any personnel supplied by the owner* shall comply with all directions of the hirer. Such personnel are still deemed to be under the hirer's control as previously, when they were specifically named as "any Driver, Operator or Flagman supplied by the Owner". The hirer is basically responsible for all personnel lent by the owner who are involved in unloading and re-loading operations, whereas it would be argued on the previous wording that the hirer was not liable for personnel sent by the owner who were not drivers, operators or flagmen; eg, fitters, mechanics, chargehands or even labourers. Incidentally, being under the hirer's control may not appear as strong as stating that the owner's employees are regarded as the employees of the hirer (see clause 8 later) but the effect is the same as control seems to be the main test of vicarious liability when employees are lent to another employer. Consequently this clause is now worded more widely against the hirer who will often find himself or herself relying on the skill and common sense of the owner's employees.

While the owner's staff should know more about unloading and loading plant than the average hirer, the point is that if such trust is misplaced and an accident occurs it is intended that the hirer should pay for the resultant expense. Thus if one employee of the owner, while loading plant on the hirer's site after the hirer has finished with it, injures another employee of the owner it would seem that the hirer's insurers are taking over the owner's employers' liability risk in this respect, which seems wrong. Similarly if the plant fell off a low-loader because of negligence by the owner's staff when unloading or loading on the hirer's site, the hirer is responsible for these people's actions, whether the result is damage to the plant and/or a third party claim.

In making the above comments it is assumed that unloading and loading are different manoeuvres from those of erection and dismantling of plant as the latter, if carried out on site under the control of the owner or his or her agent, are now the responsibility of the owner (clause 13 (c) — see later). In fact they must be separate acts otherwise clause 4 would clash with clause 13 (c).

The position (subject to the next two paragraphs) therefore seems to be that loading of the plant at the owner's depot by the owner's staff is the owner's responsibility and this is so while it is in transit to the hirer's site by these people. However unloading by the owner's staff at the site is the hirer's responsibility but erecting the same plant by the same owner's staff is the owner's responsibility.

Insurance claims people can have a difficult time handling claims when, for instance, part of a tower crane is dropped, causing general mayhem, while it is still being supported by the crane which is unloading it, but arguably is being moved into position for erection. Should the hirer's or the owner's insurers handle the claims?

There are two other aspects to be considered and the first is the common law obstacle that negligence cannot be avoided in exemption or indemnity clauses in contracts unless the word "negligence" or a synonym for it is used. This is supported by the House of Lords case of *Smith v South Wales Switchgear Ltd* (1978). Can this decision be avoided by the owner contractually passing control of his or her employees to the hirer? There is some doubt about this, particularly if in fact the hirer does not control them.

Another aspect which may alter the above situation is the effect of the Unfair Contract Terms Act 1977. See Appendix 2. If this unloading and loading of plant by the owner's employees, and the passing of responsibility to the hirer in this respect, is a method of avoiding liability for negligence for which the owner would normally be vicariously responsible, and if clause 4 is an exclusion clause, then in the cases resulting in personal injuries the clause will be void (s. 2 of the 1977 Act). In cases resulting in damage to property, in accordance with ss. 2 and 3 of the Act, the clause must be reasonable before it will be upheld. Therefore, in the event of personal injury, the hirer's insurers would not have to handle a claim, which is strictly speaking an employer's liability claim or public liability claim for the owner's insurers (although the Model Conditions are stated to have been prepared having regard to the 1977 Act). If merely property damage results, then the hirer's insurers *may* avoid handling the claim on the grounds that the clause is unreasonable.

It would seem that the legal advice given to the CPA is that clause 4 is either an indemnity clause in a contract which is nearly always made with a non-consumer, and thus s. 4 of the 1977 Act does not affect the position and clause 4 would be valid as an exclusion clause and is considered reasonable in accordance with s. 2 (2) of the 1977 Act.

Clause 8. Handling of plant

Clause 8 reads as follows:

When a driver or operator is supplied by the Owner with the plant, the Owner shall supply a person competent in operating the plant and such person shall be under the direction and control of the Hirer. Such drivers or operators shall for all purposes in connection with their employment in the working of the plant be regarded as the servants or agents of the Hirer (but without prejudice to any of the provisions of Clause 13) who alone shall be responsible for all claims arising in connection with the operation of the plant by the said drivers or operators. The Hirer shall not allow any other person to operate such plant without the Owner's previous consent to be confirmed in writing.

This clause has been amended to include the obligation on the owner that where a driver or operator is supplied with the plant, he or she shall be competent whilst retaining, as previously, control of such persons in the hands of the hirer in the operation of the plant. Probably there was always an implied condition of competence in this respect. Such operators, as before, shall for all purposes in connection with their employment in the working of the plant be regarded as the servants or agents of the hirer (but without prejudice to any of the provisions of clause 13). This statement in brackets is new and its effect will be considered when discussing clause 13. Although clause 4 still differs slightly from clause 8 in that clause 4 does not use the words "servants or agents", the practical effect is similar, thus (in the case of clause 8) the hirer is responsible for all claims arising in connection with the operation of the plant by the driver or operator.

As noted in the case of clause 4, while the driver and operator are third parties to the hirer and are in fact employees of the owner, if they are killed or injured in connection with the operation of the plant, the hirer agrees under clause 8 to be solely responsible for damages awarded to these people or their dependants, and for all legal costs. Consequently the owner, to this extent, appears to be relieved of his or her normal employer's liability risk as well as public liability risk for injury to third parties and damage to their property caused by these people. But see discussion under clause 4 concerning the Unfair Contract Terms Act. Clause 8 also saddles the hirer with responsibility for loss or damage to the plant in the circumstances mentioned, and apparently the 1977 Act requires this shifting of responsibility to be reasonable (see the commentary on clause 4), which it may be. The same remarks concerning *Smith's* case, which were made when discussing clause 4, also apply to clause 8.

In *Thompson v T Lohan (Plant Hire) and Another* (1987) the second defendants hired an excavator with a driver from the first defendants under a contract which (under clause 8) provided that such drivers, "shall for all purposes in connection with their employment in the working of the plant be regarded as the servants or agents of the hirer . . . who alone shall be responsible for all claims arising in connection with the operation of the plant". The plaintiff's husband (an employee of the first defendants) was killed as a result of the driver's negligence in operating the excavator when working for the second defendants. The plaintiff, as her husband's personal representative, obtained damages and costs against the first defendants, the driver's employers. In third party proceedings between the defendants, the judge rejected the second defendant's submission that clause 8 was contrary to s. 2 (1) of the Unfair Contract Terms Act 1977 as excluding or restricting the first defendants' liability for death or injury, and he held that the first defendants were entitled under clause 8 to an indemnity against the second defendants.

On appeal by the second defendants it was held, dismissing the appeal, that:

(a) Clause 8 was effective at common law between the parties to the contract and consequently the first defendants were entitled to be indemnified by the second defendants against the damages and costs recovered by the plaintiff.

(b) On its true construction s. 2 (1) of the Act of 1977 was concerned with protecting the victim of negligence and those who claim under him and not with arrangements between the wrongdoer and other persons regarding the sharing or bearing of the burden of compensating the victim, since such arrangements did not exclude or restrict the wrongdoers' liability and, therefore, clause 8 did not fall within the prohibition of s. 2 (1) of the 1977 Act. *Phillips Products Ltd v Hyland and Hamstead Plant Hire (1984) (1987)* was distinguished.

The interesting feature of this case is the reason why the decision in *Phillips* went the other way, ie clause 8 did not satisfy "the requirement of reasonableness" in s. 2 (2) of the Unfair Contract Terms Act 1977 and consequently the plant owners were precluded from relying on clause 8 to exempt them from liability for the driver's negligence.

The facts of *Phillips* were the same as in *Thompson* up to the point where the driver's negligence took place. In the former case, the driver negligently drove the excavator into collision with the plaintiffs' building and damaged it so there was damage to the property of one of the parties to the contract of hire. In the latter case injury was caused to a third party. Firstly, this involves the consideration of different sections of the 1977 Act. S. 2 (1) concerns personal injury and imposes invalidity. S. 2 (2) concerns damage to property and imposes the test of reasonableness. However, this is only one aspect distinguishing these two cases. Secondly, the main difference is the interpretation of clause 8 of the hire contract, bearing in mind the other facts of the cases. The effect of clause 8 in *Phillips* involved the avoidance of a common law liability in tort which would otherwise fall on the plant owner. On the facts, and in the circumstances existing at the time the contract was made, the Court of Appeal held that the judge in the court of first instance was justified in his conclusion that the plant owners had not discharged the onus placed on them by s. 11 of the Act (concerning the reasonableness test) to show, on the balance of probabilities, that clause 8 was a fair and reasonable term to include in the contract. The court took the following points into consideration.

(a) There had only been two occasions when plant had been hired by Phillips in the two years prior to the hearing.

(b) The hire was to be for a very short period with no time to discuss the agreement.

(c) There was little, if any, opportunity for the plaintiffs to arrange insurance cover for risks arising from their own negligence. A businessman or woman does not usually insure against damage caused to his or her own property by his or her own employees' negligence. They insure against common risks, eg fire. Thus to arrange cover would have required time and a special and unusual arrangement for the plaintiffs' insurers.

(d) The plaintiffs played no part in the selection of the first defendant as the operator of the JCB. They had to accept the owner's driver. The hirer could not control the driver. Indeed the driver made it perfectly plain to the plaintiffs' builder that he would brook no interference in the way he operated his machine.

(e) The necessity to comply with the clear and stern injunction issued to appellate courts by Lord Bridge, concurred with by the other members of the House of Lords, in *George Mitchell (Chesterhall) v Finney Lock Seeds* (1981) as follows:

But the several provisions of the Unfair Contract Terms Act 1977 which depend on 'the requirement of reasonableness' defined in s. 11 by reference to what is 'fair and reasonable', albeit in a different context, are likely to come before the courts with increasing frequency. It may, therefore, be appropriate to consider how an original decision as to what is "fair and reasonable" made in the application of any of these provisions should be approached by an appellate court. It would not be accurate to describe such a decision as an exercise of discretion. But a decision under any of the provisions referred to will have this in common with the exercise of a discretion that, in having regard to the various matters to which . . . s. 11 of the Act of 1977 direct(s) attention, the court must entertain a whole range of considerations, put them in the scales on one side or the other, and decide at the end of the day on which side the balance comes down. There will sometimes be room for a legitimate difference of judicial opinion as to what the answer should be, where it will be impossible to say that one view is demonstrably wrong and the other demonstrably right. It must follow, in my view, that, when asked to review such a decision on appeal, the appellate court should treat the original decision with the utmost respect and refrain from interference with it unless satisfied that it proceeded upon some erroneous principle or was plainly and obviously wrong.

The final remarks in this statement are considered by some lawyers to discourage appeals in this field. However, in *Phillips* the Court of Appeal did not interfere with the judge's finding that clause 8 was unreasonable in this particular case. Nevertheless, it emphasised the importance of appreciating that its conclusion on the particular facts of this case should not be treated as a binding precedent in other cases where similar clauses fall to be considered and where the evidence of the surrounding circumstances may be very different.

So the conclusions to be drawn are that in the first place *Thompson* was an entirely different set of circumstances, where clause 8 was considered but because the 1977 Act did not apply it cannot be assumed as in any way overruling *Phillips*. In any event the Court of Appeal in *Phillips* made it clear that it was not saying that clause 8 was unreasonable in every case. In fact, in red type at the top of the CPA Model Conditions of Plant Hire it says that the Unfair Contract Terms Act 1977 has been taken into consideration.

Clause 9. Breakdown, repairs and adjustment

This clause reads:

(a) When the plant is hired without the Owner's driver or operator any breakdown or the unsatisfactory working of any part of the plant must be notified immediately to the Owner. Any claim for breakdown time will only be considered from the time and date of notification.

(b) Full allowance will be made to the Hirer for any stoppage due to breakdown of plant caused by the development of either an inherent fault or a fault not ascertainable by reasonable examination or fair wear and tear and for all stoppages for normal running repairs in accordance with the terms of the Contract.

(c) The Hirer shall not, except for punctures, repair the plant without the written authority of the Owner. Punctures are however the responsibility of the Hirer. Allowance for hire charges and for the reasonable cost of repairs will be made by the Owner to the Hirer where repairs have been authorised.

(d) The Hirer shall be responsible for all expense involved arising from any breakdown and all loss or damage incurred by the Owner due to the Hirer's negligence, misdirection or misuse of the plant, whether by the Hirer or his servants, and for the payment of hire at the appropriate idle time rate during the period the plant is necessarily idle due to such breakdown or damage. The Owner will be responsible for the cost of repairs to the plant involved in breakdowns from all other causes and will bear the cost of providing spare parts.

Clause 9 makes the hirer responsible (as previously) for "all expense involved arising from breakdown and all loss or damage incurred by the owner due to the hirer's negligence, misdirection or misuse of the plant, whether by the hirer *or his servants*". The owner is responsible for breakdowns from all other causes and will bear the cost of providing spare parts. The onerous phrase is "or his servants" because when this phrase is read with clauses 4 and 8 in mind, clause 9 means that the hirer accepts responsibility for breakdown of the plant caused by negligence, misdirection or misuse of the plant on the part of:

(a) the driver or operator supplied by the owner to work the plant (see clause 8) and

(b) any personnel supplied by the owner provided the act causing the breakdown occurs during the unloading or loading of the plant at the site (see clause 4);

subject to the same remarks concerning *Smith's* case and the 1977 Act made under the clauses concerned.

Clause 12. Consequential losses

Save in respect of the Owner's liability if any under Clauses 5, 8 and 9, the Owner accepts no liability nor responsibility for any consequential loss or damage due to or arising through any cause beyond his control.

Under clause 12 the owner does not accept responsibility for the consequential loss suffered by the hirer through any cause beyond his or her
control save in respect of the owner's liability under clauses 5, 8 and 9.
Clauses 8 and 9 have been considered earlier and clause 5 (previously
clause 6) concerns "Delivery in Good Order and Maintenance Inspection
Reports", and is similar to the old one with a few minor exceptions
including inherent and unascertainable (by examination) faults which,
with fair wear and tear, are accepted by the owner, otherwise after the
time limits the plant is deemed to be in good order. Clause 12 no longer
contains the sweeping disclaimer of the previous clause 12 but even so
there is no certainty that it will not fall foul of *Smith's* case or the 1977 Act.

Clause 13. Hirer's responsibility for loss and damage

Clause 13 states

(a) For the avoidance of doubt it is hereby declared and agreed that nothing
     in this Clause affects the operation of Clauses 5, 8 and 9 of this Agreement.

(b) During the continuance of the hire period the Hirer shall subject to the
     provisions referred to in sub paragraph (a) make good to the Owner all
     loss of or damage to the plant from whatever cause the same may arise,
     fair wear and tear excepted, and except as provided in Clause 9 herein,
     and shall also fully and completely indemnify the Owner in respect of all
     claims by any person whatsoever for injury to person or property caused
     by or in connection with or arising out of the use of the plant and in respect
     of all costs and charges in connection therewith whether arising under
     statute or common law. In the event of loss or damage to the plant, hire
     charges shall be continued at idle time rates until settlement has been
     effected.

(c) Notwithstanding the above the Owner shall accept liability for damage,
     loss or injury due to or arising

     (i)   prior to delivery of any plant to the site of the Hirer where the plant
            is in transit by transport of the Owner or as otherwise arranged by
            the Owner.

     (ii)   during the erection of any plant, where such plant requires to be
            completely erected on the site always provided that such erection is
            under the exclusive control of the Owner or his Agent.

     (iii) during the dismantling of any plant, where plant requires to be dismantled after use prior to removal from site, always provided that such dismantling is under the exclusive control of the Owner or his Agent.

(iv) after the plant has been removed from the site and is in transit on to the Owner by transport of the Owner or as otherwise arranged by the Owner.

(v) where plant is travelling to or from a site under its own power with a driver supplied by the Owner.

This is probably the most important clause to the insurance world and where the most fundamental changes have been made. The clause:

(a) Puts beyond doubt that, notwithstanding the general responsibility placed on the hirer for all loss or damage to the plant and claims by third parties, this does not effect clauses 5, 8 and 9.

(b) Clarifies the position regarding charges where the plant is lost or damaged.

(c) Provides that the owner shall accept liability for any loss, damage, or injury due to or arising:

(i) prior to delivery of plant to the site by the owner (thus if the hirer collects the plant the owner accepts no such liability unless it is by the owner's arrangement);

(ii) where the erecting of plant is under the exclusive control of the owner or his or her agent, up to the moment of completion of the erection but not unloading (see clause 4);

(iii) where the owner is dismantling as in (ii) but not loading (see clause 4);

(iv) where the plant has been removed from the site and is in transit to the owner by his or her order;

(v) where the plant is travelling to or from the site under its own power with a driver supplied by the owner.

If the owner requests that the plant be passed on to the next hirer by the first hirer's driver this presumably comes under the heading of "as otherwise arranged by the owner" in paragraph 13 (c) (iv) and the owner remains responsible, assuming this phrase qualifies the whole paragraph. However, what is the position where the owner's driver is driving between the hirer's sites? Presumably sub-clause 13 (c) (v) applies on its wording. Nevertheless as regards clause 32 (Government regulations), observance of the Road Traffic Acts, including insurance and the other legislation mentioned in clause 32 seems to rest with the hirer as the owner is only responsible for observance during such time as the plant is travelling from owner to site and site to owner. In these circumstances (when the plant is driven by the owner's driver between sites) it seems that clause 32 is an exception to sub-clause 13 (c) (v) as it is more specific.

The main question is whether clause 13 still carries the same problem that existed in the old conditions and which has been mentioned when discussing clauses 4 and 8, namely the effect on clause 13 of making the owner's drivers and operators the servants or agents of the hirer although clause 8 now includes the statement in brackets "but without prejudice to any of the provisions of clause 13". What exactly the drafters had in mind by this statement is not certain, but taken literally it appears to refer to the acceptance of both the hirer's and the owner's responsibilities in sub-clause 13 (b) and 13 (c). Therefore in sub-clause 13 (b) as regards loss of or damage to the plant, the hirer, subject to sub-clause (a), must "make good to the Owner all loss of or damage to the plant from whatever cause the same may arise". In the light of *Smith v South Wales Switchgear* (1978) it is doubtful whether the words "from whatever cause" are sufficient to make the hirer pay for an act of negligence by the owner causing damage to the plant, and s. 2 of The Unfair Contract Terms Act 1977 makes this part of the clause subject to the test of reasonableness as it is an exemption clause. The next part of sub-clause 13 (b) concerning injury to persons and damage to property is an indemnity clause and as such would probably not be caught by s. 2 of the Unfair Contract Terms Act. Apart from the second part of clause 13 (b) being an indemnity clause, it is arguable that s. 3 of the Act has no application as the hirer is not dealing as a consumer, nor is he dealing on the *other's* standard terms, since the contract has been agreed with the FCEC. Incidentally, reference should be made to the case of *Arthur White (Contractors) Ltd v Tarmac Civil Engineering Ltd* (1967) to appreciate the considerable effect that clause 8 has on clause 13, although this case was heard before the 1977 Act was passed or *Smith's* case had been heard.

In White's case the operator of an excavator left the boom at an angle of 45° instead of lowering it to the ground. It collapsed, causing injury to the claimant for which damages were awarded. The Court of Appeal held the owners responsible for that part of the award (40%) which resulted from the failure of the driver to maintain the brakes. However, the House of Lords was satisfied that the clauses just mentioned were intended to apply to the circumstances of the accident and the hirer was 100% responsible.

It should be noted that an owner's contractual conditions may be incorporated into a contract of hire on the grounds of a common understanding between the parties that such conditions applied even though no mention was made of the owner's conditions of hire in the particular verbal contract concerned.

Prima facie clauses 8 and 13 are adverse to the hirer, but it is said that as the hirer wishes to control the operator of the plant he or she must accept all responsibility arising from operator's activities (*see British Crane Hire Corporation Ltd v Ipswich Plant Hire Ltd* (1974)).

Insurance requirements of the Conditions

None of the clauses specifically make insurance a requirement. However, if the normal procedure of plant hiring is followed through its various stages the insurance position can be considered at each stage as far as loss or damage to the plant and liabilities to others is concerned and the party responsible should check that his or her policies provide the cover necessary. Responsibility starts in stage 1 with the owner and proceeds alternately between hirer and owner at each stage thereafter.

Stage 1:   Transit from owner's depot to site. The owner is responsible (sub-clause 13 (c) (i) and (v)), but note the wording.

Stage 2:   Unloading at the hirer's site. The hirer is responsible (clause 4).

Stage 3:   Erecting plant at the hirer's site. The owner is responsible (sub-clause 13 (c) (ii), provided such erection is under the owner's exclusive control.

Stage 4:   Operating of the plant. The hirer is responsible (clauses 8 and 13 (b)).

Stage 5:   Dismantling plant at the hirer's site. As for stage 3 reading "dismantling" for "erecting" and applying 13 (c) (iii), not 13 (c) (ii).

Stage 6:   Loading at the hirer's site. As for stage 2.

Stage 7:   Transit to owner's depot from site. As for stage 1, but the sub-clauses are 13 (c) (iv) and (v).

The position at each stage shows the party usually responsible but there can be exceptions as indicated in the preceding commentary on the various clauses. Both parties are therefore advised to cover the plant and their liabilities to others at all stages. The policies concerned with the protection of the plant, apart from a separate contractors' plant policy, appear as extensions to the following:

(a) a contractors' all risks policy;

(b) a fire and special perils policy;

(c) an engineering policy;

(d) a comprehensive commercial vehicle policy if the plant is mechanically propelled.

With the exception of the ICE Conditions (clause 21), the more common standard conditions of contract used in the construction world do not require the contractors' plant or equipment to be insured. Thus it is left to the contractor to make his or her own decision in this respect, and it applies to both the contractors' own plant and that hired in. Apart from the owner of the plant, in clause 32 of the CPA Conditions agreeing to insure in conformation with the Road Traffic Act when plant is travelling to and from site under its own power with the owner's operator, there is no other requirement in these conditions on either party to insure. Incidentally, such compulsory insurance required by this statute concerns liability to third parties and not loss or damage to the plant. Even the note at the bottom of the schedule on both the "offer" and "acceptance" forms with the CPA Conditions which reads, "NB. Clause 13: The Hirer should cover by insurance the indemnity given to the Owner in this clause" is only considered to be a warning serving as a reminder which the hirer may ignore, however unwise this would be.

Policies giving the cover

Contractors' plant policy

An average clause operates and an excess applies. From the operative clause it is clear that this is a material damage policy.

The property to be covered is listed in the schedule to the policy and the protection is against loss or damage during the period of insurance "by any accident or misfortune" up to the amount of the sum insured listed in the schedule in respect of each item specified and not exceeding in the whole the total sum insured.

Most of the policy exceptions are self-explanatory, and are standard exceptions, and others concerning war and kindred risks, nuclear risks and sonic waves, already explained in earlier chapters. The following exceptions to be explained are:

(a) An exception which concerns consequential loss. (See for example under clauses 9 and 12 of the CPA Conditions mentioned earlier.)

(b) An exception which excludes loss of property unless identifiable by the insured with an occurrence which has been notified to the insurer under the appropriate policy condition. This is complementary to the limitation in the operative clause to "any accident or misfortune". Basically the purpose is to exclude unexplained shortages.

The conditions of the policy contain the usual type of condition concerning the following subjects which have been explained in Chapter 2:

(a) reasonable precautions for safety of the property insured;

(b) alterations of risk notified and the consent of the insurer obtained;

(c) subrogation;

(d) cancellation;

(e) contribution;

(f) arbitration;

(g) compliance with terms, conditions, endorsements, and truth of proposal answers shall be conditions precedent to any liability of the insurer.

The following additional conditions are particular to this type of policy:

(a) The notice of loss or damage must be given to the police as well as to the insurer.

(b) The insurer may elect to reinstate or replace property lost or damaged instead of paying the amount of the loss or damage. If the insurer elects to replace property, it does not have to be exact and complete but only substantially as nearly as circumstances permit and in a reasonably sufficient manner.

(c) Each item of, and the total value of, the property insured is subject to average. See an example of the operation of this clause in Chapter 2.

(d) If the initial premium is regulated by the estimated hiring charges, the insured has to keep an accurate record of such actual charges incurred and allow the insurer to inspect the record, and also within one month after each period of insurance, make a return to the insurers of a correct account of the charges paid or payable during that period. The premium already paid for such period is then adjusted and the difference paid or allowed to the insured accordingly.

Extension of the contractors' all risks and fire and special perils policies

Quite often contractors arrange that their contractors' all risks policy should automatically include plant and equipment. This policy usually shows a separate sum insured for plant and equipment.

In any event it is vital that this figure, together with the sum insured on the works is adequate to cover both items.

Plant and equipment should also be covered in transit and elsewhere than on site.

There is no reason why an annual contractors' all risk policy should not be extended to cover specific types of plant if a saving in premium can be obtained in this way. Similar remarks under this heading apply to a fire and special perils policy extension to cover plant.

Normally these extensions to both the contractors' all risks and the fire and special perils policies have the same exclusions as the contractors' plant policy and do not, for example, provide cover for damage to plant due to its own explosion, mechanical or electrical breakdown.

Extension of an engineering policy

In these policies it is usual to cover breakdown and to provide an inspection service unlike the plant policy and extensions just mentioned.

Sometimes in an engineering policy only "extraneous damage" cover is given which means no protection for the results of the plant's own electrical or mechanical breakdown or other inherent faults because only damage arising from outside sources is insured.

Loss or damage to contractor's own plant under a commercial vehicle policy

The own damage or material damage cover protecting special types of plant which are mechanically propelled is given under the commercial vehicle form of policy. Such plant would include angledozers, bulldozers, bullgraders, dumpers, excavators and tarsprayers.

Acknowledgements are made to George Godwin (Longman Group) for permission to use parts of the author's book *Insurance for the Construction Industry* in writing this chapter.

CHAPTER 12

Model Form of General Conditions of Contract recommended by the Institution of Mechanical Engineers — Home Contracts, With Erection

The title of this chapter is stated as it is given in the Preface of this book as part of the syllabus of the Chartered Institute of Loss Adjusters, except that in that syllabus the words "Model Form A" are added in brackets. While the Institution of Electrical Engineers, the Institution of Mechanical Engineers, and the Association of Consulting Engineers recommend this contract, the current form of contract states that it is for use with both "Home or Overseas Contracts — with Erection". This current form was published in June 1988 and is known as MF/1.

Model Form A

This form is now obsolete and its use will no longer be recommended by the above mentioned organisations to its members. Therefore the commentary thereon will be brief, on the assumption that the use of this form will gradually diminish.

This contract concerns mechanical and electrical work for use in connection with "Home Contracts — With Erection" and the relevant clauses concerning this book are clauses 21 to 23. Clause 21 deals with the allocation of risks and with indemnities by the contractor to the purchaser for liability to third parties. The purchaser is the person for whom the work is being done.

It is important to note that in sub-clause 21(i) the contractors' liability for the works is limited. Thus they are only bound to take every reasonable precaution to protect the works against loss or damage. This means that if the works are damaged despite the contractors having taken every reasonable precaution, the purchaser and not the contractors will bear the risk. Clearly it is very possible that this may happen. Thus the contractors are not at risk regarding the works unless the damage is caused by something which can be avoided by them taking reasonable precautions eg, theft and vandalism where security is at fault.

In clause 22, subject to clause 26 (which deals with delay in completion) for the deduction of liquidated damages for delay, the contractor is not liable to the purchaser for loss of use of the works.

Clause 23 deals with insurance. Again this has a limited scope since it only covers works on the site and, under this form of contract, much of the work is commonly done off the site and there is a relatively short time lag between delivery to the site and taking over. Thus in the case of the installation of a boiler, some work is done off the site and the boiler is then brought to the site and erected. The insurance is to be in the joint names of the contractor and the purchaser against "loss, damage or destruction by fire, explosion, lightning, earthquake, malicious damage, theft, flood, storm, tempest and aircraft and other aerial devices or articles dropped therefrom for the full replacement value thereof ".

Model Form MF/1

This is an entirely new Model Form suitable to both home and export contracts and replacing both Model Forms "A" and "B3" (the full title of which is Model Form of General Conditions of Contract "B3", Export Contracts — With Erection).

MF/1 recognises important changes in practice, particularly in the role of the engineer, and it incorporates special sections covering sub-contracts, and electronics hardware and software.

This book is only concerned with responsibility for and insurance of the works and in this contract there is a distinct separation of the insurance provisions from those concerning the contractor's responsibility for care of, and liability for loss or damage to, the works. Clauses 43.1 to 43.3 deal with the latter provisions and read as follows:

Care of the Works
43.1   The Contractor shall be responsible for the care of the Works or any
            Section thereof until the date of taking-over as stated in the Taking-Over

Certificate applicable thereto. The Contractor shall also be responsible for the care of any outstanding work which he has undertaken to carry out during the Defects Liability Period until all such outstanding work is complete. In the event of termination of the Contract in accordance with these Conditions, responsibility for the care of the Works shall pass to the Purchaser upon expiry of the notice of termination, whether given by the Purchaser or by the Contractor.

Making Good Loss or Damage to the Works

43.2   In the event that any part of the Works shall suffer loss or damage whilst the Contractor has responsibility for the care thereof, the same shall be made good by the Contractor at his own expense except to the extent that such loss or damage shall be caused by the Purchaser's Risks. The Contractor shall also at his own expense make good any loss or damage to the Works occasioned by him in the course of operations carried out by him for the purpose of completing any outstanding work or of complying with his obligations under Clause 36 (Defects Liability).

Damage to Works caused by Purchaser's Risks

43.3   In the event that any part of the Works shall suffer loss or damage whilst the Contractor has responsibility for the care thereof which is caused by any of the Purchaser's Risks the same shall, if required by the Purchaser within six months after the happening of the event giving rise to loss or damage, be made good by the Contractor. Such making good shall be at the expense of the Purchaser at a price to be agreed between the Contractor and the Purchaser. In default of agreement such sum as is in all the circumstances reasonable shall be determined by Arbitration under Clause 52 (Disputes and Arbitration). The price or sum so agreed or determined shall be added to the Contract Price.

Under clause 43.1 the contractors are responsible for the care of the works including outstanding work which they have undertaken to carry out during the defects liability period. This responsibility continues until the date of issue of a take over certificate or expiry of any notice of termination of the contract by either party.

Clause 43.2 emphasises the previous sub-clause 43.1 by making the contractors liable for the cost of such loss or damage to the works subject to the purchaser being responsible for loss or damage caused by the ''Purchaser's Risks'' (see below). Equally the contractors must make good at their own expense any loss or damage caused after taking-over whilst completing any outstanding work or in complying with their obligations in relation to defects under clause 36 (Defects Liability).

Purchaser's risks are defined in clause 45.1 as follows:

Purchaser's Risks

45.1   The 'Purchaser's Risks' are:-

fault, error, defect or omission in the design of any part of the Works by the Purchaser or the Engineer [responsibility for which has been disclaimed by the Contractor in the manner provided for by Sub-Clause 13.3 (Contractor's Design)];

the use or occupation of the Site by the Works, or for the purposes of the Contract; interference, whether temporary or permanent with any right of way, light, air, or water or with any easement wayleaves or right of a similar nature which is the inevitable result of the construction of the Works in accordance with the Contract;

damage (other than that resulting from the Contractor's method of construction) which is the inevitable result of the construction of the Works in accordance with the Contract;

-   use of the Works or any part thereof by the Purchaser;
-   the act, neglect or omission or breach of contract or of statutory duty of the Engineer or the Purchaser, his agents, servants or other contractors for whom the Purchaser is responsible;
-   Force Majeure except to the extent insured under the insurance policies to be effected by the Contractor in accordance with Clause 47 (Insurance).

Force Majeure

46.1   Force Majeure means:-

-   war, hostilities (whether war be declared or not), invasion, act of foreign enemies;
-   ionising radiations, or contamination by radio-activity from any nuclear fuel, or from any nuclear waste from the combustion of nuclear fuel, radio-active toxic explosive, or other hazardous properties of any explosive nuclear assembly or nuclear component thereof;
-   pressure waves caused by aircraft or other aerial devices travelling at sonic or supersonic speeds;
-   rebellion, revolution, insurrection, military or usurped power or civil war;
-   riot, civil commotion or disorder;
-   any circumstances beyond the reasonable control of either of the parties.

It will be seen that this definition follows fairly closely the ICE Conditions "excepted risks" mentioned in clause 20(3) (see Chapter 7), bearing in mind the definition of "force majeure". However, the wording is slightly different (and some of the additional wording seems to be taken from clause 22 of the ICE conditions which in that contract refers to liability to third parties) and this calls for comment. Taking these purchaser's risks in the order they appear in the definition:

(a) In the case of the first of the purchaser's risks concerning design it is necessary for the contractors to have disclaimed liability in accordance with sub-clause 13.3 for them to avoid responsibility and for this risk to fall on the purchaser.

(b) "Use or occupation of the Site by the Works, or for the purposes of the Contract" as in the case of interference with easements, is more likely to be a third party matter and less likely to concern responsibility for the works.

(c) Similarly, inevitable damage (other than that resulting from the contractors' methods of construction) which results from the construction of the works is just as likely to involve third party property as the works.

(d) "Use of the works . . . by the Purchaser" is distinguishable from "use or occupation of the Site by the Works" (see (b) above) as it includes risks within the purchaser's control, eg his or her use of the works.

(e) "The act, neglect or omission or breach of contract or of statutory duty of the Engineer or Purchaser etc" again could affect the works but is more likely to concern third parties.

(f) The definition of "force majeure" as set out in clause 46.1 follows almost word for word the first part of the "excepted risks" in clause 20(3) of the ICE Conditions and the commentary in Chapter 7 on these risks should be noted.

Clause 43.3 states that if any part of the works is damaged by reason of the "Purchaser's Risks" while the contractor has responsibility for care of the works, the purchaser has six months to require the contractors to make good the loss or damage at the purchaser's expense. If a price cannot be agreed then it is to be determined by arbitration under clause 52.

Insurance Under Form MF/1

Clauses 47.1 to 47.3 and 47.6 to 48.2 deal with the insurance of the works. Clauses 47.1 to 47.3 read as follows:

Insurance of Works

47.1 The Contractor shall, in the joint names of the Contractor and the Purchaser insure the Works and Contractor's Equipment and keep each part thereof insured for their full replacement value against all loss or damage from whatever cause arising, other than the Purchaser's Risks. Such insurance shall be effected from the date of the Letter of Acceptance, until 14 days after the date of issue of a Taking-Over Certificate in respect of the Works or any Section thereof; or if earlier, 14 days after the date when responsibility for the care of the Works passes to the Purchaser.

Extension of Works Insurance

47.2 The Contractor shall so far as reasonably possible extend the insurance under Sub-Clause 47.1 (Insurance of Works) to cover damage which the Contractor is responsible for making good pursuant to Clause 36 (Defects Liability) or which occurs whilst the Contractor is on site for the purpose of making good a defect or carrying out the Tests on Completion during the Defects Liability Period or supervising the carrying out of the Performance Tests or completing any outstanding work or which arises during the Defects Liability Period from a cause occurring prior to taking-over.

Application of Insurance Monies

47.3 All monies received under any such policy shall be applied in or towards the replacement and repair of the Works lost, damaged or destroyed but this provision shall not affect the Contractor's liabilities under the Contract.

Clause 47.1 requires a policy in the joint names of the contractor and purchaser to insure the works and the contractor's equipment for their full replacement value against all loss or damage from whatever cause arising, other than the purchaser's risks. So a CAR policy is required from the date of the letter of acceptance until 14 days after the date of issue of a taking-over certificate in respect of the works, or 14 days after the date when responsibility for the care of the works passes to the purchaser. It is relevant to point out the necessity to keep the sum insured reflecting the full replacement value. The usual escalation clause will help in this respect (see Chapter 2). "Letter of acceptance" is defined in clause 1.1.1 as meaning the formal acceptance by the purchaser of the tender incorporating any amendments or variations to the tender agreed by the purchaser and contractor.

Clause 47.2 requires the policy to cover damage which is the contractor's responsibility in accordance with clause 36 (defects liability). In fact

CAR policies provide this cover except that clause 36.2 refers to defect or damage to any part of the works which arises from any defective materials, workmanship or design. Now, the normal CAR policy would only provide a limited design cover and excludes the cost of replacing defective materials or workmanship (see Chapter 2) so this cover would have to be specially arranged. Admittedly, the contractor's obligations under the defects liability clause 36.2 do not apply to defects in designs furnished or specified by the purchaser or engineer in respect of which the contractor has disclaimed responsibility in accordance with clause 13.3 (mentioned above) nor the consequences thereof.

Clause 47.3 contains the usual requirement that insurance monies shall be applied in the replacement or repair of the works but shall not affect the contractor's other liabilities under the contract. Thus if an insured loss arises the contractor cannot just take the money and thus evade responsibility in relation to the replacement and repair of the works lost or damaged.

The remainder of the relevant insurance clauses read as follows:

General Insurance Requirements

47.6   All insurances shall be effected with an insurer and in terms to be approved by the Purchaser (such approval not to be unreasonably withheld) and the Contractor shall from time to time, when so required by the Engineer, produce the policy and receipts for the premium or other satisfactory evidence of insurance cover. The Contractor shall promptly notify the Purchaser of any alteration to the terms of the policy or in the amounts for which insurance is provided.

Exclusions from Insurance Cover

47.7   The Insurance Policies may exclude cover for any of the following:-

(a)   the cost of making good or repairing any Plant which is defective or work which is not in accordance with the Contract;

(b)   the Purchaser's Risks;

(c)   indirect or consequential loss or damage including any deductions from the Contract Price for delay;

(d)   fair wear and tear; shortages and pilferages;

(e)   risks related to mechanically propelled vehicles for which third party or other insurance is required by law.

Remedy on Failure to Insure

48.1   If the Contractor shall fail to effect and keep in force the insurances referred to in these Conditions the Purchaser may effect and keep in force any such insurance and pay such premiums as may be necessary for that purpose and from time to time deduct the amount so paid by the Purchaser from any monies due or which may become due to the Contractor under the Contract or recover the same as a debt from the Contractor.

Joint Insurances

48.2   Wherever insurance is arranged under the Conditions in the joint names of the parties, or on terms containing provisions for indemnity to principals. the party effecting such insurance shall procure that the subrogation rights of the insurers against the other party are waived and that such policy shall permit either:

(a)   the co-insured, or

(b)   the other party to the Contract

to be joined to and be a party to any negotiations, litigation or arbitration upon the terms of the policy or any claim thereunder.

Clause 47.6 is the usual requirement concerning approval of the insurer and the insurance terms plus the documentary evidence of insurance, when required, and notification to the purchaser of alteration of policy terms.

Clause 47.7 lists allowable exclusions in the policy. The question this raises is whether other exclusions (not in the above list) imposed by the insurer, make the policy a violation of the contract. Presumably specialised risks exclusions such as loss or damage by sea or water risks normally covered by a marine policy would be allowed, although not mentioned in the list in clause 47.7. In any event, perhaps the better view of these listed exclusions in clause 47.7 is that the purchaser is not entitled to object to them but can object to others if he or she so wishes. Presumably in (a) of this list, "work which is not in accordance with the Contract" includes the policy exclusion of the cost of defective workmanship and materials, which has already been mentioned when noting the contractor's responsibility for damage occurring during the defects liability period. In this connection reference should be made to exception 1 of the CAR policy in Chapter 2. The other exclusions are self-explanatory.

Clause 48.1 is the normal "failure to insure" clause, allowing the purchaser to insure if the contractor fails to do so, and deduct any

premium he or she pays from any monies due to the contractor or recover
the same as a debt.

Clause 48.2 merely makes clear the common law rule that subrogation
cannot apply against a joint insured. A subcontractor can be a co-insured
(see below).

Form of subcontract

MF/1 includes a form of subcontract suitable for use where the main
contract is under MF/1. This subcontract has been designed to dovetail
in with MF/1 and to provide the Contractor with a subcontract which fits
in with the main one. The following points are relevant to the subject
matter of this book:

(a) In accordance with clause 12 of this subcontract the subcontractor
     is to be included as a co-insured (joint insured) under the insuran-
     ces required by sub-clause 47.1 (Insurance of Works) and 47.2
     (Extension of Works Insurance) under the main contract.

(b) The subcontractor's obligations in relation to defects do not expire
     until the end of the defects liability period under the main contract.

(c) By clause 12.1 the contractor gives details of his or her CAR policy
     of insurance in respect of the works in Part I of the seventh schedule
     of this subcontract and includes the subcontractor as a co-insured.
     In accordance with clause 12.2 the subcontractor is required to
     effect insurance against such risks as are specified in Part II of the
     seventh schedule and indicate the sums insured and the persons
     to benefit. Clearly as the subcontractor is a joint insured in the main
     contractor's CAR policy such a policy will not be required from the
     subcontractor, which leaves Part II listing the liability policies
     which are required from the subcontractor.

Contractors' insurance policy

In consideration of the payment of the premium the Independent Insurance Company Ltd (the Company) will indemnify the Insured in the terms of this Policy against the events set out in the Sections operative (specified in the Schedule) and occurring in connection with the Business during the Period of Insurance or any subsequent period for which the Company agrees to accept payment of premium

The Proposal made by the Insured is the basis of and forms part of this Policy.

M J Bright
Managing Director

Definitions

1. **Proposal** shall mean any information provided by the Insured in connection with this insurance and any declaration made in connection therewith.

2. **Business** shall include
    (a) the provision and management of canteens clubs sports athletics social and welfare organisations for the benefit of the Insured's Employees
    (b) the ownership repair maintenance and decoration of the Insured's premises and the provision and management of first aid fire and ambulance services
    (c) private work carried out by an Employee of the Insured (with the consent of the Insured) for any director partner or senior official of the Insured.

3. **Employee** shall mean
    (a) any person under a

contract of service or
apprenticeship with the
Insured
(b)(i)   any labour master or
labour only subcon-
tractor or person
supplied or employed
by them
(ii)   any self-employed
person
(iii) any person hired or
borrowed by the
Insured from another
employer under an
agreement by which
the person is deemed
to be employed by the
Insured
(iv) any student or person
undertaking work for
the Insured under a
work experience or
similar scheme
while engaged in the
course of the Business.

4.   **Bodily Injury** shall include
(a) death illness or disease
(b) wrongful arrest wrongful
detention false imprison-
ment or malicious
prosecution
(c) mental injury mental
anguish or shock but not
defamation.

5.   **Damage** shall include loss.

6.   **Property** shall mean material
loss.

7.   **Territorial Limits** shall mean
(a) Great Britain Northern
Ireland the Isle of Man the
Channel Islands or off
shore installations within
the continental shelf
around those countries
(b) member countries of the
European Economic
Community where the
Insured or directors partners or Employees of the
Insured who are ordinar-
ily resident in a) above are
temporarily engaged on
the Business of the Insured
(c) elsewhere in the world
where the Insured or directors partners or
Employees of the Insured
who are ordinarily resi-
dent in a) above are on a
temporary visit for the
purpose of non-manual
work on the Business of
the Insured.

8.   **Excess** shall mean the total
amount payable by the
Insured or any other person
entitled to indemnity in
respect of any Damage to
Property or the Property
Insured arising out of any one
event or series of events arising out of one original cause
before the Company shall be
liable to make any payment.
If any payment made by the
Company shall include the
amount for which the Insured

or any other person entitled to indemnity is responsible such amount shall be repaid to the Company forthwith.

9. **Contractual Liability** shall mean liability which attaches by virtue of a contract or agreement but which would not have attached in the absence of such contract or agreement.

10. **Contract Works** means the temporary or permanent works executed or in course of execution by or on behalf of the Insured in the development of any building or site or the performance of any contract including materials supplied by reason of the contract and other materials for use in connection therewith.

11. **Principal** shall mean any person firm company ministry or authority for whom the Insured is undertaking work.

Section 1 – EMPLOYER'S LIABILITY

In the event of Bodily Injury caused to an Employee within the Territorial Limits the Company will indemnify the Insured in respect of all sums which the Insured shall be legally liable to pay as compensation for such Bodily Injury arising out of such event.

Avoidance of Certain Terms and Right of Recovery

The indemnity provided under this Section is deemed to be in accordance with such provisions as any law relating to the compulsory insurance of liability to Employees in Great Britain Northern Ireland the Isle of Man or the Channel Islands may require but the Insured shall repay to the Company all sums paid by the Company which the Company would not have been liable to pay but for the provisions of such law.

World-wide

The indemnity granted by this Section extends to include liability for Bodily Injury caused to an Employee whilst temporarily engaged in manual work outside the Territorial Limits

Provided that

(a) such Employee is ordinarily resident within Great Britain Northern Ireland the Isle of Man or the Channel Islands

(b) the Company shall not be liable to indemnify the Insured in respect of any amount payable under Workmen's Compensation Social Security or Health Insurance legislation.

Section 2 – PUBLIC LIABILITY

In the event of accidental
  (a) Bodily Injury to any
      person
  (b) Damage to property
  (c) obstruction trespass or
      nuisance
occurring within the Territorial
Limits the Company will indemnify the Insured in respect of all
sums which the Insured shall be
legally liable to pay as compensation in respect of such event.
The Company shall not be liable
for any amount exceeding the
Limit of Indemnity.

Motor Contingent Liability
Notwithstanding Exception 2 (c)
below the Company will indemnify the Insured within the terms
of this Section in respect of liability for Bodily Injury or Damage
to Property caused by or through
or in connection with any motor-
vehicle or trailer attached thereto
(not belonging to or provided by
the Insured) being used in the
course of the Business

Provided that the Company shall
not be liable for
  (a) Damage to any such
      vehicle or trailer
  (b) any claim arising whilst
      the vehicle or trailer is
      (i) engaged in racing
           pacemaking reliability
           trials or speed testing

  (ii) being driven by the
        Insured
  (iii) being driven with the
        general consent of the
        Insured or of his repre-
        sentative by any
        person who to the
        knowledge of the
        Insured or other such
        representative does
        not hold a licence to
        drive such a vehicle
        unless such a person
        has held and is not dis-
        qualified from
        holding or obtaining
        such a licence
  (iv) used elsewhere in
        Great Britain
        Northern Ireland the
        Isle of Man or the
        Channel Islands.

Defective Premises Act 1972
The indemnity provided by this
Section shall extend to include lia-
bility arising under Section 3 of
the Defective Premises Act 1972
or Section 5 of the Defective
Premises (Northern Ireland)
Order 1975 in respect of the dispo-
sal of any premises which were
occupied or owned by the
Insured in connection with the
Business

Provided that the Company shall
not be liable for the cost of remedying any defect or alleged defect
in such premises.

Movement of Obstructing Vehicles

Exception 2 (c) shall not apply to liability arising from any vehicle (not owned or hired by or lent to the Insured) being driven by the Insured or by any Employee with the Insured's permission whilst such vehicle is being moved for the purpose of allowing free movement of any vehicle owned hired by or lent to the Insured or any Employee of the Insured

Provided that
(a) movements are limited to vehicles parked on or obstructing the Insured's own premises or at any site at which the Insured are working
(b) the vehicle causing obstruction will not be driven by any person unless such person is competent to drive the vehicle
(c) the vehicle causing obstruction is driven by use of the owner's ignition key
(d) the Company shall not indemnify the Insured against
  (i) Damage to such vehicle
  (ii) liability for which compulsory insurance or security is required under any legislation governing the use of the vehicle.

Leased or Rented Premises

Exception 4 (b) shall not apply to Damage to premises leased or rented to the Insured

Provided that the Company shall not indemnify the Insured against
(a) Contractual Liability
(b) the first £100 of Damage caused otherwise than by fire or explosion.

EXCEPTIONS
The Company shall not indemnify the Insured against liability
1. in respect of Bodily Injury to any Employee arising out of and in the course of his employment by the Insured.

2. arising out of the ownership possession or use by or on behalf of the Insured of any
(a) aircraft aerospatial device or hovercraft
(b) watercraft other than hand propelled watercraft or other watercraft not exceeding 20 ft in length
(c) mechanically propelled vehicle licenced for road use including trailer attached thereto other than liability caused by or arising out of
  (i) the use of plant as a tool of trade on site or at the premises of the Insured
  (ii) the loading or unloading of such vehicle

(iii) damage to any building bridge
weighbridge road or
to anything beneath
caused by vibration or
by the weight of such
vehicle or its load
but this indemnity shall
not apply if in respect of
such liability compulsory
insurance or security is
required under any legislation governing the use of
the vehicle.

3. for Damage to Property
which comprises the Contract
Works in respect of any contract entered into by the
Insured and occurring before
practical completion or a certificate of completion has been
issued.

4. in respect of Damage to
Property
(a) belonging to the Insured
(b) in the custody or under
the control of the Insured
or any Employee (other
than property belonging
to visitors directors
partners or employees of
the Insured)

Exception 4 (b) shall not apply to
Damage to buildings (including
contents therein) which are not
owned or leased or rented by the
Insured but are temporarily
occupied by the Insured for the

purpose of maintenance alteration extension installation or
repair.

5. for the cost of and expenses
incurred in replacing or making good faulty defective or
incorrect
(a) workmanship
(b) design or specification
(c) materials goods or other
property supplied
installed or erected by or
on behalf of the Insured.

6. caused by or arising from
advice design or specification
provided by or on behalf of
the Insured for a fee.

7. for the Excess specified in the
Schedule other than for
Damage to premises leased or
rented by the Insured.

8. caused by or arising from
seepage pollution or contamination unless due to a sudden
unintended and unexpected
event.

Use of Heat
It is a condition precedent to the
liability of the Company that
when
(a) welding or flame-cutting
equipment blow lamps
blow torches or hot air
guns are used by the
Insured or any Employee
away from the Insured's

premises the Insured shall ensure that

(i) all moveable combustible materials are removed from the vicinity of the work

(ii) suitable portable fire extinguishing apparatus will be kept ready for immediate use as near as practicable to the scene of the work

(iii) before heat is applied to any wall or partition or to any material built into or passing through a wall or partition an inspection will be made prior to commencement of each period of work to make certain that there are no combustible materials which may be ignited by direct or conducted heat on the other side of the wall or partition

(iv) they are lit as short a time as possible before use and extinguished immediately after use and that they are not left unattended whilst alight

(v) blow lamps are filled and gas cylinders or cannisters are changed in the open

(vi) the area in which welding or flame-cutting equipment is used will be screened by the use of blankets or screens of incombustible material

(vii) a fire safety check is made in the vicinity of the work on completion of each period of work

(b) vessels for the heating of asphalt or bitumen are used away from the Insured's premises the Insured shall ensure that each vessel

(i) shall be kept in the open whilst heating is taking place

(ii) shall not be left unattended whilst heating is taking place.

(iii) if used on a roof shall be placed upon a surface of non-combustible material

(iv) shall be suitable for the purpose for which it is intended and be maintained and used strictly in accordance with the manufacturer's instructions.

Property in the Ground
The indemnity provided by this Section shall not apply to liability in respect of Damage to pipes cables mains and other underground services unless the Insured

1. has taken or caused to be taken all reasonable measures to identify the location of pipes cables mains and other underground services before any work is commenced which may involve a risk of Damage thereto

2. has retained a written record of the measures which were taken to comply with 1. above before such work has commenced

3. has adopted or caused to be adopted a method of work which minimises the risk of Damage to such pipes cables mains and other underground services.

Section 3 – CONTRACT WORKS

In the event of Damage to the Property Insured the Company will by payment or at its option by repair reinstatement or replacement indemnify the Insured against such Damage

Provided that
1. the Company shall not indemnify the Insured in any one period of Insurance for any amount exceeding the Limit of Indemnity in respect of each item of property Insured

2. the Property belongs to or is the responsibility of the Insured

3. the property is
   (a) on or adjacent to the site of the Contract Works or
   (b) being carried by road rail or inland waterway to or from the site of the Contract Works within the Territorial Limits.

Professional Fees
The Company will indemnify the Insured for architects' surveyors' consulting engineers and other professional fees necessarily incurred in the repair reinstatement or replacement of Damage to the Property Insured to which the indemnity provided by this Section applies

Provided that
(a) such fees shall not exceed that authorised under the scales of the appropriate professional body or institute regulating such charges
(b) the company shall not indemnify the Insured against any fees incurred by the Insured in preparing or contending any claim.

Debris Removal

The Limit of Indemnity provided in respect of Item 1 of the property Insured shall include the cost and expenses necessarily incurred by the Insured with the consent of the Company in

(a) removing and disposing of debris from or adjacent to the site of the Contract Works

(b) dismantling or demolishing

(c) shoring up or propping

(d) cleaning or clearing of drains mains services gullies manholes and the like within the site of the Contract Works

consequent upon Damage for which indemnity is provided by this Section

Provided that the Company shall not be liable in respect of seepage pollution or contamination of any Property not insured by this Section.

Off-Site Storage

The indemnity provided by this Section extends to apply to materials or goods whilst not on the site of the Contract Works but intended for incorporation therein where the Insured is responsible under contract conditions provided that the value of such materials and goods has been included in an interim certificate and they are separately stored

and identified as being designed for incorporation in the Contract Works.

Final Contract Price

In the event of an increase occurring to the original price the Limit of Indemnity in respect of Item 1 of the Property Insured shall be increased proportionally by an amount not exceeding 20%.

Tools Plant Equipment and Temporary Buildings

The Limit of Indemnity in respect of Items 2, 3 and 5 of the Property Insured is subject to average and if at the time of any Damage the total value of such Item of the Property Insured is of greater value than the Limit of Indemnity the Insured shall be considered as being his own insurer for the difference and shall bear a rateable share of the loss accordingly.

Speculative House-Building

The insurance in respect of Item 1 of the Property Insured shall not withstanding Exception 4(b) for private dwelling houses flats and maisonettes constructed by the Insured for the purpose of sale continue for a period up to 180 days beyond the date of practical completion pending completion of sale. Practical completion shall mean when the erection and finishing of the private dwelling house are complete apart from any choice of decoration fixtures and fittings which are left to be at the option of the purchaser.

Local Authorities
The Indemnity provided by this Section shall include any additional cost of reinstatement consequent upon Damage to the property Insured which is incurred solely because of the need to comply with building or other regulations made under statutory authority or with bye-laws of any Municipal or Local Authority

Provided that
1. the company shall not indemnify the Insured against the cost of complying with such regulations or bye-laws
   (a) in respect of Damage which is not insured by this Section
   (b) if notice has been served on the Insured by the appropriate authority prior to the occurrence of such Damage
   (c) in respect of any part of the Insured Property which is undamaged other than the foundations of that part which is the subject of Damage

2. the Company shall not indemnify the Insured against any rate tax duty development or other charge or assessment arising out of capital appreciation which may be payable in respect of the Property by its owner by reason of compliance with such regulations or bye-laws

3. reinstatement is commenced and carried out with reasonable despatch.

Immobilised Plant
The indemnity provided in respect of Items 2 and 4 of the Property Insured shall include the cost of recovery or withdrawal of unintentionally immobilised constructional plant or equipment provided that such recovery is not necessitated solely by reason of electrical or mechanical breakdown or derangement.

Free Materials
Property for which the Insured is responsible shall include all free materials supplied by or on behalf of the Employer (named in the contract or agreement entered into by the Insured)

Provided that the total value of all such materials shall be included in the Limit of Indemnity for Item 1 of the Property Insured and also included in the declaration made to the Company under Condition 2.

EXCEPTIONS

The Company shall not indemnify the Insured against

1. the cost and expenses of replacing or making good any of the Property Insured which is in a defective condition due to faulty defective or incorrect
   (a) workmanship
   (b) design or specification
   (c) materials goods or other property installed erected or intended for incorporation in the Contract works but this exclusion shall not apply to accidental Damage which occurs as a direct consequence to the remainder of the property Insured which is free of such defective condition.

2. Damage due to
   (a) wear tear rust or other gradual deterioration
   (b) normal upkeep or normal making good
   (c) disappearance or shortage which is only revealed when an inventory is made or is not traceable to an identifiable event.

3. Damage to
   (a) machinery plant tools or equipment due to its own explosion breakdown or derangement but this exception shall be limited to that part responsible and shall not extend to other parts which sustain direct accidental Damage therefrom
   (b) aircraft hovercraft or watercraft other than hand propelled watercraft or other watercraft not exceeding 20ft in length
   (c) any mechanically propelled vehicle licenced for road use including trailer attached thereto other than Damage which occurs to plant whilst it is on the site of the Contract Works or it is being carried to or from such site or it is stored in a premises or compound of the Insured
   (d) bank notes cheques securities for money deeds or stamps
   (e) structures (or any fixtures fittings or contents thereof) existing at the time of commencement of the Contract Works
   (f) Item 1 of the Property Insured in respect of any contract or development
       (i) the value or anticipated cost of which at the time of its commencement exceeds the Limit of Indemnity for Item 1
       (ii) the period for which

at the time of its com-
mencement exceeds
the Maximum Period.

4. Damage to the Contract
Works or any part thereof
(a) caused by or arising from
use or occupancy other
than for performance of
the contract or for completion of the Contract Works
by or on behalf of the
Insured
(b) occurring after practical
completion or in respect
of which a Certificate of
Completion has been
issued unless such
Damage arises
(i) during any period
(other than the Main-
tenance Period) not
exceeding 14 days fol-
lowing practical
completion or issue of
such Certificate in
which the Insured
shall remain respon-
sible under the terms
of the contract for the
Contract Works or the
completed part thereof
(ii) during the Mainten-
ance Period and from
an event occurring
prior to the com-
mencement thereof
(iii) by the Insured in the
course of any oper-
ations carried out in
pursuance of any obli-

gation under the con-
tract during the
Maintenance Period.

5. Damage for which the Insured is relieved of
responsibility under the
terms of any contract or agreement.

6. (a) liquidated damages or
penalties for delay or non-
completion
(b) consequential loss of any
nature.

7. Damage occasioned by pressure waves caused by aircraft
or other aerial devices travelling at sonic or supersonic
speeds.

8. the Excess specified in the
Schedule.

9. Damage in Northern Ireland
caused by or happening
through or in consequence of
(a) civil commotion
(b) any unlawful wanton or
malicious act committed
maliciously by a person or
persons acting on behalf
of or in connection with
any unlawful association

For the purpose of this exclusion

(i) unlawful association
means any organisation

which is engaged in terrorism and includes any organisation which at the relevant time is a prescribed organisation within the meaning of the Northern Ireland (Emergency Provisions) Act 1973

(ii) terrorism means the use of violence for political ends and includes any use of violence for the purpose of putting the public in fear

In any suit action or other proceedings where the Company alleges that by reason of this Exception any Damage is not covered by this Section the burden of proving that such Damage is covered shall be on the Insured.

Section 4 – 21.2.1

In the event of the Insured entering into any contract or agreement by which the Insured is required to effect insurance under the terms of Clause 21.2.1 of the Joint Contracts Tribunal Standard Form of Building Contract (or any subsequent revision or substitution thereof) or under the terms of any other contract requiring insurance of like kind the Company will indemnify the Insured and the Employer* in respect of any expense liability

loss claim or proceedings which the Employer may incur or sustain by reason of Damage to any property other than the Contract Works occurring during the period of Insurance within the Territorial Limits and caused by

(a) collapse
(b) subsidence
(c) heave
(d) vibration
(e) weakening or removal of support
(f) lowering of ground water

arising out of and in the course of or by reason of the carrying out of the Contract Works

Provided that

1. the Company shall not be liable for any amount exceeding the Limit of Indemnity

2. the Insured shall notify the Company within 21 days of entering into or commencing work under such contract or agreement whichever is the sooner together with full details of the contract

3. once notified the Company may give 14 days notice to cancel the cover granted by this Section in respect of such contract or agreement or alternatively provide a quotation which may vary the terms of this Section

*Note: the contract clause 21.2.1 only requires an indemnity to the employer. The insurer is removing the words "indemnify the insured" from their operative clause.

4. the indemnity provided by this Section in respect of such contract or agreement shall terminate 14 days from the date of issue of the quotation if the quotation has not by then been accepted by the Insured or the Employer.

Employer

For the purpose of this Section Employer shall mean any person firm company ministry or authority named as the Employer in the contract or agreement entered into by the Insured.

EXCEPTIONS

The Company shall not indemnify the Employer

1. against any expense liability loss claim or proceedings
    (a) caused by the negligence omission or default of the Insured or any agent or Employee of the Insured or of any sub-contractor or his employees or agents
    (b) which is attributable to errors or omissions in the planning or the designing of the Contract Works
    (c) arising from Damage which could reasonably be foreseen to be inevitable having regard to the nature of the work to be executed or the manner of its execution

    (d) arising from Damage to property which is at the risk of the Employer under the terms of the contract or agreement
    (e) arising from Contractual Liability
    (f) arising from Damage occasioned by pressure waves caused by aircraft or other aerial devices travelling at sonic or supersonic speeds.

2. if the contract or agreement specifies that shoring of any building or structure is required and such shoring is necessary within 35 days of commencement of the contract or agreement.

3. against any expense liability loss claim or proceedings arising from
    (a) demolition or partial demolition of any building or structure
    (b) the use of explosives
    (c) tunnelling or piling work
    (d) underpinning
    (e) deliberate dewatering of the site.

4. in respect of any sum payable under any penalty clause or by reason of breach of contract.

5. the Excess specified in the Schedule.

EXTENSIONS
Extensions to Sections 1 and 2 only

(a) Costs

The Company will in addition to the indemnity granted by each section pay

   (i) for all costs and expenses recoverable by any claimant from the Insured

  (ii) the solicitors fees incurred with the written consent of the Company for representation of the insured at

     (a) any coroner's inquest or fatal accident inquiry

     (b) proceedings in any Court arising out of any alleged breach of a statutory duty resulting in Bodily Injury or Damage to Property

  (iii) all costs and expenses incurred with the written consent of the Company in respect of a claim against the Insured to which the indemnity expressed in this Policy applies.

(b) Legal Defence

Irrespective of whether any person has sustained Bodily Injury the Company will at the request of the Insured also pay the costs and the expenses incurred in defending any director manager partner or Employee of the Insured in the event of such a person being prosecuted for an offence under the Health and Safety at Work etc. Act 1974 or the Health and Safety at Work (Northern Ireland) Order 1978.

The Company will also pay the costs incurred with its written consent in appealing against any judgement given

Provided that

  (a) the offence was committed during the Period of Insurance

  (b) the indemnity granted hereunder does not

    (i) provide for the payment of fines or penalties

    (ii) apply to prosecutions which arise out of any activity or risk excluded from this Policy

   (iii) apply to prosecutions consequent upon any deliberate act or omission

   (iv) apply to prosecutions which relate to the health safety or welfare of any Employee unless Section 1 is operative at the time when the offence was committed

    (v) apply to prosecutions which relate to the health and safety or welfare of any person not being an Employee unless Section 2 is operative at the time when the offence was committed

(c) the director manager partner or Employee shall be subject to the terms exceptions and conditions of the Policy in so far as they can apply.

(c) Indemnity to Other Persons

The Company will indemnify the following as if a separate Policy has been issued to each

(a) in the event of the death of the Insured the personal representatives of the Insured in respect of liability incurred by the Insured

(b) at the request of the Insured

   (i) any officer or member of the Insured's canteen clubs sports athletic social or welfare organisations and first aid fire security and ambulance services in his respective capacity as such

   (ii) any director partner or Employee of the Insured while acting in connection with the Business in respect of liability for which the Insured would be

entitled to indemnity under this Policy if the claim for which indemnity is being sought had been made against the Insured

Provided that

(a) any persons specified above shall as though they were the Insured be subject to the terms exceptions and conditions of this Policy in so far as they can apply

(b) nothing in this extension shall increase the liability of the Company to pay any amount exceeding the Limit of Indemnity of the operative Section(s) regardless of the number of persons claiming to be indemnified.

Extension to Sections 1, 2 and 3 only

(d) Indemnity to Principal

Where any contract or agreement entered into by the Insured for the performance of work so requires the Company will

(a) indemnify the Principal in like manner to the Insured in respect of the principal's liability arising from the performance of the work by the Insured

(b) note the interest of the

Principal in the Property Insured by Section 3 to the extent that the contract or agreement requires such interest to be noted.

Extension to Section 2 only

(e) Cross Liabilities
The Company will indemnify each insured to whom this Policy applies in the same manner and to the same extent as if a separate policy had been issued to each provided that the total amount of compensation payable shall not exceed the Limit of Indemnity regardless of the number of persons claiming to be indemnified

Provided that the Company shall not indemnify the Insured against liability for which an indemnity is or would be granted under any Employers Liability Insurance but for the existence of this Policy.

GENERAL EXCEPTIONS

The Company shall not indemnify the Insured

1. (i) for loss destruction of or damage to any property whatsoever or any loss or expense whatsoever resultng or arising there-from or any consequential loss

(ii) for any legal liability of whatsoever nature directly or indirectly caused by or contributed to by or arising from
  (a) ionising radiations or contamination by radioactivity from any nuclear waste from the combustion of nuclear fuel
  (b) the radioactive toxic explosive or other haz-ardous properties of any explosive nuclear assembly or nuclear component thereof

In respect of Bodily Injury caused to an Employee this Exception shall apply only when the Insured under a contract or agreement has undertaken to indemnify a Princi-pal or has assumed liability under contract for such Bodily Injury and which liability would have attached in the absence of such contract or agreement.

2. under Sections 1 or 2 in respect of Contractual Liability unless the sole con-duct and control of claims is vested in the Company but the Company will not in any event indemnify the Insured in respect of

  (i) liquidated damages or lia-bility under any penalty clause

(ii) Damage to Property which comprises the Contract Works and occurs after the date referred to in Exception 3 of Section 2 if liability attaches solely by reason of the contract

(iii) Damage against which the Insured is required to effect insurance under the terms of Clause 21.2.1 of the Joint Contracts Tribunal Standard Form of Building Contract (or any subsequent revision or substitution thereof) or under the terms of any other contract requiring insurance of like kind.

3. under Sections 2, 3 or 4 for any consequence of war invasion act of foreign enemy hostilities (whether war be declared or nor) civil war rebellion revolution insurrection or military or usurped power.

CONDITIONS OF THE POLICY

This policy and the Schedule shall be read together and any word or expression to which a specified meaning has been attached in any part of this Policy or of the Schedule shall bear such meaning

wherever it may appear.

1. Alteration in Risk

The Company shall not be liable under this Policy if the risk be materially increased without the written consent of the Company.

2. Premium Adjustment

If the premium for this Policy is based on estimates an accurate record containing all particulars relative thereto shall be kept by the Insured

The Insured shall at all times allow the Company to inspect such records and shall supply such particulars and information as the Company may require within one month from the expiry of each Period of Insurance and the premium shall thereupon be adjusted by the Company (subject to the Minimum Premium chargeable for the risk being retained by the Company).

3. Duties of The Insured

The Insured shall take all reasonable care

(a) to prevent any event which may give rise to a claim under this Policy

(b) to maintain the premises plant and everything used in the Business in proper repair

(c) in the selection and supervision of Employees

(d) to comply with all statutory and other obligations and regulations imposed by any authority.

4. Make Good Defects

The Insured shall make good or remedy any defect or danger which becomes apparent and take such additional precautions as circumstances may require.

5. Maximum Payments

The Company may at any time at its sole discretion pay to the Insured the Limit of Indemnity (less any sum or sums already paid in respect or in lieu of damages) or any lesser sum for which the claim or claims against the Insured can be settled and the Company shall not be under any further liability in respect of such claim or claims except for costs and expenses incurred prior to such payment.

Provided that in the event of a claim or series of claims resulting in the liability of the Insured to pay a sum in excess of the Limit of Indemnity the Company's liability for costs and expenses shall not exceed an amount being in the same proportion as the Company's payment to the Insured bears to the total payment made by or on behalf of the Insured in settlement of the claim or claims.

6. Claims

The insured or his legal personal representatives shall give notice in writing to the Company as soon as possible after any event which may give rise to liability under this Policy with full particu-

lars of such event. Every claim notice letter writ or process or other document served in the Insured shall be forwarded to the Company immediately on receipt. Notice in writing shall also be given immediately to the Company by the Insured of impending prosecution inquest or fatal inquiry in connection with any such event. No admission offer promise payment or indemnity shall be made or given by or on behalf of the Insured without the written consent of the Company. In the event of Damage by theft or malicious act the Insured shall also give immediate notice to the police.

7. Subrogation

The Company shall be entitled if it so desires to take over and conduct in the name of the Insured the defence or settlement of any claim or to prosecute in the name of the Insured for its own benefit any claim for indemnity or damages or otherwise and shall have full discretion in the conduct of any proceedings and in the settlement of any claim and the Insured shall give all such information and assistance as the Company may require.

8. Contribution

If at the time of any event to which this Policy applies there is or but for the existence of this Policy there would be any other insurance covering the same liability or Damage the Company shall not be liable under this Policy except in respect of any excess beyond the amount which would be payable under such other insurance had this Policy not been effected.

9. **Cancellation**
   The Company may cancel this Policy by giving thirty days' notice by recorded delivery letter to the last known address of the Insured. The Company shall make a return of the proportionate part of the premium in respect of the unexpired Period of Insurance or if the premium has been based wholly or partly upon estimates the premium shall be adjusted in accordance with Condition 2.

10. **Disputes**
    Any dispute concerning the interpretation of the terms of this Policy shall be resolved in accordance with the jurisdiction of the territory in which this Policy is issued.

11. **Rights**
    1. In the event of Damage for which a claim is or may be made under Section 3
       (a) the Company shall be entitled without incurring any liability under this Policy to

(i) enter any site or premises where Damage has occurred and take and keep possession of the Property Insured
(ii) deal with any salvage as they deem fit
but no property may be abandoned to the Company
(b) if the Company elects or becomes bound to reinstate or replace any property the Insured shall at their own expense produce and give to the Company all such plans and documents books and information as the Company may reasonably require. The Company shall not be bound to reinstate exactly or completely but only as circumstances permit and in reasonably sufficient manner and shall not in any case be bound to expend in respect of any one of the items of property Insured more than the Limit of Indemnity in respect of such item.

12. **Observance**
    The due observance and fulfilment of the terms exceptions conditions and endorsements of this Policy in so far as they relate to anything to be done or com-

plied with by the Insured and the truth of the statements and answers in the proposal shall be conditions precedent to the liability of the Company to make any payment under this Policy.

ENDORSEMENTS

These Endorsements apply only if the number against them appears in the Schedule to this Policy.

No.Z001 EXCLUDING WELDING OR FLAME-CUTTING EQUIPMENT
The Company shall not indemnify the Insured under Section 2 against liability caused by or arising from the use by the Insured or any Employee of welding or flame-cutting equipment away from the premises of the Insured.

No.Z002 LIMITATIONS OF WORK
For the purposes of this Policy the Business of the Insured is restricted to work on or in connection with private dwellings blocks of flats shops offices public houses guest houses or hotels not exceeding four storeys in height (including the ground floor) and attic.

No.Z003 HAZARDOUS WORK EXCLUSION
The Company shall not indem-

nify the Insured under Sections 1 or 2 against liability arising from
(a) demolition by the Insured or any Employee unless in connection with any work of erection re-construction alteration maintenance installation or repair by the Insured or any employee
(b) any work of dismantling steel structures by the Insured or any Employee other than scaffolding or machinery belonging to or hired to the Insured or undergoing maintenance repair or replacement by the Insured
(c) pile-driving water diversion or the use of explosives by the Insured or any Employee.

No.Z004 HAZARDOUS PREMISES EXCLUSION
The Company shall not indemnify the Insured under Sections 1 2 or 3 against liability or Damage arising from any work in or on or in connection with
(a) towers steeples chimney shafts blast furnaces dams canals viaducts bridges or tunnels
(b) aircraft airports ships docks piers wharves breakwaters or sea walls
(c) collieries mines chemical works gas works oil refineries or power stations
(d) offshore installations or bulk oil petrol gas or chemical storage tanks or chambers.

No.Z005 AUTOMATIC REIN-STATEMENT

The Limits of Indemnity under Section 3 will not be reduced by the amount of any claim

Provided that the Insured shall pay an additional premium at a rate to be agreed on the amount of each claim from the date Damage occurs to the date of the expiry of the Period of Insurance and that any such additional premium will be disregarded for the purpose of any adjustment of premium under Condition 2.

No.Z006 SHOWHOUSES

Exception 4(b) of Section 3 shall not apply to showhouses show-flats or showmaisonettes including the contents thereof the property of the Insured or for which they may be responsible until completion of sale takes place

Provided that the liability of the Company shall not exceed £500,000 in any one Period of Insurance nor £100,000 in respect of any one showhouse showflat or showmaisonette.

No.Z007 NEGLIGENT BREAK-DOWN

Exception 3(a) of Section 3 shall not apply to explosion breakown or derangement of machinery plant or tools hired to the Insured under the Model Conditions for the Hiring of Plant of the Contrac-

tors Plant Association or other similar conditions

Provided that
(a) such explosion breakdown or derangement is due to the negligence misuse or misdirection of the Insured or any Employee
(b) the liability of the company shall not exceed £50,000 for any one item
(c) the Company shall not provide indemnity against the first £250 of each and every occurrence.

No.Z008 CONTINUING HIRE CHARGES

The Company will indemnify the Insured under Section 3 in respect of liability assumed by the Insured under Clause 9 (d) of the Model Conditions for the Hiring of Plant of the Contractors Plant Association (or similar conditions) for the payment of hire charges arising from explosion breakdown or derangement of machinery plant or tools hired to the Insured

Provided that
(a) such explosion breakdown or derangement is due to the negligence misuse or misdirection of the Insured or any Employee
(b) the liability of the Company in any one Period of Insurance shall not exceed £10,000

(c) the company shall not provide indemnity against the
first £250 of each and every
occurrence or the hiring fee
for the first 48 hours following each and every
occurrence whichever is the
greater.

No.Z009 PLANT IMMOBI-
LISATION CONDITION

It is a condition precedent to the
liability of the Company under
Section 3 in respect of Damage
caused by theft to plant insured
by Items 2 and 4 of the Property
Insured that such plant shall be
immobilised when left
unattended.

No.Z010 PLANS

Section 3 shall extend to indemnify the Insured in respect of the
cost and expenses necessarily
incurred in re-writing or re-
drawing plans drawings or other
contract documents following
Damage thereto

Provided that the liability of the
Company shall not exceed
£25,000 in respect of any one
contract or development.

SCHEDULE

POLICY NO: _____

INSURED: _____

ADDRESS: _____

_____

_____

BUSINESS: _____

_____

PERIOD OF INSURANCE: <u>FROM</u>   <u>TO</u>

FIRST PREMIUM: _____

ANNUAL PREMIUM: _____

MINIMUM PREMIUM:
75% of the Premium for the respective Period of Insurance (see Condition 2).

MAXIMUM PERIOD:
(for the purpose of Section 3):   months plus   months Maintenance Period.

LIMITS OF INDEMNITY:

SECTION 1 EMPLOYERS' LIABILITY: _____

SECTION 2 PUBLIC LIABILITY: £ _____
This limit applies in respect of any one occurrence or series of occurrences arising out of one cause.

SECTION 3 – CONTRACT WORKS:

PROPERTY INSURED   LIMIT OF INDEMNITY

  Item 1 – Contract Works   £ _____

  Item 2 – Constructional Plant Tools and
    Equipment owned by the Insured   £ _____

  Item 3 – Temporary Buildings and Site Huts
  (including fixtures and fittings therein) £ _____

  Item 4 – Hired – in Property described in
    Items 2 and 3 not exceeding   £ _____
                            any one item

  Item 5 – Personal Effects and Tools of the
    Insureds Employees not exceeding
    £   any one Employee   £ _____

SECTION 4 21.2.1:   £ _____

This limit applies in respect of any one occurrence or series of occurrences arising out of one cause.

Where 'NIL' is inserted above that Section is inoperative and the Company shall not be under any liability therefor.

EXCESS

SECTION 2:

SECTION 3:

SECTION 4: £500 in the aggregate for any one contract or agreement

ENDORSEMENTS APPLICABLE:

AGENCY: _____

DATE OF ISSUE:_____

P.F. CI12   EXAMINED: _____

The Unfair Contract Terms Act 1977: a summary of Part I

Avoidance of liability

S. 2: FOR NEGLIGENCE

Subsection.

(1) For death or personal injury — invalid.
(2) For other loss or damage — subject to test of reasonableness.
(3) Awareness of or agreement to contract term or notice is not a voluntary acceptance of any risk.

S. 3: FOR BREACH OF CONTRACT

Subsection:

(1) Either where one deals as consumer *or* on the other's written standard terms of business.

(2) Subject to the test of reasonableness.

S. 4: BY INDEMNITY CLAUSES

Subsection:

(1) A person dealing as consumer cannot be made to indemnify another for his or her negligence or breach of contract except if reasonable.

(2) Whether the liability is
(a) direct or vicarious;
(b) to the consumer or someone else.

S. 1: DEFINES NEGLIGENCE

Subsection:

(1) Breach of
    (a) a contractual term to take reasonable care;
    (b) any common law duty to take reasonable care;
    (c) the common duty of care imposed by the Occupiers' Liability Act
        1957.

S. 12: DEFINES "DEALS AS A CONSUMER"

Subsection:

(1) (a) He or she does not make the contract in the course of a business.
    (b) The other party does make the contract in this way.
    (c) In the case of ss. 6 and 7 the goods are ordinarily supplied for
        private use or consumption.

Liability arising from sale or supply of goods

S. 5: "GUARANTEE" OF CONSUMER GOODS

Subsection:

(1) No guarantee can exclude or restrict liability for loss or damage to
    goods supplied which results from
    (a) defects while in consumer use;
    (b) negligence of a manufacturer or distributor.
(2) Defines
    (a) "in consumer use";
    (b) a guarantee.
(3) Excludes guarantees between parties to a contract under which
    possession or ownership of the goods passed.

S. 6: SALE AND HIRE PURCHASE

Subsection:

(1) Liability from breach of obligations arising from
    (a) s. 12 of the Sale of Goods Act 1893;
    (b) s. 8 of the Supply of Goods (Implied Terms) Act 1973
    cannot be excluded or restricted by any contract term.

(2) Liability against a person dealing as consumer from
     (a) ss. 13, 14, 15 of the 1893 Act
     (b) ss. 9, 10, 11 of the 1973 Act
     cannot be excluded or restricted by any contract terms.
(3) Liability in (2) against a non-consumer is subject to the requirements
     of reasonableness.

S. 7: MISCELLANEOUS CONTRACTS UNDER WHICH GOODS PASS

Subsection:

(1) Contracts other than sale of goods or hire purchase with contract
     terms excluding or restricting liability for breach of obligation arising
     by implication of law:
(2) As against a consumer (in respect of correspondence of goods with
     description or sample, or quality or fitness for purpose) are invalid.
(3) As against a non-consumer are subject to a requirement of reasonable-
     ness.

Other provisions

S. 8: MISREPRESENTATION

Subsection:

(1) Amends s. 3 of the Misrepresentation Act 1967.

S. 9: EFFECT OF BREACH

Subsection:

(1) Amends the law concerning fundamental breach.

S. 10: EVASION BY MEANS OF SECONDARY CONTRACT

Not possible.

S. 11: THE "REASONABLENESS" TEST

(1) The time to consider this in the case of a contract term is when the
     contract was made.
(2) In the case of ss. 6 and 7 consider the guidelines in schedule 2.
(3) The time to consider this in the case of notice (not having contractual

effect) is when the liability arose or (but for the notice) would have
arisen.

(4) Where a contract term or notice restricts liability to a specified sum
    consider
    (a) the resources available to meet the liability;
    (b) the availability of insurance.

(5) It is for those claiming a contract term or notice satisfies the
    "reasonableness" test to show that it does.

S. 13: VARIETIES OF EXEMPTION CLAUSE TO WHICH PART I APPLIES

S. 14: DEFINITIONS FOR PART I

Includes:

"Business" includes a profession and the activities of any government
department or local or public authority. "Notice" includes an
announcement, whether or not in writing, and any other communication
or pretended communication. "Personal injury" includes any disease and
any impairment of physical or mental condition.

Trinity Insurance Company Limited — Policy of Insurance for Employer's Loss of Liquidated Damages JCT 1980 Clause 22D

In consideration of the Contractor and/or the Employer

(a) having made a proposal or supplied information which shall form the basis of this policy
and
(b) having paid or agreed to pay the Premium

to the Trinity Insurance Company Limited (hereinafter called the Company)

The Company agrees (subject to the terms, conditions, exceptions and limitations contained herein or endorsed hereon) that if during the Period of Insurance or any further period for which the Contractor or the Employer have requested cover and agreed to pay and the Company to accept the appropriate additional premium

Practical Completion of the Works be delayed directly in consequence of loss or damage by one or more of the Insured Perils as defined in the Specification forming part of this policy of or to

the permanent works, temporary works, unfixed materials and goods intended for incorporation in the Works (hereinafter referred to as the Property) or any temporary buildings, plant, tools or equipment for use in connection with the Works

all whilst at or adjacent to the Site of the Works (loss or damage so caused being hereinafter termed Damage)

then provided that an extension of time therefor has been granted by the Architect in accordance with the Contract in consequence of the Damage the Company will pay to the Employer the Nominated Amount during the Payment Period less the Policy Excess in accordance with the provisions and definitions contained in the Schedule and Specification forming part of this policy

provided that

(1) at the time of the happening of the Damage there shall be in force an insurance on the Property arranged in accordance with the appropriate part of Clause 22A, B or C of the Contract and that liability for Damage thereto (where applicable) has been admitted thereunder (or would have been but for the operation of a proviso excluding liability for losses below a specified amount)

(2) the liability of the Company shall in no case exceed the Nominated Amount set out in the said Schedule nor in total the Sum Insured hereby (or such other sum or sums as may hereafter be substituted therefor by memorandum signed by or on behalf of the Company)

On behalf of the Company

....

THE SCHEDULE

(Forming part of Policy No.   )

The Employer:

The Contractor:

The Architect:

The Works:

The Site of the Works:

Practical Completion of the Works: as defined in the Contract

The Insured Perils: as detailed in the Specification attached
hereto

The Nominated Amount: £   per
or such other lesser amount which shall be
substituted by reason of Clause 18.1.4. of
The Contract

The Sum Insured: £

Payment Period: the period during which Practical Completion of the Works is delayed directly in
consequence of the Damage
(1) beginning with the date upon which but
for the Damage Practical Completion of the
Works would have been achieved
and
(2) ending not later than
    (a) the maximum period thereafter for
    which an extension of time has been
    granted
    or
    (b) the Maximum Payment Period
    thereafter
    whichever is the less

Maximum Payment Period:

The Policy Excess: £   each and every occurrence

The Contract: The JCT Standard Form of Building Contract 1980 Edition entered into by the Employer and the Contractor for the Works

The Period of Insurance: From   to
                                 both days inclusive

The Premium: £

THE SPECIFICATION

(Forming part of Policy No.   )

The Insured Perils:

1. Fire

2. Lightning

3. Explosion
   For the purpose of this insurance pressure waves caused by aircraft or other aerial devices travelling at sonic or supersonic speeds shall not be deemed explosion

4. Aircraft and other aerial devices or articles dropped therefrom excluding damage occasioned by pressure waves caused by aircraft or other aerial devices travelling at sonic or supersonic speeds

5. Earthquake

6. Riot Civil Commotion Strikers Locked-Out Workers or Persons taking part in labour disturbances or Malicious Persons acting on behalf of or in connection with any political organisation excluding damage resulting from cessation of work

   provided that full details of such Damage shall be furnished to the Company within seven days of its happening

7. Storm or Tempest or Flood
   excluding damage by frost

8. Bursting or overflowing of water tanks apparatus or pipes

EXCEPTIONS

This policy does not cover payments resulting directly or indirectly from any of the following causes:

(i)   war invasion act of foreign enemy hostilities (whether war be declared or not) civil war rebellion revolution insurrection or military or usurped power

(ii) confiscation requisition acquisition or destruction by order of any government or other authority

(iii) loss or destruction of or damage to any property whatsoever or any loss or expense whatsoever resulting or arising therefrom or any consequential loss directly or indirectly caused by or contributed by or arising from:

(a) ionising radiations or contamination by radioactivity from any nuclear fuel or from any nuclear waste from the combustion of nuclear fuel

(b) the radioactive toxic explosive or other hazardous properties of any explosive nuclear assembly or nuclear component thereof

(iv) loss or destruction of or damage to any property in Northern Ireland or loss resulting therefrom caused by or happening through or in consequence of:

(i) civil commotion

(ii) any unlawful wanton or malicious act committed maliciously be a person or persons acting on behalf of or in connection with any unlawful association.

For the purpose of this Exception:

'Unlawful association' means any organisation which is engaged in terrorism and includes an organisation which at any relevant time is a proscribed organisation within the meaning of the Northern Ireland (Emergency Provisions) Act, 1973.

In any action, suit or other proceedings where the Company alleges that by reason on the provisions of this Exception any loss, destruction or damage is not covered by this policy the burden of proving that such loss, destruction or damage is covered shall be upon the Contractor and/or the Employer.

MEMORANDA

(The clause numbers mentioned are those specified in The Contract)

1. Payments made under this policy shall be subject to the Contractor in accordance with Clause 25.2 giving written notice to the Architect that the Works are likely to be delayed and the Architect granting an extension of time in accordance with Clause 25.3.

2. Where the Relevant Events stated by the Architect in accordance with Clause 25.3.1.3 are not limited specifically to the Damage insured by this policy the Company shall agree with the Employer that part of such extension which is due to the Damage and thereafter the Company shall pay to the Employer the Nominated Amount for the Payment Period so agreed.

3. Where agreement cannot be reached as to that part of an extension of time which has resulted from the Damage the Employer and the Company hereby agree to refer at the cost of the Company to an architect (other than the Architect named in the Schedule) whose decision shall be binding.

   The architect shall be a practising member of the Royal Institute of British Architects acceptable to both the Employer and the Company or otherwise as nominated by the President for the time being of that Institute.

4. Notwithstanding the Contractor's obligations under Clause 25.3.4.1 necessary and reasonable additional expenditure may be incurred with the approval of the Company for the sole purpose of avoiding or diminishing the payments which but for that expenditure would have been made under this policy but not exceeding the amount of the payments thereby avoided.

CONDITIONS

1. This policy shall be voidable in the event of misrepresentation misdescription or non-disclosure in any material particular

2. If at any time after the commencement of this insurance

    (a) the Contractor's or Employer's business be wound up or carried
        on by a liquidator or receiver or permanently discontinued
    or
    (b) the Contractor or Employer become bankrupt or make a compo-
        sition or enter into any deed of arrangement with creditors
    or
    (c) the Contractor's or Employer's interest cease otherwise than by
        death
    or
    (d) any alteration be made either in the Works or the Property where-
        by the risk of Damage is increased

    this policy shall be avoided unless its continuance be admitted by
    endorsement signed by or on behalf of the Company.

3. The Contractor and Employer shall take all reasonable precautions to
    prevent loss or damage and the Company's representatives shall have
    access to the Site of the Works at all reasonable times.

4. On the happening of any event giving rise or likely to give rise to a
    claim under this policy the Employer or the Contractor on the
    Employer's instructions shall

    (a) forthwith give notice thereof in writing to the Company

    (b) allow immediate access to the Site of the Works for the purpose
        of inspecting the Works and provide all evidence as may be
        required to a loss adjuster appointed by the Company

    (c) so far as may reasonably be practicable take precautions to
        preserve any things which might prove necessary or useful by
        way of evidence in connection with any claim

    (d) do and concur in doing and permit to be done all things which
        may be reasonably practicable to minimise the delay in the
        completion of the contract or to avoid or diminish the loss

    (e) in the event of a claim being made under this policy at the
        Employer's expense deliver in writing to the Company not later
        than thirty days after the expiry of the Payment Period or within
        such further time as the Company may in writing allow a state-

ment setting forth particulars of the Employer's claim together with details of all other insurances covering the Damage or consequential loss of any kind resulting therefrom

(f) forthwith at the request and expense of the Company do and concur in doing all such acts and things as the Company may reasonably require for the purpose of enforcing any rights and remedies or obtaining relief or indemnity from other parties (other than the Contractor or any sub-contractor thereof against whom or which any existing rights of subrogation are waived) to which the Company shall be or would become subrogated upon its making payment under this policy whether such acts and things shall be or become necessary or required before or after payment by the Company

No claim under this policy shall be payable unless the terms of this condition have been complied with and in the event of non-compliance therewith in any respect any payment on account of the claim already made shall be repaid to the Company forthwith.

5. If any claim be in any respect fraudulent or if any fraudulent means or devices be used by the Employer or anyone acting on his behalf to obtain any benefit under this policy or if any Damage be occasioned by the wilful act of or with the connivance of the Employer all benefit under this policy shall be forfeited.

6. If at the time of any Damage resulting in a loss covered by this policy there be any other insurance effected by or on behalf of the Employer covering such loss or any part of it the liability of the Company hereunder shall be limited to its rateable proportion of such loss.

7. If any difference shall arise as to the amount to be paid under this policy (liability being otherwise admitted) such difference shall be referred to an arbitrator to be appointed by the parties in accordance with the statutory provisions in that behalf for the time being in force. Where any difference is by this condition to be referred to arbitration the making of an award shall be a condition precedent to any right of action against the Company.

8. Without prejudice to the Contractor's obligations pursuant to Conditions 3 and 4 of this policy the Contractor in taking out this insurance is acting as the agent of the Employer.

APPENDIX 4

Further details of certain cases

Computer & Systems Engineering plc v John Lelliott (Ilford) Ltd and EWG Stoddart Ltd

The contractor, under clause 22C of JCT 1980, bears the risk of damage from a subcontractor's negligent fracture of a water pipe —in contribution proceedings within the main action the subcontractor was ordered to indemnify the contractor.

Computer & Systems Engineering plc entered into a JCT 1980 contract with the contractor John Lelliott (Ilford) Ltd for work at the former's premises. EWG Stoddart Ltd was the subcontractor required to install metal purlins.

While a purlin was being lifted into position by the subcontractor, it fell and fractured one of the pipes of the sprinkler system. Water emerged at high pressure and damaged the goods of the employer. The incident was caused by the negligence of the subcontractor which was joined in the action as second defendant and by the contractor, the first defendant, as third party.

It was claimed that the employer could not recover damages against the contractor or the subcontractor by reason of clause 22C.1 of JCT 80. This reads:

The existing structures together with the contents thereof . . . shall be at the sole risk of the employer as regards loss or damage by the clause 22 perils.

The clause 22 perils are defined in clause 1.3 as including:

flood, bursting or overflowing of water tanks, apparatus or pipes . . .

It was contended by the contractor and subcontractor that, under the contract, the incident was a "bursting or overflowing of water tanks, apparatus or pipes" and therefore the responsibility of the employer.

It was held that:

(a) The employers were not liable under clause 22.

(b) " The words are to given their ordinary meaning, bearing in mind the context in which they occur and the general nature of the contractual provision."

(c) " The court should not be astute to construe a contractual term which in effect completely absolves a wholly and solely guilty tortfeasor from the consequences of his wrong."

(d) " Bursting or overflowing" were to be construed intransitively — involving some disruption of a pipe from within: *Commonwealth Smelting Ltd v Guardian Royal Exchange* (1986) 1 Lloyds Rep 121.

(e) John Lelliot (Ilford) Ltd was liable in damages to Computer & Systems Engineering plc but was entitled to an indemnity from the subcontractors, EWG Stoddard Ltd.

Glasgow Training Group (Motor Trade) Ltd v Lombard Continental plc

The collapse of a building roof caused by a heavy fall of snow, was damage caused by a "storm" covered by an insurance policy. The word "storm" was properly used where the precipitation was of an extreme or unusual intensity, particularly as policy had to be construed *contra proferentum*.

The pursuers were the heritable proprietors of a building covered by a policy of insurance effected with the defenders in respect of, *inter alia*, damage by storm or tempest. On 14.1.87 part of the roof of the building collapsed following a period during which a considerable quantity of snow landed on the roof.

The question before the judge was whether the defenders were bound to indemnify the pursuers under the policy in respect of the damage which was then suffered.

The particular risk to which the pursuers looked for the basis of their claim was that of damage by storm. There was no dispute on the cause of the collapse of the roof of the building, which was the additional loading imposed by the accumulation of snow on the roof.

It was not suggested that any wind was a factor in the mechanism of the collapse. The only question was whether the circumstances whereby the snow came to be on the roof were circumstances which fell within the expression "storm" in the policy.

Certain evidence was led with a view to establishing the weather conditions in the area of the building over the period of the few days preceding the collapse.

In construing the word "storm", it was submitted by both parties that the word fell to be construed in its ordinary sense according to the ordinary usage of the English language. The word should not be given the particular technical significance which it had in the Beaufort scale for the particular purpose for which that scale of windspeed had been devised.

It was not suggested that the word had any special or peculiar meaning in the insurance industry. The defenders did not argue that wind, at least at ground level, was always an essential for the existence of a storm.

The defenders submitted that an essential ingredient for a storm was some form of violence in the atmosphere or in the vicinity of the structure. Even if the collapse was sudden or startling, there was no violence in the weather conditions and accordingly no storm.

The pursuers submitted that the term "storm" applied if the snowfall was of sufficient severity even if there was no wind. The prolonged period of severe weather constituted a storm.

The *Shorter Oxford Dictionary* primary definition of storm was "a violent disturbance of the atmosphere, manifested by high winds, often accompanied by heavy falls of rain, hail or snow, by thunder and lightning, and at sea by turbulence of the waves. Hence sometimes applied to a heavy fall of rain, hail or snow, or to a violent outbreak of thunder and lightning, unaccompanied by strong wind".

Certain Scottish meanings of "storm" indicated that the word was used simply to mean snow or wintry weather.

That did not seem to be a modern general usage and his Lordship, preferred the primary definition. The juxtaposition of the words "storm" and "tempest" in the insured perils clause gave no unusual colour to the word "storm".

Although it was accepted that the presence of wind was not always an essential for a "storm", to define the word simply as adverse weather was not sufficiently precise.

It was held that:

(a) While "storm" might involve an element of violence in the sense of rapid movement of air or liquid, it was also properly to be used where the precipitation was of an extreme or unusual intensity.

(b) In the particular case of snow, as opposed to rain or hail, the precipitation might be in itself of a less impetuous or rapid nature but if the snow fell with a significant degree of intensity the event was properly to be described as a snow storm. Thus the definition in the *Shorter Oxford Dictionary*, of a heavy fall of snow was reiterated.

(c) In deciding the meaning of "heavy", fallen snow and duration were relevant factors.

(d) In considering "violence", the intensity and severity of the incident as well as its suddenness or speed of impact might be characterised as violence.

(e) The expression "storm", could be considered ambiguous and on the principle of construing the policy *contra proferentum*, preference should be given to including a heavy fall of snow.

(f) In the case in question in common parlance the weather conditions would properly be described as storm conditions. There was a significant falling of snow over a relatively short period and a degree of turbulence. The general evidence and picture of the conditions confirmed that the description "storm" was appropriate.

(g) In the whole circumstances the loss or damage in question was caused by storm within the meaning of the policy.

Petrofina (UK) Ltd and Others v Magnaload Ltd and Others

Subrogation and contribution. The meaning of subcontractor.

This trial of a preliminary issue arose out of an accident in September 1978 while an extension was being carried out to an oil refinery. The first and second plaintiffs benefit from the operation of the refinery by the third plaintiffs, the Lindsey Oil Refinery Co Ltd. The fourth plaintiffs, Omnium Leasing Co, are a consortium of companies which financed the extension. The main contractor, Foster Wheeler Ltd, subcontracted the installation of a catalytic cracking unit to Greenham (Plant Hire) Ltd, which obtained lifting equipment from Mammoet Stoof BV, the second defendant. The accident occurred after the installation of the unit while dismantling the lifting equipment.

The first defendants (partly owned by the second defendants) had employees involved in the installation operation. Greenham was joined as the third party to the proceedings.

It had to be assumed for the purposes of the preliminary issue that the first and second defendants were negligent and that their negligence caused the accident.

The contract works were insured with the second third party, the New Hampshire Insurance Co, for £92 million. A claim under that insurance by Lindsey was settled for £1^1/4 million. Having paid that claim the insurer now wished to exercise its subrogation right by suing the defendants. The defendants maintained that the insurer had no right of subrogation because the defendant was itself insured under the same policy. The main question for determination in this preliminary issue was whether that contention was correct, but other additional points for decision were also involved, *viz* that the defendants were not "sub-contractors" within the meaning of the policy and therefore not insured at all; it was only insured in respect of its own property or that for which it was responsible; as it had other insurances a non-contributory exception applied.

It was held that:

(a) Strictly speaking Magnaload was not a subcontractor but a sub-subcontractor. It was, nevertheless, a subcontractor within the definition in the contracts and within the ordinary meaning of the word "subcontractors" as contained in the policy. On the true construction of the policy Magnaload and Mammoet were both subcontractors and both insured under the policy.

(b) A subcontractor who is engaged in contract works may insure the entire contract works as well as its own property and the defendants on this case were each so insured and this follows *Commonwealth Construction Co Ltd v Imperial Oil Ltd* (1977) 69 DLR 3rd 588.

(c) Whether the rule that insurers can never sue one co-insured in the name of another is a fundamental principle or whether it rests on the principles of circuity, there is no doubt as to its existence and its application in the case of contractors and subcontractors engaged in a common enterprise under a building or engineering contract. Following the *Commonwealth Construction* case.

(d) A general exception in a policy repudiating liability in the event of another policy operating except in respect of any excess beyond the amount payable under that other policy, does not apply to policies on property, where the additional policy is a liability policy. It only applies to true double insurance (the same insured, covered in respect of the same property against the same risks). Therefore the exception does not apply to the defendants' liability policies.

Leave to appeal was granted.

Pioneer Concrete (UK) Ltd v National Employers' Mutual General

Public liability policy exception — Condition requiring immediate notification to insurers of proceedings — Failure to give such notification — Plaintiff obtaining judgement in default against insured — Whether insurers liable to pay adjudged sum in spite of failure to give above notification — Whether insurers required to show prejudice in order to rely on breach of condition — Third Parties (Rights Against Insurers) Act 1930.

The insured, East London Concrete Ltd, was employed by the plaintiff to dismantle, transport and re-erect the latter's plant. Ten months after doing so a hopper (part of the plant) collapsed, the main reason being that the feet of the metal structure supporting the hopper were inadequately secured to the concrete foundations on which they stood. East London was insured with the defendant under a public liability policy which was subject to certain exceptions and conditions which provided, *inter alia:* "This policy does not cover . . . (iv)(a) the making good of faulty workmanship . . ." and "The insured shall give written notice to the Head Office or Branch Office of the Association of any accident or claim proceedings immediately the same shall have come to the knowledge of the insured or his representative".

The plaintiff's solicitor informed the insurer of the accident and the plaintiff's intention to claim against East London. By the time the plaintiff's issued a writ against East London, the latter was in liquidation but notification of the issue of the writ never reached the insurer. The plaintiff obtained judgement against East London but the insurer refused indemnity to East London on the grounds that it had not been notified of the proceedings as required by a policy condition. The plaintiff brought an action against the insurer under s. 1 of the Third Parties (Rights Against Insurers) Act 1930, claiming the sum for which East London had been adjudged to be liable and contending that the insurer was not entitled merely to rely on a breach of the policy condition to avoid indemnity but had also to show that it had been prejudiced by the breach.

There was also a dispute as to the extent of the operation of the policy exception. The items of the claim were as follows:

(a) £5200 in respect of repairs to the aggregate bins and associated machinery;

(b) £580 for additional work to replace the holding down bolts fasten-

ing the site to the foundations, the wrong bolts having been fitted
in the first place;

(c) £57.90 for recalibration of scales;

(d) £74.79 for replacement of rollers.

It was held, firstly, regarding the policy exception, that it only operated
to exclude item (b) as the other items had nothing to do with the making
good of faulty workmanship. This exception referred to the cost of redoing
or patching up work which had been done inadequately or defectively on
the first occasion. It was entirely different from damage caused to the plant
itself as a result of accidental collapse caused by negligent erection of the
plant.

Secondly, the notification condition required the insurer to be notified
not only of the accident and claim but also of any proceedings, thus
notification only of the accident and of the plaintiff's claim was not
sufficient to satisfy the condition since the insurers had never been notified of the proceedings.

Thirdly, the insurers were entitled to rely on the breach of the notification condition in the policy even if they had not been prejudiced by the
lack of notification because the condition expressed in clear terms that
notification was a condition precedent to the insurers' liability to make
payment under the policy. In any event, the insurer had been prejudiced,
although only slightly, by the lack of notification of the proceedings since
it had been allowed no opportunity to consider how to deal with the
litigation and once the plaintiff had entered judgement the insurer's
position in the litigation inevitably had been weakened.

Redland Bricks Ltd v Morris and Another

Mandatory injunction — Order in general terms not specifying details of work to be done — Injunction requiring defendants to take all necessary steps to restore the support to the plaintiffs' land.

Mandatory injunction — Discretion over grant of remedy — Principles on which exercised — Loss of support of plaintiffs' land by reason of defendants' excavation on neighbouring land — Order requiring expenditure of £30,000 for benefit of land, etc, worth not more than £12,000, and an offer to buy was refused.

The respondents were market gardeners who farmed eight acres of land; this was adjoined by the appellant's land which the appellant used to dig for clay. In 1964 some of the respondents' land slipped, due to lack of support, into the appellant's land. Slip occurred again in 1965 and 1966. It was likely that further slips would occur rendering a large part of the respondents' land unworkable as a market garden. To remedy the slipping was estimated to cost about £30,000. The respondents' land was worth £12,000. In October 1966 a country judge (upheld by the Court of Appeal) granted two injunctions in favour of the respondents: (a) an injunction restraining the appellants from withdrawing support; and (b) a mandatory injunction "that the [appellants] do take all necessary steps to restore the support to the [respondents'] land within a period of six months". On appeal against the mandatory injunction, it was held that although there was a strong probability that grave damage would, in the future, accrue to the respondents, the injunction would be discharged because in its terms it did not inform the appellant exactly what it had to do.

Note: as the appellant had behaved, although wrongly, not unreasonably, it would have been wrong to have imposed on it the obligation of remedying the slip at a cost of £30,000, which would have been unreasonably expensive. The judge would, however, have been justified in imposing an obligation to do some reasonable and not too expensive works which might have had a fair chance of preventing further damage. Thus the decision of the Court of Appeal was reversed on this point.

These legal aspects must be considered by insurers in the event of a claim under any policy they issue covering the perils mentioned in sub-clause 21.2.1 of the JCT contract.

Saint Line Ltd v Richardsons, Westgarth & Co Ltd

Contract — Breach — Measure of damages — "Indirect or consequential"
damages.

By a clause in a contract for the provision of engines for a ship limiting the
liability of the engine builder in certain events it was provided (*inter alia*)
"nor shall their liability ever or in any case . . . extend to any indirect or
consequential damages or claims whatsoever". The contract was broken
by the engine builder, and the shipowner claimed damages

(a) for loss of profit during the time it was deprived of the use of the
vessel;

(b) expenses of wages, stores, etc;

(c) fees paid to experts for superintendence.

It was held, that inasmuch as the damages claimed were recoverable only
in so far as they were the direct and natural result of the breaches, the
plaintiff's rights were not cut down by the clause in the contract, since all
these heads of damage were direct and immediate, and not "indirect or
consequential".

APPENDIX 5

Form of ICE subcontract

Designed for use in conjunction with the ICE General Conditions of Contract: Fifth Schedule.

Example 1: Insurances

Part I: Subcontractor's insurances

Employers' liability — unlimited in amount.
Third party (public) liability — minimum on any one occurrence £1,000,000 (number of occurrences unlimited).
Plant and equipment — to the full value.
Subcontract works — to the full value.

The Subcontractor shall effect the above insurance in such a manner in the name of himself and such others as are required under the Main Contract that he assumes in respect of the Subcontract all the obligations and liabilities required of the Contractor under the Main Contract.

Part II: Contractor's policy of insurance
No benefit under the Contractor's policies of insurance is available to the Subcontractor.

Example 2: Insurances

Part I: Subcontractor's insurances

Employers' liability
Plant and equipment

Part II: Contractor's policy of insurance
The Subcontractor shall have the benefit of the Contractor's 'Contractor's All Risks' and 'Public Liability' insurance (subject to policy excesses).

Note: The public liability insurance will be included where it is part of the Contractor's all risks policy.

APPENDIX 6

Specification forming part of an advance profits policy

SPECIFICATION referred to in Business Interruption Policy No
in the name of

Item no		Sum Insured
1	On Anticipated Rent	£

The Insurance under Item No 1 is limited to the loss sustained by the Insured in consequence of the Accident and the amount payable as indemnity thereunder shall be

(a) the loss of Anticipated Rent suffered by the Insured during the Indemnity Period

(b) the additional expenditure necessarily and reasonably incurred for the sole purpose of avoiding or diminishing the loss of Anticipated Rent which but for that expenditure would have taken place during the Indemnity Period but not exceeding the amount of the reduction in Anticipated Rent thereby avoided

less any sum saved during the Indemnity Period in respect of such charges of the Business that would have been payable out of anticipated Rent as may cease or be reduced in consequence of the Accident

provided that if the Sum Insured by this Item be less than   the Annual Anticipated Rent the amount payable shall be proportionately reduced

Note 1 — Unless the Insured can provide evidence that it was the intention to lease or rent the Premises to one tenant only then should the Contract be completed and the Premises vacant at the time of the Accident the Company shall be liable for loss in respect only of the portion or portions of the Premises physically affected by the Accident

but in as far as the loss of Anticipated Rent in respect of

(i)   the portion or portions of the Premises unaffected by the Accident

(ii) an Accident to portion or portions of the Premises not capable of direct occupation but providing services or access within the Premises

payment will be made on the provision of evidence that occupation of the Premises in whole or in part would have taken place during the Indemnity Period

Note 2 — If at the time of the Accident it is established that it was the Insured's sole intention to sell the leasehold or freehold of the Premises this Insurance shall remain valid and the Indemnity will be based on the application of the Percentage Rate of Interest per annum to the proposed selling price of the leasehold or freehold of the Premises (agreed or assessed by the Professional Valuer as appropriate) calculated pro rata for the length of the Indemnity Period but not exceeding in all the indemnity that would have been granted if it had been the Insured's intention to lease or rent the Premises or the Sum Insured whichever shall be the less

In assessing the actual amount on which interest will be paid consideration will be given to any amounts saved by the Insured in consequence of the Accident

DEFINITIONS

The Business — Property Owners and Developers

The Premises — The site of the Contract and/or the completed buildings at

The Contract — The erection and/or reconstruction and/or redevelopment of buildings at the premises

Anticipated Rent (if evidence is provided of an agreement with a prospective tenant) — The money that would have been paid or payable to the Insured in respect of accommodation provided in course of the Business at the Premises

Anticipated Rent (if evidence is not provided of an agreement with a prospective tenant and the Contract is not complete) — The money that would have been paid or payable to the Insured in respect of accommodation provided in course of the Business at the Premises assessed by the Professional Valuer at the rates deemed to apply to the Premises at the date upon which but for the Accident the Contract would have been completed

Anticipated Rent (if evidence is not provided of an agreement with a prospective tenant and the Contract is complete) — The money that would have been paid or payable to the Insured in respect of accommodation provided in course of the Business at the Premises assessed by the Professional Valuer on a charge for area basis at the rates deemed to apply to the Premises at the date of the Accident

Indemnity Period (if evidence is provided of an agreement with a prospective tenant) — The period beginning with the date upon which but for the Accident the Premises would have been let and occupied and ending not later than   months thereafter during which the results of the Business shall be affected in consequence of the Accident

Indemnity Period (if evidence is not provided of an agreement with a prospective tenant and the Contract is not complete) — The period beginning with the date upon which but for the Accident the Contract would have been completed and ending not later than   months thereafter during which the completion of the Contract is delayed in consequence of the Accident

Indemnity Period (if evidence is not provided of an agreement with a prospective tenant and the Contract is complete) — The period beginning with the occurrence of the Accident and ending when that part of the Premises capable of direct occupation and affected by the Accident is restored to its predamaged condition but not later than   months after the occurrence of the Accident

Indemnity Period (if the terms of Note 2 apply) — the three previous definitions shall apply as appropriate except that the word "purchaser"

is substituted for "tenant" and the word "sold" is substituted for "let and occupied"

Annual Anticipated Rent — The proportional equivalent for a period of twelve months of the Anticipated Rent (as defined) during the Indemnity Period

Percentage Rate of Interest — The actual rate of Interest payable by the Insured during the Indemnity Period in respect of Capital borrowed to finance the Contract adjusted in respect of the non-borrowed portion of the proposed selling price of the leasehold or freehold of the Premises to the ninety-day money market rate pertaining during the Indemnity Period

The Professional Valuer — A practising member of the Royal Institution of Chartered Surveyors whose appointment shall be satisfactory to both the Insured and the Insurers or otherwise by nomination of the President for the time being of the Royal Institution of Chartered Surveyors

Note — The fees payable to the Professional Valuer shall be paid by the Company

Memo: 1 — In the settlement of any loss under this Policy account will be taken of any factor which might affect the trend of the business and consideration will be given to any variations in or special circumstances affecting the business either before or after the Accident or which would have affected the business had the Accident not occurred so that the final settlement of the loss shall represent as nearly as may be reasonably practicable the results which but for the Accident would have been obtained during the Indemnity Period in accordance with the terms of this Policy

Memo: 2 — If during the Indemnity Period in consequence of the Accident alternate premises be made available to secure to the Insured Rental or other income which would otherwise have been received by the Business at the Premises account shall be taken thereof in arriving at the Indemnity hereunder

Memo: 3 — Payments on account will be made to the Insured monthly during the Indemnity Period if desired

Memo: 4 — Any particulars or details contained in the Insured's books of account or other business books or documents which may be required by the Insurers under Condition 3 of this Policy for the purpose of investigating or verifying any claim hereunder may be produced and certified by the Insured's Auditors and their certificate shall be prima facie evidence of the particulars and details to which such certificate relates

The Company will pay to the Insured the reasonable charges payable by the Insured to their Auditors for producing such particulars or details or any other proofs information or evidence as may be required by the Company under the terms of Condition 3 of this policy and reporting that such particulars or details are in accordance with the Insured's books of account or other business books or documents
provided that the sum of the amount payable under this clause and the amount otherwise payable under the policy shall in no case exceed the total sum insured by the policy.

Eurotunnel Channel Fixed Link Project construction policy

The Thames Barrier insurance mentioned in Chapter 3 was a policy arranged by the main contractors for the civil engineering works lying at the heart of the project. That policy was complemented by separate construction insurances on an equally wide basis for the installation of gates and other equipment. The Eurotunnel Project insurance however goes one stage further in covering, under one single policy, all the works, equipment and rolling stock that make up the complete Eurotunnel Project both in France and in the United Kingdom.

The more parties involved and the more complex the project, the more sensible it becomes for construction insurance to be arranged on a comprehensive project basis. Eurotunnel's policy is a good example of this concept used sensibly and correctly. Its principle claim to fame is that it may well be the first truly Franco-British single contract of insurance.

Comprehensive project (sometimes referred to as wrap-up or omnibus) insurance usually covers at least public liability and all risks insurance of the works for all parties involved, or as many as possible. This avoids the time and trouble spent by all parties involved in any loss, damage or liability claims blaming the other parties to the contract or subcontract. See the other advantages and disadvantages of project insurance given in Chapter 8 of the author's book on *Insurance Under the JCT Forms* published by Collins (now BSP Ltd).

The product that the construction industry wants from insurers is one policy covering the project and protecting all the parties involved in its construction, not separate policies covering the liability of its producers. This is difficult to achieve because of the structure of the insurance market, the risks involved and the general unwillingness of insurers to provide latent defects insurance where there is a lack of claims data or other statistics on building defects on which to base an appraisal of risk, and, in a small market, selection against the insurer. But, the report produced by the Insurance Feasibility Steering Committee through the National Economic Development Office (NEDO) entitled *Building User's Insurance Against Latent Defects* (BUILD), is seen by some as the answer to the problem. However, this report only applies to commercial buildings and not to civil engineering projects. Probably the main obstacle to a full project insurance is the small size of, and bad experience suffered by, the professional indemnity insurance market in the construction industry.

The policy

The first thing that strikes the reader of this policy is its bilingual form and that the co-insurers subscribing directly represent a broad cross-section of both British and French companies as well as Lloyds Underwriters.

The insured parties are listed separately depending upon their French or British identity, but taken together the comprehensive list includes:

(a) all companies in the Eurotunnel Group as principals (ie project owners) and any eventual successors;

(b) the banks and the other parties providing the finance to Eurotunnel under the latter's credit agreement;

(c) the Governments of United Kingdom and France and their appointed representatives;

(d) the consultant companies acting in the supervisory role of maitre d'oeuvre;

(e) the ten British and French construction companies who in joint venture collectively constitute Transmanche Link as main contractor together with the parent and subsidiary companies of the individual firms;

   (i) any consultants, subcontractors of any tier or suppliers engaged by the contractors as well as any Government departments or authorities providing services to the project.

(f) Any other person or firm engaged by the principal.

CAR cover is granted for the nearly six year period of construction up to mid-1993 with extensions of period held covered, followed by a mainten-ance period not exceeding 24 months.

Cover is in respect of the whole project defined as "the design, procure-ment, construction, testing, commissioning and maintenance of the works for the Fixed Link between the United Kingdom and France".

The insured property is defined under two items as:

1. Works comprising permanent works and temporary works... including unfixed materials, goods and all other property for incorporation therein (which encompasses the shuttle trains, locomotives and spares ordered for Eurotunnel).
2. All plant and equipment and temporary buildings together with their contents and all other property owned by or for which the insured accepts responsibility as well as tools, equipment, clothing and personal effects of employees of the insured.

The combined sum insured on a first loss basis is £500 million, any one occurrence.

(At this point, it is worth noting that the same policy also contains a public liability section with a primary limit of £25 million, any one occurrence, as well as a third section covering additional interest charges payable in the event of prolonged delay directly caused by damage to works or plant insured for CAR risks.)

Coverage applies equally to all construction sites in France or England including transit between sites. Subject to certain restrictions regarding the manufacture and delivery of external supplies, the territorial limits are world-wide, excluding USA and Canada, and provision is also made for a modest amount of cover in respect of marine and/or air sendings if required subject to declaration.

The operative clause reads "The Insurers will indemnify the Insured against physical loss of or damage to the Insured Property howsoever caused subject to the following Exclusions..."

The exclusions themselves are those normally found in a CAR policy but many with qualifications negotiated to reflect the needs of a project policy covering both principal main contractors and subcontractors on an equal footing.

(a) Aircraft are excluded but only boats in excess of 10 metres.

(b) Insurers are not liable for any item of constructional plant or equipment due to its own mechanical or electrical breakdown, failure or derangement but this exclusion does not apply to specified types of resultant damage and does not apply to the machinery which is installed as part of the works.

(c) The normal defects exclusion is re-worded to exclude "the costs necessary to replace, repair or rectify any defect in design, plan, specification, materials or workmanship but should unintended damage result from such defect, this Exclusion shall be limited to the additional costs of improvement to the original design, plan or specification including the costs of carrying out such improvements".

(d) On the other hand, an increased deductible of £250,000 applies to each occurrence, or series of occurrences, arising out of one event consequent upon defective design, materials or workmanship insofar as concerns damage to the works.

Insurers exclude:

costs and expenses in respect of tunnel and shaft excavations relating to:

.1 dewatering except where such cost results from an incident which suddenly produces water flows exceeding those which could reasonably be anticipated

.2 overbreak excavation in excess of the maximum excavation provided for in the plans and the additional expenses resulting therefrom for refilling of cavities

.3 loss destruction or damage in advance of the tunnel face

There is also a deductible of £100,000 each occurrence in respect of offshore activities, tunnelling and shaft operations.

In respect of all other loss or damage affecting the works (temporary works or materials), the deductible is £25,000 each occurrence.

In respect of constructional plant and equipment, the deductibles are:

(a) £100,000 each occurrence in respect of tunnelling machinery whilst in the running or service tunnels or whilst being placed below ground or whilst being removed therefrom

(b) £2,500 in respect of all other loss or damage.

French law requires that separate decennale insurance be effected in respect of buildings (as opposed to civil engineering works) on French soil and the policy therefore excludes such damage occurring after completion which is compulsorily insurable.

Full all risks cover continues on the whole of the permanent works until the (single) completion certificate is issued to the contractors or until the works are put into commercial operation, whichever first occurs.

During the subsequent maintenance period of 12 months (or 24 months in respect of electrical and mechanical equipment) cover is granted in respect of physical loss or damage to:

(a) any outstanding work;

(b) the permanent works arising out of maintenance operations;

(c) the permanent works occurring during the maintenance period and arising from a cause happening prior to commencement of such period.

This latter broad coverage is however restricted to the extent that it does not benefit manufacturers of the rolling stock in respect of damage caused by any defect in design plan, specification, materials or workmanship in such equipment.

The CAR section of the combined project policy also contains explanatory memoranda dealing inter alia with:

(a) professional fees;

(b) debris removal and loss minimisation expenses;

(c) marine/non-marine loss sharing

(d) the previously mentioned facility for transit by sea or air anywhere in Europe and general average;

(e) hired in constructional plant and liability for continuing hire charges;

(f) expediting expenses not exceeding 50% of "normal" indemnity;

(g) 72 hour clause in respect of the application of deductibles to storm, flood or earthquake.

The CAR coverage must, of course, be read in the context of the detailed clauses and also in the context of the general memoranda and general conditions applicable to a policy issued in three sections. It is not possible to reproduce these in full, particularly since they are repeated in both English and French.

This bilingual aspect, as well as the dual nationality of the policy itself is underlined by the general memorandum which states that the construction, validity and performance of the insurance shall be governed by and interpreted in accordance with French law to the extent that the claimant is French (or with English law to the extent that the claimant is English). In either case, as appropriate, it is the French or English version of the wording which is deemed to be authentic, although in the event of dispute as to interpretation, meanings and definitions in both languages may be taken into consideration to assist the resolution of any dispute.

To the extent that French law applies, the provisions of the French Code des Assurances are incorporated into the policy which also provides for arbitration on disputes as to the amount of indemnity payable (liability being otherwise admitted). Eventually however, the mixture of French and English insurers do clearly agree to submit to the jurisdiction of the French or English courts as applicable.

The leading insurers are jointly Commercial Union in London and Union des Assurances de Paris, with the policy having been placed jointly by Sedgwick Limited and Gras Savoye/Faugère & Juteau in Paris.

APPENDIX 8

Clauses 8A, B and C of JCT (NSC/4) — Nominated Subcontract Works

[e] 8A   **Sub-Contract Works in New Buildings —
Main Contract Conditions Clause 22A**

Benefit of Main
Contract Joint
Names Policy for
loss or damage by
the Specified Perils

8A.1   The Contractor shall, prior to the commencement of the Sub-contract Works, ensure that
the Joint Names Policy referred to in clause
22A of the Main Contract Conditions shall be
so issued or so endorsed that, in respect of
loss or damage by the Specified Perils to the
Main Contract Works and Site Materials insured thereunder, the Sub-Contractor is
either recognised as an insured under the
Joint Names Policy or the insurers waive any
rights of subrogation they may have against
the Sub-Contractor; and that this recognition
or waiver shall continue up to and including
whichever is the earlier of the Terminal
Dates.

Responsibility of
Sub-Contractor —
loss or damage to
Sub-Contract Works
and Sub-Contract
Site Materials

8A.2 .1   Before whichever is the earlier of the
Terminal Dates the Sub-Contractor shall
(subject to clause 8A.2.2) be responsible
for the cost of restoration of Sub-Contract
work lost or damaged, replacement or
repair of Sub-Contract Site Materials and

before practical
completion of the
Sub-Contract Works

removal and disposal of any debris arising therefrom in accordance with clause
8A.3 except to the extent that the loss or
damage to the Sub-Contract Works or
Sub- Contract Site Materials is due to:

one or more of the Specified Perils
(whether or not caused by the negligence, breach of statutory duty,
omission or default of the Sub-Contractor or of any person for whom the
Sub-Contractor is responsible) or

any negligence, breach of statutory
duty, omission or default of the Contractor or of any person for whom the
Contractor is responsible or of the
Employer or any person engaged,
employed or authorised by him or by
any local authority or statutory undertaker executing work solely in pursuance of its statutory rights or
obligations.

.2 Where during the progress of the Sub-
contract Works sub-contract materials or
goods have been fully, finally and properly incorporated into the Works before
practical completion of the Sub-Contract
Works, the Sub-Contractor shall be
responsible, in respect of loss or damage
to sub-contract work comprising the materials or goods so incorporated caused by
the occurrence of a peril other than a Specified Peril, for the cost of restoration of
such work lost or damaged and removal
and disposal of any debris arising therefrom in accordance with clause 8A.3 but
only to the extent that such loss or damage
is caused by the negligence, breach of
statutory duty, omission or default of the

Sub-Contractor or any person for whom the sub-Contractor is responsible.

Loss or damage occurring to Sub-Contract Works and Sub-Contract Site Materials before practical completion of the Sub-Contract Works — Sub-Contractor's obligation to restore etc. such loss or damage

8A.3 If before the earlier of the Terminal Dates any loss or damage affecting the Sub-Contract Works or Sub-Contract Site Materials is occasioned, whether by one or more of the Specified Perils or otherwise, then, upon discovering the loss or damage, the Sub-Contractor shall forthwith give notice in writing to the Contractor of the extent, nature and location thereof. The Sub-Contractor shall, in accordance with any instructions of the Architect or directions of the Contractor, with due diligence restore Sub-Contract work lost or damaged, replace or repair any Sub-Contract Site Materials which have been lost or damaged, remove and dispose of any debris arising therefrom and proceed with the carrying out and completion of the Sub-Contract Works.

Payment for restoration etc. of work done under clause 8A.3 by Sub-Contractor

8A.4 Where under clause 8A.2 the Sub-Contractor is not responsible for the cost of compliance with clause 8A.3, such compliance shall be treated as it if were a Variation required by an instruction of the Architect to which clause 4.2 refers and valued under clause 16 or clause 17 whichever is applicable. The amount of the valuation under clause 16 shall not be added to the Sub-Contract Sum and the amount of the valuation under clause 17 shall not be included in the gross valuation referred to in clause 21.4 but such amounts shall be paid by the Contractor to the Sub-Contractor or recoverable by the Sub-Contractor from the Contractor as a debt.

Loss or damage occurring to the

8A.5 On or after the earlier of the Terminal Dates the Sub-Contractor shall not be responsible

Sub-Contract Works after their practical completion — responsibility of Sub-Contractor	for loss or damage to the Sub-Contract Works except to the extent of any loss or damage caused thereto by the negligence, breach of statutory duty, omission or default of the Sub-Contractor or of any person for whom the Sub-Contractor is responsible.

Footnote	[e]	The Sub-Contractor should consider whether he should take out insurance to cover any risks for which he is not covered under clause 8A.1 e.g. impact, subsidence, theft, vandalism.

[e]8B   Sub-Contract Works in new buildings — Main Contract Conditions clause 22B

Benefit of Main Contract Joint Names Policy for loss or damage by the Specified Perils	8B.1	The Contractor shall, prior to the commencement of the Sub-Contract Works, ensure that the Employer arranges that the Joint Names Policy referred to in clause 22B.1 of the Main Contract Conditions shall be so issued or so endorsed that, in respect of loss or damage by the Specified Perils to the Main Contract Works and Site Materials insured thereunder, the Sub-Contractor is either recognised as an insured under the Joint Names Policy or the insurers waive any rights of subrogation they may have against the Sub-Contractor; and that this recognition or waiver shall continue up to and including whichever is the earlier of the Terminal Dates.

Responsibility of Sub-Contractor — loss or damage to Sub-Contract Works and Sub-Contract	8B.2	.1 Before whichever is the earlier of the Terminal Dates the Sub-Contractor shall (subject to clause 8B.2.2) be responsible for the cost of restoration of Sub-Contract work lost or damaged, replacement

Site Materials before
practical completion
of the Sub-Contract
Works

or repair of Sub-Contract Site Materials
and removal and disposal of any debris
arising therefrom in accordance with
clause 8B.3 except to the extent that the
loss or damage to the Sub-Contract Works
or Sub-Contract Site Materials is due to:

one or more of the Specified Perils
(whether or not caused by the negligence, breach of statutory duty,
omission or default of the Sub-Contractor or of any person for whom the
Sub-Contractor is responsible) or

any negligence, breach of statutory
duty, omission or default of the Contractor or of any person for whom the
Contractor is responsible or of the
Employer or any person employed,
engaged or authorised by him or by
any local authority or statutory undertaker executing work solely in pursuance of its statutory rights or
obligations.

.2 Where during the progress of the Sub-
Contract Works sub-contract materials or
goods have been fully, finally and properly incorporated into the Works before
practical completion of the Sub-Contract
Works, the Sub-Contractor shall be responsible, in respect of loss or damage to
sub-contract work comprising the materials or goods so incorporated caused by
the occurrence of a peril other than a Specified Peril, for the cost of restoration of
such work lost or damaged and removal
and disposal of any debris arising therefrom in accordance with clause 8B.3 but
only to the extent that such loss or damage

is caused by the negligence, breach of statutory duty, omission or default of the Sub-Contractor or any person for whom the Sub-Contractor is responsible.

Loss or damage occurring to Sub-Contract Works and Sub-Contract Site Materials before practical completion of the Sub-Contract Works — Sub-Contractor's obligation to restore etc. such loss or damage

8B.3 If before the earlier of the Terminal Dates any loss or damage affecting the Sub-Contract Works or Sub-Contract Site Materials is occasioned, whether by one or more of the Specified Perils or otherwise, then, upon discovering the loss or damage, the Sub-Contractor shall forthwith give notice in writing to the Contractor of the extent, nature and location thereof. The Sub-Contractor shall, in accordance with any instructions of the Architect or directions of the Contractor, with due diligence restore Sub-Contract work lost or damaged, replace or repair any Sub-Contract Site materials which have been lost or damaged, remove and dispose of any debris arising therefrom and proceed with the carrying out and completion of the Sub-Contract Works.

Payment for restoration etc. of work done under clause 8B.3 by Sub-Contractor

8B.4 Where under clause 8B.2 the Sub-Contractor is not responsible for the cost of compliance with clause 8B.3, such compliance shall be treated as if it were a Variation required by an instruction of the Architect to which clause 4.2 refers and valued under clause 16 or clause 17 whichever is applicable.

Loss or damage occurring to the Sub-Contract Works after their practical completion — responsibility of Sub-Contractor

8B.5 On or after the earlier of the Terminal Dates the Sub-Contractor shall not be responsible for loss or damage to the Sub-Contract Works except to the extent of any loss or damage caused thereto by the negligence, breach of statutory duty, omission or default of the Sub-Contractor or of any person for whom the Sub-Contractor is responsible.

Footnote [e] The Sub-Contractor should consider whether he should take out insurance to cover any risks for which he is not covered under clause 8B e.g. impact, subsidence, theft, vandalism.

[e] 8C **Sub-Contract Works in existing structures — Main Contract Conditions clause 22C**

Benefit of Main Contract Joint Names Policy for loss or damage by the Specified Perils

8C.1 The Contractor shall, prior to the commencement of the Sub-Contract Works, ensure

.1 that the Employer arranges that the Joint Names Policy referred to in clause 22C.1 of the Main Contract Conditions shall be so issued or so endorsed that, in respect of loss or damage by the Specified Perils to the existing structures and the contents thereof owned by the Employer or for which the Employer is responsible and which are insured thereunder, the Sub-Contracter is either recognised as an insured under the Joint Names Policy or the insurers waive any rights of subrogation they may have against the Sub-Contractor; and

.2 that the Employer arranges that the Joint Names Policy referred to in clause 22C.2 of the Main Contract Conditions shall be so issued or so endorsed that, in respect of loss or damage by the Specified Perils to the Main Contract Works and Site Materials insured thereunder, the Sub-Contractor is either recognised as an insured under the Joint Names Policy or the insurers waive any rights of subrogation they may have against the Sub-Contractor; and

.3 that the recognition or waiver referred to

in clauses 8C.1.1 and 8C.1.2 shall continue
up to and including whichever is the earlier of the Terminal Dates

Responsibility of　　**8C.2 1.** Before whichever is the earlier of the
Sub-Contractor —　　　　Terminal Dates the Sub-Contractor shall
loss or damage to　　　　(subject to clause 8C.2.2) be responsible
Sub-Contract Works　　　for the cost of restoration of Sub-Contract
and Sub-Contract　　　　Work lost or damaged, replacement or
Site Materials before　　repair of Sub-Contract Site Materials and
practical completion　　removal and disposal of any debris aris-
of the Sub-Contract　　ing therefrom in accordance with clause
Works　　　　　　　　　8C.3.3 except to the extent that the loss or
damage to the Sub-Contract Works or
Sub-Contract Site Materials is due to:

one or more of the Specified Perils
(whether or not caused by the negligence, breach of statutory duty,
omission or default of the Sub-Contractor or of any person for whom the
Sub-Contractor is responsible) or

any negligence, breach of statutory
duty, omission or default of the Contractor or of any person for whom the
Contractor is responsible or of the
Employer or any person employed,
engaged or authorised by him or by
any local authority or statutory undertaker executing work solely in pursuance of its statutory rights or
obligations.

.2 Where during the progress of the Sub-
Contract Works sub-contract materials or
goods have been fully, finally and properly incorporated into the Works before
practical completion of the Sub-Contract
Works, the Sub-Contractor shall be responsible, in respect of loss or damage to

sub-contract work comprising the materials or goods so incorporated caused by the occurrence of a peril other than a Specified Peril, for the cost of restoration of such work lost or damaged and removal and disposal of any debris arising therefrom in accordance with clause 8C.3.3 but only to the extent that such loss or damage is caused by the negligence, breach of statutory duty, omission or default of the Sub-Contractor or any person for whom the Sub-Contractor is responsible.

Loss or damage occurring to Sub-Contract Works and Sub-Contract Site Materials before practical completion of the Sub-Contract Works — Sub Contractor's obligation to restore etc. such loss or damage

8C.3 **.1** If before the earlier of the Terminal Dates any loss or damage affecting the Sub-Contract Works or Sub-Contract Site Materials is occasioned, whether by one or more of the Specified Perils or otherwise, then, upon discovering the loss or damage, the Sub-Contractor shall forthwith give notice in writing to the Contractor of the extent, nature and location thereof.

.2 If the occurrence of such loss or damage or any other loss or damage gives rise to a determination of the employment of the Contractor under clause 22C.4 of the Main Contract Conditions clause 31.2 shall apply as if the employment of the Contractor had been determined under clause 28 of the Main Contract Conditions but subject to the exception in regard to the application of clause 28.2.2.6 of the Main Contract Conditions referred to in clause 22C.4.3.2 of the Main Contract Conditions.

.3 If the employment of the Main Contractor is not determined under clause 22C.4 of the Main Contract Conditions the Sub-

Contractor shall, in accordance with any
instructions of the Architect or directions
of the Contractor, with due diligence
restore Sub-Contract work lost or
damaged, replace or repair any Sub-
Contract Site Materials which have been
lost or damaged, remove and dispose of
any debris arising therefrom and proceed
with the carrying out and completion of
the Sub-Contract Works.

Payment for   **8C.4** Where under clause 8C.2 the Sub-Contractor
restoration etc. of   is not responsible for the cost of compliance
work done under   with clause 8C.3.3 such compliance shall be
clause 8C.3.3 by   treated as if it were a Variation required by
Sub-Contractor   an instruction of the Architect to which
                               clause 4.2 refers and valued under clause 16
                               or clause 17 whichever is applicable.

Loss or damage   **8C.5** On or after the earlier of the Terminal Dates
occurring to the   the Sub-Contractor shall not be responsible
Sub-Contract Works   for loss or damage to the Sub-Contract Works
after their practical   except to the extent of any loss or damage
completion —   cause thereto by the negligence, breach of
responsibility of   statutory duty, omission or default of the
Sub-Contractor   Sub-Contractor or of any person for whom
                               the Sub-Contractor is responsible.

Footnote   **[e]**   The Sub-Contractor should consider whether
                               he should take out insurance to cover any
                               risks for which he is not covered under clause
                               8C.1.2 e.g. impact, subsidence, theft, vandal-
                               ism.

APPENDIX 9

Summary of essential insurance requirements — to be read in conjunction with Condition 8 of the General Conditions of Contract GC/Works/1 edition 3

EMPLOYERS'
LIABILITY
INSURANCE

The insurance to be completely free from any monetary limitation as to the amount of indemnity provided.

COMBINED CONTRACTORS "ALL RISKS"/PUBLIC LIABILITY INSURANCE

INSURED

1. The Property Services Agency or any client body for whom it acts.

2. The Contractor and/or Sub-Contractor.

3. Professional Consultants to 1 above for their respective rights and interests.

INSURED PERIOD:

to represent the total construction/erection period plus the maintenance period stated in the Contract.

CONSTRUCTION "ALL RISKS"

Risks Insured:

All Risks of physical loss or damage.

Property Insured: 1.   All Permanent Works and materials or
equipment for incorporation therein
including free supplied items:

2.   Temporary Works, i.e. those other things
erected or constructed for the purposes of
making possible the erection or installation
of the Permanent Works and which it is
intended shall not pass to the ownership of
the Authority:

AMOUNT INSURED

The full Contract Sum of the Insured Project including an allowance for
variations and free supplied items.

TERRITORIAL LIMITS OF COVER

While on the Site of the Insured Project or in transit thereto or therefrom (other than by sea or air), including loss or damage occurring during any deviation therein or storage in the course of transit, temporary
off-site storage or temporary removal from the Site for any purpose
whatsoever (including any loading transit or unloading incidental
thereto) or while held for the purpose of the Insured Project at the
premises of the Insured or anywhere in the United Kingdom.

INSURED'S RETAINED LIABILITY

The Insured's retained liability shall not exceed:

(i)   £2,500 each and every occurrence in respect of loss or damage
caused by Storm, Tempest, Flooding, Water, Subsidence or Collapse.

(ii)   £1,000 each and every occurrence in respect of any other Insured
loss or damage.

and *if insured by the Contractor* (see Note 2)

(iii)   £50 each and every occurrence in respect of Employees' Personal
Effects, Tools or other property except when caused by Fire or
Explosion when there shall be no retained liability.

(iv) Loss of or damage to Temporary Buildings, Constructional Plant and Equipment; the first £500 of each and every claim arising from any single occurrence or series of occurrences constituting a single event.

PUBLIC LIABILITY

RISKS INSURED

All sums for which the Insured shall become legally liable to pay (including claimants costs and expenses) as damages in respect of:

(i) death of or bodily injury to or illness or disease contracted by any person, not being a person who at the time of suffering such death, bodily injury or disease was in the Insured's employment and where the same arose out of and in the course of such employment:

(ii) loss of or damage to property;

(iii) interference to property or the enjoyment of use thereof by obstruction, trespass, loss of amenities, nuisance or any like cause;

happening during the Insured Period and arising out of or in connection with the Insured Project.

TERRITORIAL LIMITS OF COVER

(i) anywhere in the United Kingdom in connection with the Insured Project:

(ii) elsewhere in the course of commercial visits by the Insured and / or his employees in connection with the Insured Project.

INSURED'S RETAINED LIABILITY

The Insured's retained liability shall not exceed:

£1,000 each and every occurrence (in respect of property damage claims only — personal injury claims will be paid in full).

NOTES

1. Your attention is specifically drawn to the fact that insurance is to be effected in respect of those matters described in Condition 8. The

insurance should indemnify the Contractor and nominated and domestic Sub-Contractors. Your tender should therefore reflect the likely savings in Sub-Contract prices.

2. Your attention is particularly drawn to the fact that if the policy effected to meet these Requirements and Condition 8 does not provide cover in respect of loss of or damage to Temporary Buildings, Constructional Plant and Equipment and employees' personal effects and tools, you should price the risk in respect of Temporary Buildings, Construction Plant/Equipment etc within the BQs in the normal way.

CERTIFICATE OF INSURANCE (ALTERNATIVE A) IN RESPECT OF CONDITION 8 OF THE GENERAL CONDITIONS OF CONTRACT (GC/WORKS/1-EDITION 3)

1. This certificate relates to Contract No. . . . . with respect to work at (Short title of the Works), ...

. . . .

2. A tender has been accepted from (name of contractor) . . . . for execution of the above contract.

3. The Contract requires under Condition 8 confirmation that within 21 days from acceptance of the tender there be in force as described in the Contract:

   a. Employers Liability Insurance
   b. Contractors All Risks Insurance
   c. Public Liability Insurance

4. Signature and return of this Certificate is to be deemed due confirmation by either the contractor's Insurance Brokers or Insurers that the above described insurance requirements have been fully complied with.

   ON BEHALF OF THE CONTRACTOR'S INSURANCE BROKERS

   (i) Name of Insurance Brokers:-

   . . . .

   (ii) Signed on behalf of (i)

   . . . .

   ON BEHALF OF THE CONTRACTOR'S INSURERS

   (i) Name of Insurers

   . . . .

   (ii) Signed on behalf of (i)

   . . . .

CERTIFICATE OF INSURANCE   (ALTERNATIVE B)
IN RESPECT OF CONDITION 8
OF THE GENERAL CONDITIONS
OF CONTRACT (GC/WORKS/1 — EDITION 3)

1.   This certificate relates to Contract No. . . . . with

respect to work at (Short Title of the Works), ...

. . . .

. . . .

2.   A tender has been accepted from (name of Contractor) . . . .
for execution of the above Contract.

3.   The Contractor requires under Condition 8 confirmation that
within 21 days from acceptance of the tender there be in force as
described in the Contract:

(a) Employers Liability Insurance
(b) Contractors All Risks Insurance
(c) Public Liability Insurance

The policy or policies effected by the Contractor under (b) and (c)
above shall jointly indemnify for their respective rights and
interests:-

(a) The Property Services Agency or any client body for which it
      may work
(b) The Contractor
(c) All Sub-Contractors
(d) Professional Consultants to (a) above

4.   Signature and return of this Certificate is to be deemed due confirmation by either the Contractor's Insurance Brokers or Insurers
that the above described insurance requirements have been fully
complied with.

ON BEHALF OF THE CONTRACTOR'S INSURANCE BROKERS

(i)   Name of Insurance Brokers:-

. . . .

(ii) Signed on behalf of (i)

. . . .

ON BEHALF OF THE CONTRACTOR'S INSURERS

(i)   Name of Insurers

. . . .

(ii) Signed on behalf of (i)

. . . .

APPENDIX 10

Table of cases

Index